Introductory Relational Database Design for Business, with Microsoft Access

Introductory Relational Database Design for Business, with Microsoft Access

Jonathan Eckstein

MSIS Department
Rutgers Business School
United States

Bonnie R. Schultz

Schultz Writing Services
Princeton, New Jersey
United States

This edition first published 2018
© 2018 John Wiley & Sons Ltd

Registered Office(s)
John Wiley & Sons, Inc., 111 River Street, Hoboken, NJ 07030, USA
John Wiley & Sons Ltd, The Atrium, Southern Gate, Chichester, West Sussex, PO19 8SQ, UK

Editorial Office
9600 Garsington Road, Oxford, OX4 2DQ, UK

For details of our global editorial offices, customer services, and more information about Wiley products visit us at www.wiley.com.

Wiley also publishes its books in a variety of electronic formats and by print-on-demand. Some content that appears in standard print versions of this book may not be available in other formats.

Library of Congress Cataloging-in-Publication Data

Names: Eckstein, Jonathan, author. | Schultz, Bonnie R., author.
Title: Introductory relational database design for business, with Microsoft Access / by Jonathan Eckstein and Bonnie R. Schultz.
Description: Hoboken : Wiley, 2017. | Includes bibliographical references and index. | Identifiers: LCCN 2017019748 (print) | LCCN 2017028117 (ebook) | ISBN 9781119329428 (pdf) | ISBN 9781119329442 (epub) | ISBN 9781119329411 (hardback)
Subjects: LCSH: Relational databases. | Microsoft Access. | BISAC: BUSINESS & ECONOMICS / Statistics. | COMPUTERS / Management Information Systems.
Classification: LCC QA76.9.D3 (ebook) | LCC QA76.9.D3 E325 2017 (print) | DDC 005.75/65—dc23
LC record available at https://lccn.loc.gov/2017019748

Cover Design: Wiley
Cover Image: Relationships Windows: Courtesy of Jonathan Eckstein

Set in 10/12pt Warnock by SPi Global, Pondicherry, India

Contents

Preface *ix*

1 Basic Definitions and Concepts *1*
Basic Terms and Definitions *1*
Types of Information Systems *3*

2 Beginning Fundamentals of Relational Databases and MS Access *7*
Beginning Fundamentals of MS Access *8*
A "Hands-On" Example *9*
Introduction to Forms *15*
Another Method to Create Forms *18*
Introduction to Reports *22*
Introduction to Queries *26*
Common Datatypes in MS Access *32*
Exercises *34*

3 Introduction to Data Management and Database Design *43*
Introduction to Data Management *43*
General Data Management Issues *43*
Classifying Information Systems Tasks: Transaction and Analytical
Processing *45*
What Is Wrong with Just One Table? *46*
Repeating Groups *47*
An Illustration of Multiple Tables and Foreign Keys *48*

4 Basic Relational Database Theory *53*
Tables and Their Characteristics *53*
Primary Keys and Composite Keys *55*
Foreign Keys and Outline Notation *57*
Creating Entity-Relationship (ER) Diagrams *59*
Functional Dependency *60*

Dependency Diagrams *61*
Partial Dependency *62*
Transitive Dependency *63*
Database Anomalies *63*
What Causes Anomalies? *64*
How to Fix Anomalies *65*
Good Database Design Principles *66*
Normalization and Zip Codes *67*
Expanding the Customer Loans Database *68*
DVD Lending Library Example without Loan History *71*
The DVD Lending Library Example with Loan History *75*
Subtypes *78*
Exercises *85*

5 Multiple Tables in Access *95*
The Relationships Window and Referential Integrity *95*
Nested Table View *100*
Nested Forms *101*
Queries with Multiple Tables *103*
Multiple Joins and Aggregation *108*
Personnel: Database Design with Multiple Paths between Tables *115*
Creating the Database in Access using Autonumber Keys *119*
A Simple Query and a Different Way to Express Joins in SQL *120*
Exercises *123*

6 More about Forms and Navigation *127*
More Capabilities of Forms *127*
Packaging it Up – Navigation *132*
Exercises *135*

7 Many-to-Many Relationships *139*
Focus Groups Example *139*
The Plumbing Store: Many-to-Many with an Additional
    Quantity Field *143*
Hands-On Exercise and More About Queries and SQL *146*
Project Teams: Many-to-Many with "Flavors" of Membership *154*
The Library *159*
Exercises *163*

8 Multiple Relationships between the Same Pair of Tables *171*
Commuter Airline Example *171*
The College *177*

Sports League Example   *181*
Multiple Relationships in Access   *183*
Exercises   *184*

9   Normalization   *189*
First Normal Form   *189*
Second Normal Form   *192*
Third Normal Form   *194*
More Normal Forms   *197*
Key Factors to Recognize 3NF   *198*
Example with Multiple Candidate Keys   *198*
Normalizing an Office Supplies Database   *198*
Summary of Guidelines for Database Design   *202*
Exercises   *203*

10   Basic Structured Query Language (SQL)   *215*
Using SQL in Access   *215*
The SELECT ... FROM Statement   *215*
WHERE Conditions   *217*
Inner Joins   *218*
Cartesian Joins and a Different Way to Express
    Inner Joins   *221*
Aggregation   *228*
GROUP BY   *231*
HAVING   *237*
ORDER BY   *238*
The Overall Conceptual Structure of Queries   *240*
Exercises   *243*

11   Advanced Query Techniques   *253*
Outer Joins   *253*
Outer Joins and Aggregation   *256*
Joining Multiple Records from the Same Table: AS in the FROM
    Clause   *260*
Another Use for AS in the FROM Clause   *262*
An Introduction to Query Chaining and Nesting   *262*
A More Complicated Example of Query Chaining: The League
    Standings   *265*
Subqueries and Back to the Plumbing Store Database   *270*
Practical Considerations and "Bending the Rules" Against
    Redundancy   *274*
Exercises   *275*

12 Unary Relationships *279*
Employee Database *279*
Setting Up and Querying a Unary Relationship in Access *283*
The Course Catalog Database *291*
Exercises *294*

Further Reading *301*
Index *303*

Preface

Why Did We Write this Book?

This book arose from the first author's experience of teaching an undergraduate management information systems (MIS) course in the business school of Rutgers University in Piscataway, NJ, United States. This experience consisted of teaching 20 different sections in 12 different semesters, spread over a 20-year time span.

Rutgers' undergraduate New Brunswick business program's approach to teaching MIS differs from that of most business schools. Typically, MIS courses and textbooks stress superficial familiarity with dozens or even hundreds of aspects of information technology. The Rutgers approach, even before the first author arrived there, was different. At least two thirds of the course is spent achieving a relatively deep understanding of one of the most pervasive, durable, and persistent technologies in information technology: relational databases. Finding suitable textbooks was difficult, however. For some time, we used two books, one being a traditional MIS book and the other covering the Microsoft Access relational database product. This solution was expensive and not entirely satisfactory, and became less so over time. With each release of Access, the available Access books became increasingly focused on details of the user interface, and shied away from explaining the underlying design issues of how to structure databases. Giving such a book to somebody without solid prior experience in designing databases is like having somebody without a driver's license read the owner's manual of a feature-laden luxury car: while they might learn how to set the climate control to keep the passenger and driver at different temperatures, they would be no closer to being able to properly use the car for its fundamental task of transportation. Books specifically about database design also exist but are primarily aimed at computer science majors. They are overly abstract and too technical for business students just beginning to learn about information technology.

This book, which began as a set of class notes, takes a different approach. It develops an understanding of relational databases step by step, through numerous compact but realistic examples that gradually build in complexity. While readers will not necessarily gain enough experience to design large-scale organizational systems with hundreds or thousands of tables, they do get a thorough grounding in the technology and its applications, enough to build useful systems with dozens of tables. At every stage, the technology is presented through application examples from business, as well as other fields, giving the reader a chance to concretely think through the details and issues that often arise.

One may well ask, "why should one teach an introductory MIS course this way?" The main reasons are as follows:

- Relatively lasting hands-on knowledge of a pervasive and useful technology
- Acquisition of immediately marketable skills
- Development of analytical thinking and problem solving

The currently prevalent approach to teaching MIS stresses "buzzword"-level knowledge of numerous currently popular technologies. But without the foundation of hands-on application and problem solving, such material is quickly forgotten. Such knowledge may be useful for those in high-level decision-making positions, but by the time most undergraduate students might reach such positions, the knowledge will most likely be largely forgotten and outdated.

Relational databases are one of the most durable technologies in information systems. For decades, they have been the dominant way most organizations store most of their operational data. While databases have grown larger and data are being gathered at ever-increasing rates, the basic concepts and techniques of the technology have remained stable (much more stable, in fact, than procedural programming languages). Once one is comfortable with basic productivity software such as e-mail clients, word processors, spreadsheets, and presentation packages, there could scarcely be a more important or foundational technology to learn, even for manipulating data on one's own personal computer. By designing dozens of (albeit relatively simple) databases and formulating dozens of queries, students using this book acquire an understanding of relational databases in a way that should be more durable than knowledge acquired by memorizing facts or concepts.

Being able to understand and work with relational databases is a marketable skill that students can put to work at the beginning of their careers in almost any industry. While we first introduce queries using Microsoft Access' QBE (query-by-example) grid, most of this book's coverage of queries is through SQL (Structured Query Language), which is used with minor variations in nearly all relational database systems. We have received positive feedback from students who used earlier versions of this text distributed as class notes, to the effect that they were able to "hit the ground running" in jobs or internships because they already understood how to formulate complex database queries in SQL. Superficial "survey" MIS courses do not provide such skills.

Designing a database is a highly analytical skill, involving breaking down a situation into its critical components such as things, people, and events, and clearly elucidating the relationships between these components. Learning such a skill develops the mind generally, fostering abilities in critical thinking and problem solving. Developing such abilities is an important component of any college education, regardless of students' fields of study. Just because a course is in a business school does not mean it should convey only facts – students in business programs deserve to develop their fundamental thinking skills just as much as (for example) majors in philosophy, mathematics, or chemistry. Such considerations motivate our approach of not teaching just facts and trends, but of also covering relevant material that helps students learn new ways of thinking and solving problems. Relational database design is an ideal vehicle for such mental development. Compared to other cognitively demanding IT-related skills like procedural computer programming, we have found that relational databases are relatively accessible and easily related to a wide range of nontrivial applications. The somewhat widespread notion that only computer scientists can or should design databases is simply not true. Almost any business student can learn how to design databases with up to a dozen or so tables, and for most people it is a much less frustrating means of cognitive development than learning, for example, Python or Java.

When embedded in packages such as Microsoft Access, relational database technology now allows the production of relatively sophisticated software applications with little or no computer programming in the traditional procedural sense. In fact, Access' Form, Report, Navigation, and Query features allow construction of professional-looking and useful applications without any "classical" programming whatsoever. Chapter 6 explores these abilities of Access, and its exercises provide a number of different mini-projects for student assignments. Being able to completely build such an application gives students a feeling of mastery and accomplishment.

This book uses Microsoft Access as a vehicle for learning about relational databases because it is widely available and relatively easy to use. But this is *not* "an Access book." We leave many features of Access uncovered and focus on basic skills that largely transfer to other relational database settings. Students need "hands-on" experience, and Access is simply the most logical vehicle to use. For more exhaustive coverage of the many "nooks and crannies" of Access, numerous books are already available. However, they all assume that their readers already know how to design a database.

When we teach MIS, we also cover some material not included in this book. In the course of a typical 28-class semester, we might have 6–7 lectures on other topics such as spreadsheets, network technology, security, and ethics. We chose not to include such material in this text because it is amply covered in other textbooks, especially at the level of detail that only 6–7 classes permit. Instead, this book focuses on what is unique about our approach to teaching MIS. Instructors are encouraged to combine this book with other books, excerpts from other books, or their own notes and lectures on topics not covered here.

Finally, while this book was conceived as a textbook for undergraduate business students, it could also be used in other educational situations or even outside the context of a graded course, as a relatively "friendly" introduction to database technology. We are not aware of other books, textbooks or otherwise, that develop relational database technology in the incremental, example-rich manner that has proved effective at Rutgers over the past two decades.

1

Basic Definitions and Concepts

This chapter covers the following topics:

- Basic definitions and concepts in database technology
- The role of computers and network technology in helping run businesses and other organizations
- Common types of information processing systems in current use

Basic Terms and Definitions

There are some basic definitions and concepts that should provide useful context for understanding database design. Some of the terms we define are in common use but take on specific meaning in the information technology field.

Datum is a singular word, and *data* is its plural. A datum (sometimes called a "data item") is a "particle" of information like "12" or "Q."

Information refers to data that are structured and organized to be useful in making a decision or performing some task. Relational databases are currently the most common way data are organized into information; hence this book's focus on relational databases.

Knowledge denotes understanding or evaluating information. An example could be when Casleton Corporation analyzes its recruiting data and concludes that recruits from Driftwood College tend to have good performance evaluations only if their GPAs are at least 3.0. Based on this "knowledge," Casleton's managers might choose to screen applicants from Driftwood College by their GPAs, interviewing only those graduates with at least a 3.0 GPA.

For this book, we will focus on representing information within computer systems. Note, however, that knowledge can also be represented within computers. One common kind of knowledge representation (KR) within computers is part of the field of *artificial intelligence* (AI). One common business application of AI in business is in automated *business rules* systems. Another

Introductory Relational Database Design for Business, with Microsoft Access, First Edition.
Jonathan Eckstein and Bonnie R. Schultz.
© 2018 John Wiley & Sons Ltd. Published 2018 by John Wiley & Sons Ltd.

recently popularized AI application is the "Siri" personal assistant on iPhones and iPads, or the similar "Google Voice" app on Android devices. Although its business uses are substantial and gradually expanding, we will not discuss AI, as relational database systems are simpler and far more ubiquitous.

Information systems consist of the ways that organizations store, move, organize, and manipulate/process their information. The components that implement information systems – in other words, *information technology* – consist of the following:

- Hardware – physical tools: computer and network hardware, but also low-tech objects such as pens and paper
- Software – (changeable) instructions for the hardware (when applicable; the simplest hardware does not need software)
- People
- Procedures – instructions for people
- Data/databases

Information systems existed before computers and networks – they just used relatively simple hardware that usually did not need software (at least as we know it today). For example, filing all sales receipts alphabetically by customer in a filing cabinet is a form of information system, although it is not electronic. Tax records kept on clay tablets by ancient civilizations were also a form of information system. Strictly speaking, this book is about an aspect of CBISs (computer-based information systems). Because of the present ubiquity of computers in information systems, we usually leave out the "CB," treating it as implicit.

Present-day CBISs have the following advantages over older, manual information systems:

- They can perform numerical computations and other data processing much more quickly, accurately, and cheaply than people.
- They can communicate very quickly and accurately.
- They can store large amounts of information quickly and cheaply, and information retrieval can often be very rapid.
- They can, to varying degrees, automate tasks and processes that previously required human labor.
- Information no longer needs to be "stuck" with particular things, locations, or people.

However, increasingly, automated systems can have drawbacks, such as the following:

- Small errors can have a much wider impact than in a less automated system. For example, in March 2003, a minor software bug in some airport data collection code – which programmers were aware of but considered too small to cause operational problems – grounded all aircraft in Japan for two days.

- Fewer people in the organization understand exactly how information is processed.
- Sometimes, malfunctions may go unnoticed. For example, American Airlines once discovered a serious bug in its "yield management" software only after reporting quarterly results that were significantly lower than expected. ("Yield management" refers to the process of deciding how many aircraft seats to make available for sale at different fare levels.)

Information architecture is the particular way an organization has arranged its information systems: for example, a particular network of computers running particular software might support a firm's marketing organization, while another network of computers running different software might support its production facilities, and so forth.

Information infrastructure consists of the hardware and software that support an organization's information architecture, together with the personnel and services dedicated primarily to maintaining and developing that hardware and software.

Application and *application program* (nowadays sometimes simply "app") are somewhat ill-defined terms but typically denote computer software and databases supporting a particular task or group of tasks. For example, a firm's human resource department might use one application to analyze benefit costs and usage, and another to monitor employee turnover.

A classic business IT problem is that applications, especially those used by different parts of an organization, may not communicate with one another effectively – for example, a new hire or retirement might have to be separately entered into both of the human resources systems described above because they do not communicate or share a common database.

Types of Information Systems

Particular information systems may be intended for use at one or more *levels* of an organization, as follows (Figure 1.1):

- The operational level – day-to-day operations and routine decisions. In an airline, for example, an operational decision is whether to cancel a particular flight on a particular day, or what type of aircraft to schedule on a particular flight during the summer flying season. Operational events that that might need to be recorded could include a customer scanning her boarding pass as she boards a flight, or an aircraft arriving at its destination gate.
- The strategic level – the highest-level, "big picture" decisions. In the example of an airline, whether to serve the Asia–US market, or whether to emphasize cost over service quality.

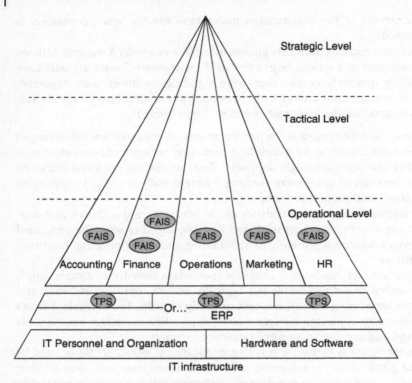

Figure 1.1 Information systems and the levels of an organization.

- The tactical level – decisions in between operational and strategic levels; for an airline, such a decision might be whether to increase or decrease service to a particular city.

In reality, the boundaries between these levels are typically somewhat indistinct: the levels form a continuous "spectrum." But labeling different segments of this spectrum as "levels" is useful conceptually.

Organizations are also typically divided into *functional areas*, meaning that different parts of the organization have different functions (that is, they do different things). These divisions vary by organization, but Figure 1.1 shows a fairly standard division into accounting, finance, operations, marketing, and human resources.

Transaction processing systems (TPSs) gather data about everyday business events in "real time" as they occur. Examples:

- You buy three items at a local store.
- A shipment of coffee beans arrives at a local distribution center.
- A passenger checks in for a flight.
- A package is unloaded from a FedEx or UPS aircraft.

Although only one of the above events is a transaction in the classical economic sense, from an information systems perspective all of these events are examples of *transactions* that may be immediately tracked by a TPS. Often, technology like barcodes and scanners makes tracking such transactions quicker, cheaper, and more detailed than if their associated data were to be keypunched manually. TPS systems are always operational-level systems, but they may also be used at other levels, or feed information to other systems at higher levels.

Functional area information systems (FAISs), also called *departmental information systems* (DISs), are designed to be operated within a single traditional functional department of an organization such as sales, human resources, or accounting. In the early days of CBIS, these were often the only kind of systems that were practical, because managing the data from more than one functional area would have required too much storage or computing power for a single system.

When an organization has multiple functional area systems, properly coordinating them becomes a potentially difficult issue. The systems may require overlapping data and can therefore become "out of sync" with one another. *ERP (enterprise resource planning) systems* are a relatively extreme reaction to the problem of poorly coordinated functional area systems, and are offered by vendors such as SAP and Oracle. They aim to support the entire organization's needs with essentially one single integrated system. They have enormous potential benefits but are also notoriously tricky and expensive to configure and install. Note that the only really meaningful word in the ERP acronym is "enterprise," denoting a system for the entire enterprise, and the reasons for "resource planning" in the acronym are historical. Such systems can perform resource planning but not particularly more than any other business function.

Some other common terms, some of which we will define in more detail later in the book, include the following:

- MIS – *management information system* – refers to a standard system that consolidates operational data into reports useful to managers.
- DSS – *decision support system* – refers to a system designed to help analyze and make specific kinds of decisions (at any level of the management hierarchy).
- ES – *expert system* – refers to a system that mimics the knowledge and behavior of human experts in particular domains, such as diagnosing problems with complicated equipment.
- EIS – *executive information system* – refers to a system that is designed to provide executives with information to assist them in making high-level (strategic or tactical) decisions.
- An *interorganizational system* (IOS) is a system that connects two organizations – for example, it may allow a company to automatically share inventory and backlog data with suppliers or customers.
- *Electronic commerce* or *e-commerce* refers to sales transactions in which at least one side of the transaction (buyer or seller), and perhaps both, is performed by a CBIS without direct human intervention.

2

Beginning Fundamentals of Relational Databases and MS Access

Microsoft Access is an example of *relational database* software, usually called a *relational database management system* (RDBMS). Access is just one of many relational database offerings in the software marketplace. Others include packages such as Oracle and Ingres. Some database software, such as MySQL, is available free of cost, while other packages are sold by commercial vendors such as Oracle and IBM.

All of these database packages are conceptually similar to MS Access. The greatest difference is in the scale of operation each package supports, in terms of both the volume of data and the number of simultaneous users. User interfaces also differ from package to package.

It is important to note that not all databases are relational. Some older technologies are still in use in the business environment, and other modern approaches exist, such as *object databases*. However, relational databases are by far the most commonly used today, especially in business applications, which is why this textbook focuses on them.

In relational databases, all data are kept in *tables*, also called *relations*. Most relational databases contain more than one table, but for now we will keep things simple and consider only a single table. A database with only one table is often called a *flat file* database.

Table 2.1 shows an example of a data table pertaining to students.

The *rows* of the table, also called *tuples* or *records*, correspond to things or events that we wish to store information about, such as people, orders, or products. In Table 2.1, each row corresponds to a student.

The *columns* of the table, also called *attributes* or *fields*, record various properties of the things or events being described. In this example, the attributes are the ID number, first name, last name, and zip code of each student.

Other kinds of software can store tables of data. For example, spreadsheet programs such as Microsoft Excel can store data tables. The biggest different between Excel and Access is in the way in which Access allows for relationships between multiple tables. However, other differences exist. For instance, each

Introductory Relational Database Design for Business, with Microsoft Access, First Edition.
Jonathan Eckstein and Bonnie R. Schultz.
© 2018 John Wiley & Sons Ltd. Published 2018 by John Wiley & Sons Ltd.

Table 2.1 Example table of student data.

ID#	FirstName	LastName	ZipCode
14758993	Joseph	Ho	08765
23458902	Karen	Leigh	21678
89312199	Max	Saperstein	11572
90926431	Alex	Holmes	08743
82938475	Meera	Rajani	99371
19284857	Evan	Chu	34012

column in a relational database table has a *fixed datatype*. Here "datatype" refers to the kind of data being stored: for example, an amount of money, some other kind of number, or a character string like a person's name. In a relational database, every datum stored in a column must have the same datatype; that is, every entry in the column must be a percentage, or every entry must be a character string, and so forth. In spreadsheets, you can have data of different types within the same column. For example, a name might be stored in a particular cell, but another cell in the same column might contain a percentage.

Another difference is that in relational databases, one identifies columns by a user-specified attribute name (such as *ID#* or *FirstName* above) rather than by sequential letters (A, B, C,...), or column numbers as in a spreadsheet.

One more difference is that in spreadsheets, rows and columns are essentially symmetrical in their basic function. For example, it is no harder to add a column to a spreadsheet than it is to add a row. In relational database tables, rows and columns have fundamentally different roles. In relational databases, you can add or delete rows easily and quickly, whereas columns are largely static. Depending on the specific relational database software one is using, one might be able to add or delete columns in a table after it has been created, but if the table already contains a large amount of data, such an operation may be very time consuming and require significant computing resources.

Beginning Fundamentals of MS Access

Microsoft Access is both of the following:

- A relational database system
- A graphical, object-oriented software development environment (but not an object database or object-oriented database, which would imply a different, more flexible data-storage model)

To develop an Access application, one uses various tools and "wizards" to create, customize, and link "objects" to suit one's needs. It is also possible

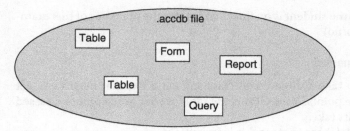

Figure 2.1 Objects within an Access file.

to write segments of computer programming code in the Visual Basic language and combine them with objects, but doing so is often unnecessary for simple Access applications. Thus, Access allows someone to build fairly sophisticated applications without engaging in classic text-based computer programming.

Access' most frequently used kinds of objects are *tables, forms, queries,* and *reports*. Access stores all the objects for a database in a single file with the type ".accdb" (or ".mdb" in earlier versions of Access).

Typically, Access keeps each database and its entire constituent objects inside a single operating-system file (Figure 2.1). For different database software or operating systems other than Microsoft Windows, the situation might be different: the database or even a single table might be spread across multiple operating-system files.

Access allows you to link objects in useful ways. We will start by examining the simplest such linkage, between a *table* and a *form*. Essentially, the table provides a way to store your basic data, and the form provides an alternative way to view that data on the screen. Information can flow in both directions between the table and form (Figure 2.2).

Figure 2.2 A table interacting with a form.

A "Hands-On" Example

Let us suppose we want to track information about students at a small college. We want to keep the following information for each student:

- ID number (9 digits)
- Name (First, Last, and Middle name or initial)
- Address, consisting of street address, city, state, and zip code
- Major
- Gender
- Birth date (question: why is it better to store a person's birth date than their age?)

- Whether or not the student is on financial aid (for the purposes of this example, a simple yes/no)
- Credits taken
- Grade points amassed

Note that if you take a three-credit class and get a B+, that means you get $3 \times 3.5 = 10.5$ grade points. Your GPA is the ratio of your grade points amassed to your total credits taken.

Let us create a database to store this information:

1) Open Microsoft Access from the "Start" or Windows menu at the bottom left of the screen (Figure 2.3).

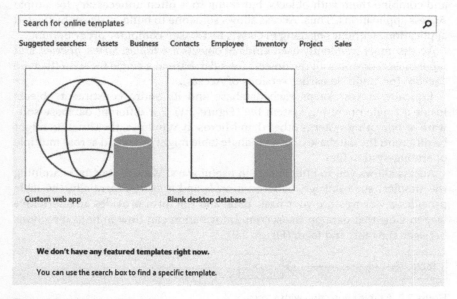

Figure 2.3 When Access opens.

2) Click the "Blank desktop database" icon ("Blank database" in earlier versions of Access).
3) In the resulting dialog box, provide a file name, for example, "students" (if Windows is configured not to display file types) or "students.accdb" (if Windows is configured to display file types).
4) Click "Create."

Access assumes that the first thing we want to do is to create a table. We see an empty table called "Table1." Now, we want to define what information resides in this table. This step is called *table design* (Figure 2.4).

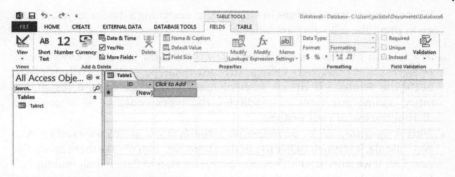

Figure 2.4 A new Access table.

5) Accordingly, we click the "View" button at the top left (make sure you have the "FIELDS" tab selected), and select "Design View."
6) A small dialog box appears requiring us to give the table a name – we call the table STUDENT and then click OK (Figure 2.5).

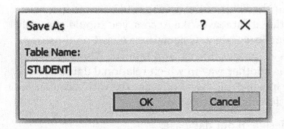

Figure 2.5 Naming a table in Access.

We now see a list of the attributes in the table (somewhat counterintuitively, the columns of the table appear as *rows* in this view; Figure 2.6).

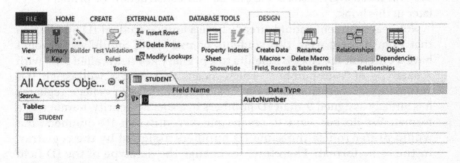

Figure 2.6 Table design view.

We now specify the columns in our table. In designing a database, you should keep in mind the following guidelines:

- *Try to plan for the future and include all the data you are likely to need.* In Access, it is possible to change attribute datatypes or add attributes later, but if the database is already large or many people are using it simultaneously, adding attributes or modifying datatypes could be slow or could disrupt the use of your system.
- *Have a separate field for each division of the data you anticipate needing.* As a general rule, it is much easier to put data together than to take them apart. For example, if we store student's names as three different fields (first, middle, and last names) then we can easily form a student's whole name by concatenating (placing end-to-end) the contents of these fields. If we just store the name as one large field, then certain tasks, such as sorting students by their first or last names, may become unnecessarily difficult and prone to error.
- *Avoid storing calculated fields.* If you have already stored the total credits and grade points amassed, you can easily calculate GPA. There is no need to redundantly store the students' GPAs. That will take up unnecessary space and create an opportunity for the fields of the database to become inconsistent with one another. In relational databases like Access, you should generally use table objects only for your "base" data. Calculations based on those data reside in other objects, such as queries, forms, and reports. This separation of base and calculated data is another way in which relational databases are different from spreadsheets, in which all "base" data coexist with calculations within the same two-dimensional grid of cells.

Let us now proceed with the design of our database:

1) Access has already provided a field called "ID," in keeping with the standard procedure of every table including a *primary key* attribute whose value uniquely identifies each row of a table. This is another difference from spreadsheets, which identify rows by simply numbering them sequentially. We will extensively discuss the choice and construction of primary keys later in this book.

   Now, each student should already have a unique student ID number, so that even if there were two students named "John Smith," each would have a different ID. Access defaults to a primary key field called "ID" with a datatype of "Autonumber," which means that Access will assign IDs automatically. Let us assume for this example that the college registrar has already assigned 9-digit ID numbers in a social-security-number-like format. We do not want to create our own different ID numbers, but would prefer to use the same ID numbers assigned by the registrar, in the same format. Therefore, we change the datatype of the ID field to text, rather than Autonumber, by selecting "Short Text" (for Access 2013) or "Text" (for earlier versions) from the pull-down menu under "Data Type." Note that it is generally customary to use text fields to represent ID numbers and the like, which do not have any specific arithmetic meaning – for example, it makes no sense to add or subtract two students' ID numbers.

Versions of Access prior to 2013 had two kinds of text fields, "Text" for standard, fixed-length fields and "Memo" for potentially very long, free-form, variable-length fields. In Access 2013 the terminology for these two kinds of fields was changed to "Short Text" and "Long Text," respectively. This terminology can be a bit confusing because "Short Text" has the potential to be quite long (255 characters), and a "Long Text" field does not necessarily have to be long. In this textbook, we will use the term "Text" to refer to standard, "short" text fields, and we will not use "Long Text" fields in our exercises. Therefore, we will refer to "Short Text" fields simply as "Text" from this point forward.

In the "field properties" at the bottom of the screen, we enter "9" in "field size" (to set the ID length to nine characters) and "000\-00\-0000" under "input mask." This input mask allows you to enter only numbers (because of the "0" characters), and the placement of the "\-" characters causes the IDs to display in a social-security-number-like format. Note that the hyphens in the input mask are not actually stored in the database. Instead of just typing in the input mask, we can instead click on the "..." button in the input mask property, and select from commonly used input masks in the "input mask wizard" that then pops up. Finally, we can enter an explanation like "Student ID number from registrar" in the "description" area.

2) In the next row, we create a "FirstName" field by typing "FirstName". The datatype defaults to "Short Text" (or, equivalently, "Text" in older versions of Access), with a length of 255 characters. Here, we may select a shorter length, like 40. Here and below, we will select some reasonable lengths for text fields, but there is nothing magical or "best" about the lengths chosen.

3) Create a "MiddleName" text field; set the length to 20.

4) Create a "LastName" text field; set its length to 50.

5) Create a "StreetAddress" text field; set its length 80.

6) Create a "City" text field; set its length to 50.

7) Create a "State" text field, and set its length to 2 (assuming we will use standard postal two-letter codes for states).

8) Create a "ZipCode" text field, and set its length to 9 (for modern zip + 4 codes). We can click the "..." box on the right of "input mask," and after saving the table, select a standard mask for zip codes. Note that adding or multiplying zip codes makes no sense, so we store them as text.

9) Create a "Gender" text field; set its length to 1. We will just store "M" or "F" in this field. Later in this chapter we will see how to ensure that a user does not enter other letters.

10) Create a "Major" text field; set its length to 30 (later in this book, we will see how to allow only real majors to be entered in situation like this).

11) Create a "BirthDate" field. Access has a special datatype for dates and times, called "Date/Time," which can store combined dates/times with an accuracy of seconds. Select this datatype. Under "field properties," we can also select a format to use to display this information – for example, "short date." Note that it is much better to store a student's birth date, which is static, than their age, which would have to be periodically updated.

12) Create a "FinancialAid" field. Assume that we just want the database to remember whether the student has any financial aid. In this case, we have an example of a "yes/no" field; select the "Yes/No" datatype. We can set the format to "Yes/No" instead of the default "True/False" (this change affects only how the field is displayed).

13) Create a "Credits" field. Note that a student's tally of credits is a number on which it makes sense to perform addition and other arithmetic operations. Select the "number" datatype. In "field properties," select a "Field Size" of either "Long Integer" or "Integer" for the "field size" (an "Integer" means a whole number). Note that "Integer" can hold whole numbers in the range −32,768 through +32,767, which should be more than sufficient to hold a tally of credits. If the school were to allow fractions of credits, it would have to make this field a "Single" or "Double," datatypes that can hold numbers containing fractions.

14) Create a "GradePoints" field. Grade points amassed can be fractional, so select "number" and a field size of "Double," which can store arbitrary numbers including fractions. "Single" can store fractional values with about 6 digits of accuracy and "Double" about 14. "Double" is generally recommended over "Single" unless you anticipate having a gigantic database and need to worry about how much storage it will consume.

15) The table design process is now complete (Figure 2.7). Finally, we save the table design by clicking the small disk icon in the top left corner, next to the Access logo. Note that "saving" in Access saves an object within the overall Access file; in other Microsoft Office applications, "save" has the different meaning of saving the whole file. In Access, the database file as a whole is continuously saved.

Next, we switch the "view" to "datasheet" instead of "design," and enter some data (we can just invent some information for now; Table 2.2).

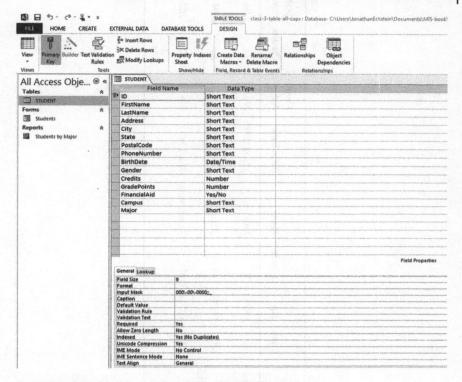

Figure 2.7 Completed Design View for the STUDENT table.

Introduction to Forms

We will now create a form to view our table in a more visually pleasing way.

With the table open, select the "Create" tab and push the "Form" button. Access then creates a form automatically linked to the STUDENT table. Note that we can enter data into the form, and it is immediately reflected in the table, and vice versa. The form first appears in "Layout View." If we choose "Form View," we can enter and change data.

We can now choose the "Design View" of the form and make changes. For example, we can change the font in the header, resize the text boxes, and so forth. To make changes to the widths and positions of the individual text boxes, we must first remove the "layout" that initially links them together. To remove this linking, choose the "arrange" tab, click the small handle on the upper left area of the form that looks like a box with a "+" sign in it, and click "Remove Layout."

Table 2.2 Sample data entered into the STUDENT table.

ID	First Name	Middle Name	Last Name	Street Address	City	State	Zip	Gender	Major	Birth Date	Financial Aid	Credits	Grade Points
547-89-9399	Bella	Q	Amati	393 West Boulevard	Piscataway	NJ	08854-	F	Marketing	12/22/1986	No	35	90
784-57-8483	Matthew	F	Short	23 Greene Circle	East Brunswick	NJ	08750-	M	Finance	3/12/1987	Yes	38	94
129-34-8900	Yu-Ping		Chen	177 Whitcomb Lane	Sparta	NJ	07768-	M	Accounting	4/4/1987	No	30	102.5

If you want to view forms and tables as sub-windows rather than tabs, select the "File" tab (or click the Office icon in Access 2007), click "Options," select the "Current Database" tab, and select "Overlapping Windows" under "Document Window Options." You then see a message stating "You must close and reopen the database for the specified option to take place." Close and reopen the database.

In Design View, our form should look approximately as in Figure 2.8.

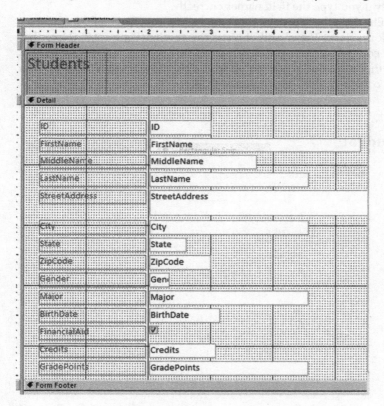

Figure 2.8 Design View of a form linked to the STUDENT table.

We can now add a box to display each student's GPA:

16) Select "Design View" again, if it is not already selected.
17) If desired, make space on the form by dragging the "Form Footer" boundary down.
18) In the "design" tab, click the "text box" tool ("ab |" near the left of the ribbon).
19) Draw the text box somewhere on the form.
20) After aligning the text box and its label, type "GPA" in the label.

- Next, view the properties of the text box (if you do not see them on the right of the screen, right-click the box and select "properties"). In these properties, perform the following operations:
  - Enter "=[GradePoints]/[Credits]" in "Control Source" – note that the names are case sensitive: "Credits" is not the same as "credits." The square brackets indicate to Access that it should use the values of fields in the linked table, in this case *Students*. Access should insert the brackets automatically if you type the field names correctly.
  - Select "Fixed" in the "Format" property and "3" for "Decimal Places."
  - Go back to "Form View," and observe the results (Figure 2.9). Note that GPA is computed from the other fields in the same record when you display the form, but is not stored in the database itself. Therefore, it is called a *computed field* or *calculated field*.

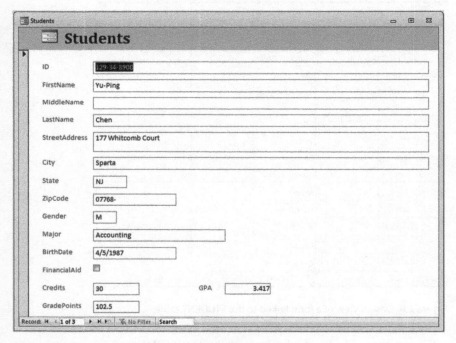

Figure 2.9 Completed student form with GPA display.

Another Method to Create Forms

We now present a method to create forms that gives the user a bit more control. To begin with, we download a slightly different version of the database we created earlier, class-3-base.accdb, from the book website.

This file is similar to the one we just created, but contains some preloaded data. After downloading, you may need to click the "Enable Content" and/ or "Save As" buttons in order to have full ability to modify the database file. To explore the alternative means of creating forms, perform the following steps:

1) Select the "Create" tab from the ribbon.
2) Click "Form Wizard" (one of the smaller buttons). A "wizard" dialog box should then appear (Figure 2.10). By default, the form we are about to produce is based on the only other object in the database, the table STUDENT.

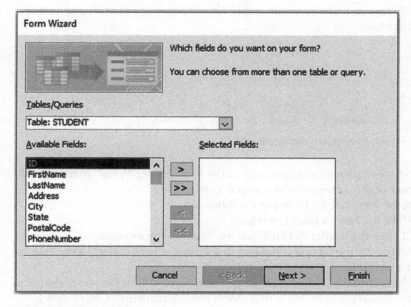

Figure 2.10 The Form Wizard.

3) Move all available fields to the form by pressing ">>". Note that in future we may use the ">" button to move fields one by one to the form. This technique allows you to hide some fields from the form if you do not want to include them.
4) Then press "Next >".
5) Choose the "Columnar" (standard) design (Figure 2.11), then press "Next >" and give the form a name (it can have same name as a table). Then press "Finish." A new form should appear.
6) Note that "Major" was automatically generated as a "combo box" with a pull-down menu because this version of the database contains some hidden information about the allowed values of "Major." Note that the same is not true for the "Gender" field, which appears as a regular text box.

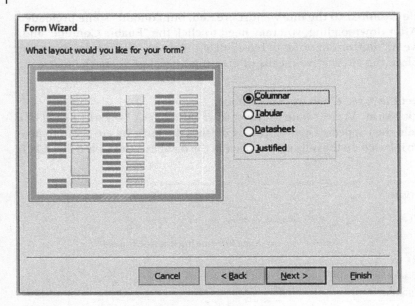

Figure 2.11 Selecting "columnar" form layout.

7) Next, we improve the appearance of the form. Under "View" in the top left corner of the Access window, select "Design View."
8) Edit the form header by doing the following:
   - Make the header label box wider.
   - Change the header "STUDENT" to "Student Information."
   - Adjust the font size and bolding in the header (under the "Home" tab in the ribbon).
   - Check the form's appearance with "Form View." Adjust the size of the form if necessary (it is better to make form size adjustments in Form View).
9) Edit some of the labels generated by the wizard to include spaces for readability: change "GradePoints" to "Grade Points," and "FinancialAid" to "Financial Aid."
10) Our next major step is to change the "Gender" text box to a "combo box" with a pull-down menu, into which you are only allowed to enter "M" or "F":
   - Make sure you are back in "Design View."
   - Select and delete (by pressing the "delete" key) the current text box and label for "Gender."
   - Choose "Design" in the ribbon, and then click the "combo box" tool, which looks like ▦. Draw the new combo box where the old "Gender" box used to be.
     If you cannot see the "combo box" tool, you may need to click the scroll arrow under DESIGN to find it, then click on the ▦ symbol (Figure 2.12).

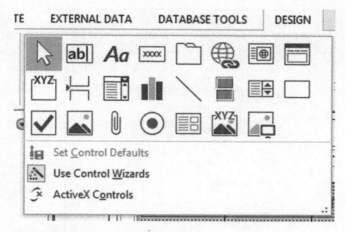

Figure 2.12 Finding the combo box tool.

- Once you have drawn the combo box, a "wizard" window should immediately appear. In this window, select "I will type in the values I want" and click "Next >".
- Type "M" and "F" in the first column of the next pane, then "Next >".
- Select "store that value in this field," and select "Gender." Press "Next >".
- Type "Gender" for "what label would you like," then click "Finish."
- Adjust the alignment of the combo box and label.
- Check the results in "Form View."

11) Review: Add the calculated field for GPA:
- Select the text box tool from the "Design" tab in the ribbon (the button looks like ⓐⓑⓛ).
- Draw a new text box on the form.
- Enter "=GradePoints/Credits" into the box. Access will insert square brackets around "GradePoints" and "Credits" if it recognizes the field names – otherwise, check for misspellings, extra spaces, or non-matching uppercase/lowercase letters. You can enter this formula either into the text box itself, or into the "Control Source" property on the property sheet (see below).
- If the object properties are not visible on the right of the screen, right-click and select "Properties."
- Select the "All" or "Format" tab within the properties pane.
- Set the format to fixed.
- Set decimal points to 3.
- In the label, type "GPA".
- Adjust the sizes and positions of the combo box and its label.
- Back in "Form View," adjust the size of the window (Figure 2.13).
- Save the resulting form by clicking the "Save" (floppy-disk-like) icon near the top left of the Access window.

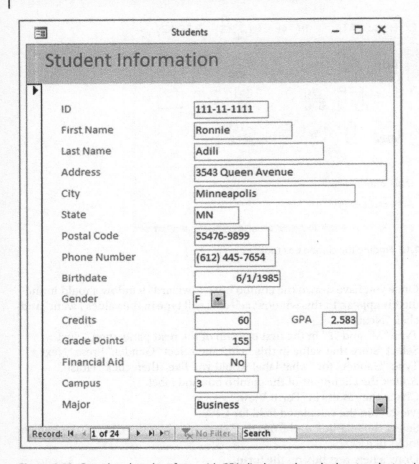

Figure 2.13 Completed student form with GPA display and combo box to select majors.

Introduction to Reports

Reports are a way of extracting information from Access databases. Reports are a feature that is not present in every RDBMS and can vary substantially in implementation between different systems.

Access reports are similar to forms, with the following differences:

- They are specifically designed for printing or non-interactive viewing.
- Consequently, they are "one-way." They display data but do not let you enter it.
- They have some sorting and grouping capabilities not found in forms (later, we will see how to accomplish something similar to grouping with nested forms, but that is more complicated).

Suppose we want to create a report as follows:

- The report should present a master list of all students with just the first name, last name, gender, and phone number, in that order.
- The students should be grouped by major.
- Students should be sorted alphabetically within each group by last name and then by first name (that is, students with the same last name are sorted by their first names).
- At the end of each group, there is a count of the number of students in the major.

The steps required to create this report are as follows:

1) Select the "Create" tab in the ribbon.
2) Click "Report Wizard" in the "Reports" group.
3) A "wizard" similar to the "Form Wizard" appears. Use the STUDENT table.
4) Put each field specified for inclusion, as well as "Major," into the report by clicking ">" (one by one, since we do not want all the fields). Then click "Next >". We need to include "Major" because we are going to use it to group records, and we also need to display a header for each group.
5) The next wizard window controls grouping (Figure 2.14). Select "Major" and click ">" to group by major; then press "Next>".

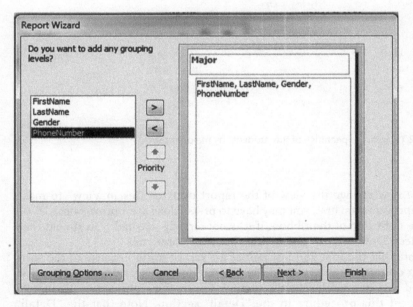

Figure 2.14 Grouping control in the Report Wizard.

6) The next wizard window controls sorting. Select *LastName* in the first box and *FirstName* in the second box, then "Next >" ("Ascending" means alphabetical order, which is what we want; you would choose "Descending" for reverse alphabetical order, starting with Z).
7) In the next window, choose "Outline" format and press "Next >".
8) Give the report a name, for example, "Students by Major," and press "Finish." The report should now appear (Figure 2.15).

Students by Major

Major		Business		
Last Name		First Name	Gender	Phone Number
Adili		Ronnie	F	(612) 445-7654
DiGiacomo		Kevin	M	(305) 531-7652
Gibson		Christopher	M	(305) 235-4563
Ramsay		Robert	M	(212) 223-9889
Watson		Ana	F	(305) 561-2334
Major		Communications		
Last Name		First Name	Gender	Phone Number
Faulkner		Eileen	F	(305) 489-8876
Joseph		Cedric	M	(404) 667-8955
Ortiz		Frances	F	(303) 575-3211
Price		Lori	F	(310) 961-2323
Slater		Erica	F	(312) 545-6978

Figure 2.15 Initial appearance of the "students by major" report.

9) We now change the view of the report over to "Design View" to make improvements: first, you may have to press "close print preview mode" on the right side of the ribbon. If it is not already selected, you should then select "Design View" under "View" in the "Home" tab.
10) Note that the first and last names are out of order because of the sorting options we selected. In the "Major Header" section, move the first and last name label boxes so they are in the right order. To match, repeat this procedure in the "Detail" section. Note that the "Detail"

section appears for each record in the report. If necessary, we may also need to perform a similar procedure to put the gender and phone number fields in the order requested. Note that moving fields on the report canvas will not change the sorting order that was already established by the wizard.

11) Select the "Home" tab or the ribbon, and then "Report View" under "View" to view the results.

12) We now need to create a group section footer for the count of the number of students in each major. Go back to design view, and click "Group & Sort" under the "Design" tab in the ribbon. Next to "Group on Major" near the bottom of the screen, click "more…" and then change "without a footer section" to "with a footer section." A "Major footer" section should appear in the report.

13) Create a text box, and place it in the footer we just created (we have already performed a similar task with a form instead of a report).

14) Put "Number of students in major" in the text box label. Resize and realign the text box and its label to make the appearance of the report acceptable (you may check its appearance in "Report View").

15) In the text box itself, enter "=Count(ID)". You can also enter this formula in the field's "Control Source" property, and in either case square brackets should appear around "ID" to indicate Access recognized "ID" as a field name. If not, check for typos, spaces, or errors in capitalization. The "Count" function does not count unique values, just the total number of input items that are not blank. Thus, we could just have well have counted "Gender," or any other field that cannot be blank. Note that the scope of "Count" or "Sum" or any similar aggregation function is determined by the header or footer you put it in. If you use the function in the "major" footer, its scope will be all records with a given major.

16) Examine the results in "Report View."

17) Back in "Design View," adjust the size and positioning of the items in the footer, and use the property sheet to set the "Border Style" property (under the "All" or "Format" tabs) of the count box to "Transparent" for consistency. While borders around boxes are nice for on-screen data entry, they are distracting when viewing a full report.

18) Finally, we add a report footer showing the total number of students across all majors. To accomplish this, first drag the report footer section end line down to create a nonempty footer. Next, copy the objects from the major footer to this new footer and change the label to "Total number of students." Once we have copied the objects to the report footer, the scope of "Count" will be the whole report, since it is in the report footer instead of the group footer. Thus, we will get a simple footer at the end of the whole report, and it will show the total number of students (Figure 2.16).

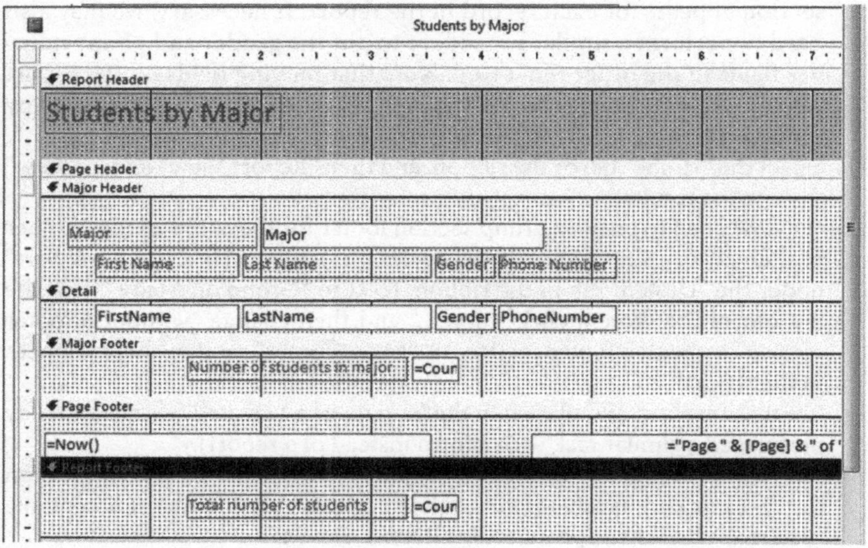

Figure 2.16 Adding a report footer.

Introduction to Queries

Queries are a standard feature of all relational database management systems and are represented in some form of the SQL language, with minor variations between different systems.

Queries retrieve specific information from a database. Unlike reports, queries are concerned with the basic manipulation of data and not with the visual appearance of the result. Queries place the extracted information in temporary tables variously called:

- Ephemeral tables
- Views
- Dynasets

All these terms have the same meaning. Such tables are *not* permanently stored in the database. As soon as the underlying data from the source objects changes, they immediately change to match, because they are automatically recomputed functions of the underlying data. In Access, you can attach forms or reports to a query rather than directly to tables. This feature allows you to combine the features of forms or reports with data manipulation and processing features that are only (or more conveniently) available in queries. However, in this chapter we will concentrate on simple queries directly connected only to a single table.

One feature of queries, not readily accessible in forms or reports, is the ability to extract only data matching specific criteria. In addition, queries can generate computed fields and sort and aggregate values in much the same manner as a report. "Aggregating" values refers to computing summary information over groups of records, such as the counts of students calculated in the report example above. Another example of aggregation (for a chain of retail stores) is computing total quarterly sales amounts over geographical regions or product lines.

On the same database we have been using, let us try our first query:

1) Go to the "Create" tab in the ribbon, and select "Query Design" (the "wizard" is not particularly helpful for making queries).
2) Select the STUDENT table in the "add table" box that immediately pops up, click "add," and then click "close." We should now see Access' standard "query grid" (Figure 2.17).

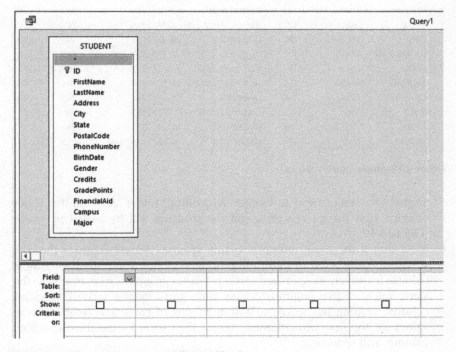

Figure 2.17 The Access query grid (Design View).

3) Drag the following fields from the STUDENT table to the "Field" row of the query grid in order: *LastName, FirstName, State, Major, BirthDate, FinancialAid,* and *Credits.*
4) To view the results of the query, click the "!" (Run) button (next to the "View" button at the top left) or select "Datasheet View" under "View" (Figure 2.18).

Last Name ▾	First Name ▾	Stat ▾	Major ▾	BirthDat ▾	FinancialAi ▾	Credit ▾
Adili	Ronnie	MN	Business	6/1/1985	No	60
Heltzer	Peter	FL	Engineering	3/8/1983	No	25
Gibson	Christopher	FL	Business	3/12/1983	Yes	35
Zimmerman	Kimberly	TX	Education	4/18/1980	No	120
Ramsay	Robert	NY	Business	5/1/1984	Yes	50
Frazier	Steven	MD	Undecided	9/9/1978	No	35
Korba	Nickolas	CA	Education	11/11/1981	No	100
Weissman	Kimberly	FL	Liberal Arts	11/11/1984	Yes	63
Parulis	Christa	MD	Liberal Arts	7/15/1982	No	50
Berlin	Jared	SC	Engineering	1/15/1982	Yes	100
Camejo	Oscar	NY	Liberal Arts	3/10/1979	Yes	100
Solomon	Wendy	FL	Engineering	1/31/1985	No	50
Watson	Ana	FL	Business	4/18/1985	No	30
Faulkner	Eileen	FL	Communication	9/12/1985	No	30
Watson	Ana	FL	Liberal Arts	8/1/1985	Yes	70
Ortiz	Frances	CO	Communication	2/3/1984	Yes	28
Coe	Bradley	CA	Undecided	8/22/1981	No	52
DiGiacomo	Kevin	FL	Business	5/31/1982	Yes	105
Slater	Erica	IL	Communication	5/1/1982	Yes	105
Joseph	Cedric	GA	Communication	4/12/1984	Yes	45
Cornell	Ryan	GA	Undecided	9/30/1984	No	45
Price	Lori	CA	Communication	7/1/1982	Yes	24
Zacco	Michelle	MA	Undecided	10/24/1985	No	21
Huerta	Carlos	NY	Undecided	6/18/1985	No	15

Figure 2.18 Student query results.

5) Go back to design view, and select "Ascending" under "Sort" in the *Major* column. Run the query again, and the students will be sorted by major (Figure 2.19).

6) Note that if there are multiple sorting criteria, Access assumes that the sorting priority is left to right – that is, data are first sorted by the leftmost column for which we specified sorting. Within groups of rows that have the same value of this column, Access then sorts by the second specified column, reading left to right. Within groups of rows that have identical values for the first two columns, Access then sorts by the third specified column, and so forth.

7) Suppose we wanted to sort by major first, then sort by state, but we would like the state to display to the left of the major. To accomplish this, we may drag an additional *State* field to the right end of the grid, and sort ascending by major and by this second state field. We do not sort by the first state field. To avoid the state from appearing twice in the output, we may uncheck the "show" box under the second *State* field.

Last Name ▾	First Name ▾	Stat ▾	Major ▾	BirthDat ▾	FinancialAi ▾	Credit ▾
Watson	Ana	FL	Business	4/18/1985	No	30
Gibson	Christopher	FL	Business	3/12/1983	Yes	35
DiGiacomo	Kevin	FL	Business	5/31/1982	Yes	105
Ramsay	Robert	NY	Business	5/1/1984	Yes	50
Adili	Ronnie	MN	Business	6/1/1985	No	60
Price	Lori	CA	Communication	7/1/1982	Yes	24
Joseph	Cedric	GA	Communication	4/12/1984	Yes	45
Slater	Erica	IL	Communication	5/1/1982	Yes	105
Ortiz	Frances	CO	Communication	2/3/1984	Yes	28
Faulkner	Eileen	FL	Communication	9/12/1985	No	30
Zimmerman	Kimberly	TX	Education	4/18/1980	No	120
Korba	Nickolas	CA	Education	11/11/1981	No	100
Heltzer	Peter	FL	Engineering	3/8/1983	No	25
Berlin	Jared	SC	Engineering	1/15/1982	Yes	100
Solomon	Wendy	FL	Engineering	1/31/1985	No	50
Parulis	Christa	MD	Liberal Arts	7/15/1982	No	50
Weissman	Kimberly	FL	Liberal Arts	11/11/1984	Yes	63
Watson	Ana	FL	Liberal Arts	8/1/1985	Yes	70
Camejo	Oscar	NY	Liberal Arts	3/10/1979	Yes	100
Huerta	Carlos	NY	Undecided	6/18/1985	No	15
Frazier	Steven	MD	Undecided	9/9/1978	No	35
Coe	Bradley	CA	Undecided	8/22/1981	No	52
Cornell	Ryan	GA	Undecided	9/30/1984	No	45
Zacco	Michelle	MA	Undecided	10/24/1985	No	21

Figure 2.19 Sorted student query results.

8) Note that an alternative solution is to drag a second *Major* field to the left of the grid, sort on it, and uncheck its "show" box. This field comes first in the sort order, but it does not appear in the output, so the result looks as we want.

9) Suppose we want the query to include GPAs. In an empty field at the end of the grid, enter "GPA: =GradePoints/Credits". Make sure the capitalization and spelling in this formula exactly match the field names. If "[]" automatically appears around a field name, it is correct. Note that the "GPA:" at the beginning of the expression specifies that the name of the calculated field is "GPA."

10) Press "!/Run" to view the results (Figure 2.20). If Access asks you to enter a parameter value when you run the query, then you misspelled or miscapitalized one of the names. The formatting capabilities of queries are much more limited than for forms and reports, but it is possible to right-click a column in design view to bring up its property sheet, and select an output format. For example, we can select the "Fixed" format with three digits to output the GPA.

Last Name ▾	First Name ▾	Stat ▾	Major ▾	BirthDat ▾	FinancialAi ▾	Credit ▾	GPA ▾
Watson	Ana	FL	Business	4/18/1985	No	30	2.500
Gibson	Christopher	FL	Business	3/12/1983	Yes	35	1.714
DiGiacomo	Kevin	FL	Business	5/31/1982	Yes	105	3.571
Adili	Ronnie	MN	Business	6/1/1985	No	60	2.583
Ramsay	Robert	NY	Business	5/1/1984	Yes	50	3.240
Price	Lori	CA	Communication	7/1/1982	Yes	24	1.750
Ortiz	Frances	CO	Communication	2/3/1984	Yes	28	2.143
Faulkner	Eileen	FL	Communication	9/12/1985	No	30	2.667
Joseph	Cedric	GA	Communication	4/12/1984	Yes	45	3.778
Slater	Erica	IL	Communication	5/1/1982	Yes	105	3.714
Korba	Nickolas	CA	Education	11/11/1981	No	100	1.660
Zimmerman	Kimberly	TX	Education	4/18/1980	No	120	3.292
Heltzer	Peter	FL	Engineering	3/8/1983	No	25	4.000
Solomon	Wendy	FL	Engineering	1/31/1985	No	50	3.500
Berlin	Jared	SC	Engineering	1/15/1982	Yes	100	2.500
Weissman	Kimberly	FL	Liberal Arts	11/11/1984	Yes	63	2.635
Watson	Ana	FL	Liberal Arts	8/1/1985	Yes	70	2.786
Parulis	Christa	MD	Liberal Arts	7/15/1982	No	50	1.800
Camejo	Oscar	NY	Liberal Arts	3/10/1979	Yes	100	2.800
Coe	Bradley	CA	Undecided	8/22/1981	No	52	2.750
Cornell	Ryan	GA	Undecided	9/30/1984	No	45	1.778
Zacco	Michelle	MA	Undecided	10/24/1985	No	21	3.238
Frazier	Steven	MD	Undecided	9/9/1978	No	35	1.286
Huerta	Carlos	NY	Undecided	6/18/1985	No	15	2.667

Figure 2.20 Student query results with a calculated field.

11) Remove all prior sort directives by changing them to "not sorted," and then sort "Descending" by GPA. When we run the query, we now see a list of students sorted from best to worst GPA.

12) We now explore applying data selection criteria. First return to design view, then type "Business" in the "Criteria" row under "Major." Note that Access will insert the quotes automatically because the *Major* attribute has the (short) text datatype. However, you can also type the quotes manually (Figure 2.21).

Field:	FirstName	State	Major	BirthDate	FinancialAid	Credits	GPA: [GradePoints]/[Credits]
Table:	Students	Students	Students	Students	Students	Students	
Sort:							Descending
Show:	☑	☑	☑	☑	☑	☑	☑
Criteria:			"Business"				
or:							

Figure 2.21 Adding selection criteria to the query grid.

Specifying this criterion reduces the output to business majors only.

13) Since we know the major is business, we could uncheck "Show" under "Major" – note that we can still apply a criterion to a field we are not showing. Try this, then check "show" again to get the major back in the output.

14) Now type "FL" in the "State" criterion on the same row. Note that criteria on the same row are combined with a logical AND operation. We now get only business majors from Florida.

15) If we want business majors *or* students from Florida (or both), we put "FL" on a different row. Access first combines each criterion row with AND, and then combines the rows with OR. This setup allows for complex criteria such as:

```
((Major="Business") AND (State="FL"))
            OR
((Major="Communications") AND (FinancialAid=Yes))
```

There are a number of additional ways of specifying criteria in each individual query cell. For example:

- We can also use the criterion "Not *value*," as in "Not Communications."
- Other criterion formats for are possible, for example, for a numeric field like *Credits* or GPA:
  o < *number*
  o <= *number*
  o > *number*
  o > = *number*
  o < > *number* (meaning "not equal")
  o = *number* (equivalent to just "*number*")
  o "Between *number1* And *number2*" (this could be done by combining the > = and < = criteria above, but that would involve extra non-shown fields, so "between" is more compact. Note that "between" includes the specified range values, that is, Between 10 and 20 includes the values 10 and 20.
  o Dates are treated like numbers, but should be quoted with the "#" character. For example, all dates in 1984 or 1985 may be selected through the criterion Between #1/1/1984# And #12/31/1985#.
- You may embed an "or" operation within a cell to force "or" to be evaluated before "and". For example, if you put "Business" Or "Communications" within a single cell, it will force the "or" operation to occur before performing "and" with any other criteria on the same row.

Note that, in addition to datasheet view and design view, there is a third way to view a query called "SQL view" (in the IT world, "SQL" is often pronounced "sequel"). SQL is a standard computer language for describing queries and is embedded (with minor variations in syntax) in nearly all relational database systems. When you run a query formulated with Access' query design view, Access translates the query specification into SQL and then executes it. We will examine SQL more closely later in this book. SQL can be valuable to know because it can be used with essentially any database system, not just Access. You may use the SQL View to see how some of your queries look when translated into SQL.

Common Datatypes in MS Access

We have already covered, by example, most of the principal datatypes in Microsoft Access. This section summarizes the properties of datatypes we have already learned about, and introduces a few more that are often useful. Table 2.3 summarizes the most common Access datatypes.

The Short Text datatype is perhaps the most commonly used in Access and is for holding relatively small pieces of text up to 255 characters long. In older versions of Access, this datatype is simply called "Text." Throughout this book, we will refer to this datatype simply as "text." For each Short Text field, you specify a "Field Size," which indicates the maximum number of characters allowed. The storage consumed per record is $n + 1$ bytes, where n is the number of characters entered. Therefore, the amount of storage used can vary

Table 2.3 Common MS Access datatypes.

Datatype	Part of main datatype	Purpose	Storage consumed per record
Short Text		Limited-length text up to 255 characters	$n + 1$ bytes, where n is the number of stored characters
Long Text		Free-form text	8–10 bytes, plus one byte per character actually used
Byte	Number	Whole numbers in the range 0–255	1 byte
Integer	Number	Whole numbers in the range −32,768 and 32,767	2 bytes
Long Integer	Number	Whole numbers in the range −2,147,483,648 and 2,147,483,647	4 bytes
Single	Number	Numbers containing fractions, up to about 6 digits of accuracy	4 bytes
Double	Number	Numbers containing fractions, up to about 14 digits of accuracy	8 bytes
Date/Time		Points in time or lengths of time	8 bytes
Currency		Amounts of money	8 bytes
Autonumber		Synthetic keys (see Chapters 4–5)	4 bytes in the most common case
Yes/No		True/false or yes/no values	1 byte

from record to record. In other database software, the amount of storage consumed per row might simply be *s* or *s* + 1 bytes for every row, where *s* is the field size.

The Long Text datatype can store essentially unlimited amounts of text, such as commentaries or narratives. In older versions of Access, it was called the "Memo" datatype. A Memo field uses 8–10 bytes of space in each record, plus one additional byte for each character of text actually entered. This datatype cannot be sorted and cannot be used for primary keys.

The Byte datatype can store whole numbers between 0 and 255. It cannot store negative numbers. To use this datatype, select the principal datatype "Number" and then select a field size of "Byte" in the properties pane. As its name suggests, this datatype uses one byte of storage per table record.

The Integer datatype can store whole numbers between −32,768 and 32,767. To use this datatype, select the principal datatype "Number" and then select a field size of "Integer" in the properties pane. In other computer environments, this datatype is often referred to as a "short integer." It uses two bytes of storage per table row.

The Long Integer datatype is the most common way to store whole numbers, and can store numbers in the range -2^{31} through $2^{31} - 1$, which is approximately plus or minus two billion. To use this datatype, select the principal datatype "Number" and then select a field size of "Long Integer" in the properties pane. A Long Integer field consumes four bytes of storage per table row.

The Single datatype can store essentially arbitrary numbers that may contain fractions. A "Single" field uses four bytes of storage per table row. Internally, the Single datatype stores numbers using a system resembling scientific notation with approximately six decimal digits of precision. To use this datatype, select the principal datatype "Number" and then select a field size of "Single" in the properties pane. Because of the somewhat limited arithmetic precision of the Single datatype, it is more customary to use the Double datatype (see immediately below), which has far greater precision at the cost of using more storage.

The Double datatype, like the Single datatype, can store numbers containing fractions. However, it has an arithmetic precision of about 14 decimal digits, and can thus be far more precise than the Single datatype. The Double datatype's higher accuracy comes at a cost of consuming eight bytes of storage per table row, as opposed to the four bytes per table row consumed by the Single datatype. In the current era of inexpensive storage, the Double datatype is the most common way to store numbers that might be extremely large or contain fractions, with the exception of amounts of money, for which the Currency datatype (see below) is recommended. To use the Double datatype, select the principal datatype "Number" and then select a field size of "Double" in the properties pane.

The Date/Time datatype is the preferred way to store dates, instants in time, or spans of time. To an accuracy of one second, it can represent any moment in time between the beginning of January 1 of the year 100 to the end of the year 9999. A Date/Time field consumes eight bytes per table row.

The Currency datatype is the preferred way to store amounts of money. It resembles the Double number datatype, but its arithmetic accuracy properties are somewhat different: it can store only 4 digits after the decimal point and 15 digits before the decimal point. On the other hand, when performing calculations on very large numbers or large sets of numbers, it is less susceptible to small rounding errors than the Double datatype. A Currency field consumes eight bytes of storage per table row.

The Autonumber datatype is often used for primary key fields when the data themselves do not contain convenient primary key attributes. This topic will be discussed in detail in Chapters 4 and 5. In the typical case, an Autonumber is essentially a variant of the Long Integer datatype.

The Yes/No datatype holds simple Yes/No, True/False, or On/Off values. In other computer environments, this kind of datatype is often called "logical" or "Boolean." A Yes/No field consumes one byte of storage per table row.

Exercises

2.1 Create a database called "countries.accdb" that contains a single table COUNTRY. The fields in this table should be as follows:
- An ID number (Number/Integer; this field should be the primary key)
- Country name (text/50 characters)
- Total area in square kilometers (Number/Double)
- Land area in square kilometers (Number/Double)
- Population (Number/Double)
- GDP (Number/Double)
- Oil consumption (Number/Double)

Note that total area and land area are different, because land area does not include lakes, rivers, and coastal waters claimed as part of the country's territory. GDP is measured in US dollars per year and oil consumption in barrels per day.

Once you have saved this table, close it and select the COUNTRY table in the left panel Access window, select the DATABASE TOOLS tab, and then click "Database Documenter." In the resulting dialog box, check the box next to COUNTRY in the "Tables" pane, and click OK. An "Object Definition" window should then appear, containing a report.

2.2 Download and save the file countrydata.txt from the textbook website. Then load it into the COUNTRY table you created in the previous exercise by selecting the EXTERNAL DATA tab and pressing the "Text File" button. Use the "Browse" button to navigate to the previously saved `countrydata.txt` file, and select the "Append a copy of the records to the table" option. Click through the resulting wizard by pressing "Next" or "Finish" at each step to import the data (the file is delimited by the character "tab," which is the default). View the resulting table.

2.3 Consider the database you created in Exercise 2.2. Using the form wizard (or by any other method you like), construct a form linked to this table that looks approximately like Figure 2.22.

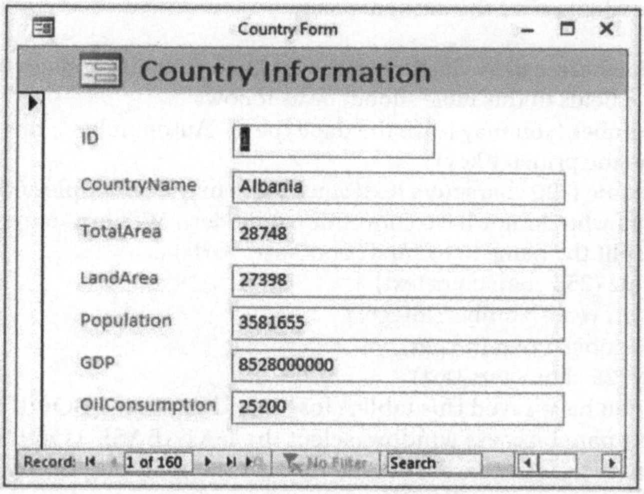

Figure 2.22 Desired appearance of the country form.

2.4 Perform the following queries on the database you created in Exercise 2.2. Make sure that the fields appear in the same order as requested.

A Show the name and total area of all countries having at least 2 million square km *total* area. List the countries from largest to smallest total area.

B For each country that has at least 1 million square km *land* area *and* at least 20 million people, show the country name, land area, population, and population density, which is the population divided by the land area. Display the population density column in the "Fixed" format with two decimal places. Sort the results from the least densely populated to the most densely populated.

C Show the name, land area, total area, and population of each country with a population of at least 1 million, along with the fraction of the total area that is made up of land. Display this last calculated field in the "Percent" format with two digits after the decimal point. Sort from the smallest to largest fraction of land, and only show countries that are less than 95% land.

D A country's "oil per capita" is its amount of oil consumed per person per *year*, divided by its population (to convert barrels per day to barrels per year, assume that a year is exactly 365 days). For each country with at least 40 million people *or* at least 2 million barrels per day consumption, show the country name, oil consumption, population, and oil per capita. Sort the results so that the highest oil per capita appears at the top of the output and display this field in "Fixed" format with two digits after the decimal place.

2.5 Create a database called "histbooks.accdb" that contains a single table BOOK. The fields in this table should be as follows:
- An ID number (you may leave the datatype as "Autonumber"; this field should be the primary key)
- Author name (120 characters text; since there may be multiple authors, or authors who do not have conventional modern Western names, we will not split the name in to "first" and "last" parts)
- Book name (255 characters text)
- Publication year (Number/Integer)
- Pages (Number/Long Integer)
- Category (25 characters text)

Once you have saved this table, close it and select the BOOK table in the left panel Access window, select the DATABASE TOOLS tab, and then click "Database Documenter." In the resulting dialog box, check the box next to BOOK in the "Tables" pane, and click OK. An "Object Definition" window should then appear, containing a report.

2.6 Download and save the file `BooksData.txt` from the textbook website. Then load it into BOOK table of the database you created in Exercise 2.5 by selecting the "External Data" tab and pressing the "Text File" button. Use the "Browse" button to navigate to the saved `BooksData.txt` file, click "Open," and then select the "Append a copy of the records to the table" option. Click through the resulting wizard to import the data. View the resulting table in "Datasheet View."

2.7 Create a form linked to the BOOK table and then make minor modifications until it looks approximately like Figure 2.23. Make sure the form has a header like "History Book Database" in Figure 2.23 (and not just "BOOK").

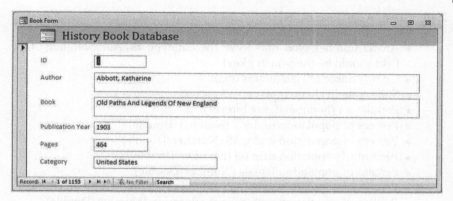

Figure 2.23 Desired appearance of the history book form.

2.8 Using the history books database from Problem 2.6, perform the following queries. Make sure the fields are displayed in the same order as they are requested. In these exercises, "title" should be considered synonymous with "book name."

  A Show the author, title, year, and pages of all books with less than 20 pages.

  B Show the author and title and year of all "Ancient" books published in 1970 or after. Do not display the category.

  C Show the author, title, pages, and year for all "United States" books published in the 1920s. Do not display the category.

  D Show the title, pages, year, and category of all "Ancient" books published in the 1940s, along with all "England & Empire" books published in the 1930s. Sort the results alphabetically by title.

  E Show the title, author, pages, and category for all books with at least 800 pages. Sort alphabetically by category; within each category, sort by number of pages, with the largest number of pages first. Note that the category should be displayed after the number of pages.

2.9 From the database of Problem 2.6, produce a report showing all the fields except the ID number. It should be grouped by author; the author should not appear in the detail section, but only in the header for each group. Within each author, books should be sorted chronologically by publication year (earliest books first). At the end of the section for each author, show the average number of pages for books by that author, rounded to the nearest whole number of pages. Make sure no box or border is visible around the average number of pages (note that the Access function for averaging is called Avg). Make sure the entirety of each column label is visible, and insert spaces into column names so they are readable, for example "Publication Year" instead of "PublicationYear."

2.10 Create a database called `counties.accdb` that contains a single table COUNTY. The fields in this table should be as follows:
- An ID number (you may leave the datatype as "AutoNumber"; this field should be the primary key)
- County name (30 characters text)
- State code (2 characters text)
- Population (Number/Long Integer)
- Percent of population under 5 (Number/Double)
- Percent of population under 18 (Number/Double)
- Percent of population over 65 (Number/Double)
- Percent of population female (Number/Double)
- Percent of population with high-school education (Number/Double)
- Percent of population with college education (Number/Double)
- Per capita income (Currency)
- Land area in square miles (Number/Double)

  Once you have saved this table, close it and select the COUNTY table in the left panel Access window, select the DATABASE TOOLS tab, and then click "Database Documenter." In the resulting dialog box, check the box next to COUNTY in the "Tables" pane, and click OK. An "Object Definition" window should then appear, containing a report.

2.11 Download and save the file `counties-a-through-d.txt` from the book website. This file contains all counties in the United States in states whose names start with the letters "A" through "D." Load this file into the COUNTY table of the database you created in the previous problem by selecting the "External Data" tab and pressing the left-hand "Text File" button (the right-hand "Text File" button is for transferring data out of the database; we want to transfer in). Use the "Browse" button to navigate to the saved `counties-a-through-d.txt` file, and select the "Append a copy of the records to the table" option. Click through the resulting wizard to import the data. View the resulting table in "Datasheet View."

2.12 Consider the database you created in the previous exercise. Using the form wizard, or any other method you like, construct a form for this table that looks approximately like Figure 2.24. Make sure the form has a header like "County Database" in Figure 2.24.

2.13 Perform the following queries on the database you constructed in Exercise 2.11. For each query, paste both the query results and a screen shot of the query grid into an MS Word document.

  A Show the name, state, population, and land area for all counties with at least 1 million people.

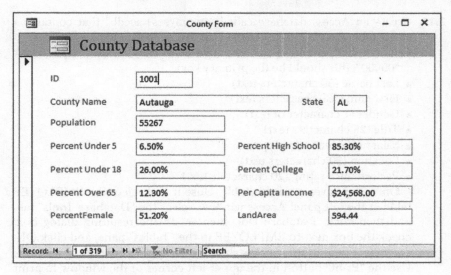

Figure 2.24 Desired appearance of the county form.

B Show the name, population, and per capita income of all counties in Delaware ("DE"). Do not display the state.

C Show the name, population, and per capita income for all Arizona ("AR") counties whose per capita income is at least $20,000. Do not display the state.

D Show the name, state, percentage of the population under five, and percentage of females for all counties that have more than 10% of the population under five, or less than 40% of the population female. Note that you should enter 10% as "0.1" and 40% as "0.4."

E For all counties that have a land area of at least 5000 square miles and are not in Alaska ("AK"), show the county name, state, population, land area, and percentage of the population with a college degree. Sort the results by population, with the largest populations coming first.

2.14 Produce a report showing each county's name, population, percentage of population under 18, percentage of population over 65, per capita income, and land area (in that order). It should be grouped by state; the state abbreviation need not appear in the detail section, but only in the header for each group. Within each state, counties should be sorted by population, with the largest population first. At the end of each state, show the total population of the state. Make sure no box or border is visible around the total population. Print enough of the report so that all the information related to the first state ("AK") is included. Make sure the entire contents of the population field are visible.

2.15 Create an Access database called "employees1.accdb" that contains a single table EMPLOYEE. The fields in this table should be as follows:
- A five-digit employee ID (use five characters of text, input mask "00000"; this should be the primary key)
- Last name (50 characters text)
- First name (30 characters text)
- Gender (1 character of text)
- Title (25 characters text)
- Salary (Currency datatype)
- Location (30 characters text)
- Performance rating (20 characters text)

Once you have saved this table, close it and select the EMPLOYEE table in the left panel Access window, select the "Database Tools" tab, and then click "Database Documenter." In the resulting dialog box, check the box next to EMPLOYEE in the "Tables" pane, and click OK. An "object definition" window should then appear, containing a report. Use the "Print" button in the upper left corner of the window to print this report.

2.16 Download and save the file employees-data.txt from the book website. Then load it into the EMPLOYEE table of the database you created in the previous problem by selecting the "External Data" tab and pressing the left-hand "Text File" button (the right-hand "Text File" button is for transferring data out of the database; we want to transfer data in). Use the "Browse" button to navigate to the saved employees-data.txt file, and select the "Append a copy of the records to the table" option. Click through the resulting wizard to import the data. View the resulting table in "Datasheet View."

2.17 In the database you created in Exercise 2.16, use the form wizard to construct a simple form for viewing/editing the employee table you created in the previous exercise. Add a form header reading "Employee Information."

2.18 Perform the following queries on the database you constructed in Exercise 2.16.
- **A** First name, last name, title, and salary of all employees making at least $50,000.
- **B** First name, last name, gender, and salary for all Boston employees who make less than $30,000. The location field should not appear in the output, and the output rows should be sorted alphabetically by last name.

C First name, last name, title, and salary for all senior account reps who make at least $60,000 and all account reps who make at least $45,000. The rows should be sorted from highest salary to lowest. Employees with the same salary should be sorted alphabetically by last name (but the columns should appear in the order specified). For both account reps and senior account reps, only include employees with "Excellent" performance ratings.

2.19 Using the same database from Exercise 2.16, create a query that shows the ID, first name, last name, salary, location, and performance rating for all female employees whose performance rating is either "Excellent" or "Good." Use this query to produce a report that groups these employees by location and presents them alphabetically by last name within each location. Each detail line of the report should show the employees' attributes in the following order: ID, first name, last name, salary, and performance rating. At the end of each location, there should be a "footer" that gives the number of such employees at the location and their average salary rounded to the nearest dollar (to obtain this rounding, set the appropriate text box to use the "currency" format with its decimal places property set to "0"). At the end of the report, include a similar footer given the total number of such employees and their average salary.

3

Introduction to Data Management
and Database Design

Introduction to Data Management

We have learned a bit about some of the basic properties of the relational database tables in which business data are typically stored. We will now discuss *data management*, which refers to how data are organized within database systems and across multiple database systems. Proper organization of a database, for example, allows users to readily perform actions such as adding, updating, or erasing information. Included under the topic of data management are issues such as the following:

- How many tables should an information system's database have?
- What data should be stored in each table?
- How should the tables be linked to one another?
- How many different information systems should an organization have?
- What should be the function of each system?
- What information should each system contain?
- How should the systems interact?

This textbook will focus on the data management issue of how tables should be organized within a single database system. This area is well understood, and its basic concepts are not too difficult. As to how entire systems should interact, this book takes a more descriptive, superficial approach. This subject is a less well-developed area of database theory, sometimes called *information architecture*, and is generally considered an advanced topic.

General Data Management Issues

One common data management problem facing modern organizations is a *massive and increasing amount of data*. Historical data are often kept for extended periods, so typically data arrive faster than they are deleted. New

Introductory Relational Database Design for Business, with Microsoft Access, First Edition.
Jonathan Eckstein and Bonnie R. Schultz.
© 2018 John Wiley & Sons Ltd. Published 2018 by John Wiley & Sons Ltd.

technologies mean that gathering new data becomes progressively easier and faster. So, not only is the total volume of data increasing, it tends to accumulate at an accelerating rate.

One question to consider is whether a firm should take advantage of every possible opportunity to gather data. For example, any website can gather "clickstream" data: records of exactly how users moved around the site, and even how long they let the mouse hover near certain objects on screen. This information may or may not be of much value, but it can accumulate quickly.

Modern organizations may accumulate some kinds of data with little idea of how they might be useful. Business consultants are now frequently hired with instructions to find value in data that have already been collected, without a specific purpose in mind. Traditionally, organizations tended to gather data only after they had identified a specific operational question or problem to which the data might pertain.

Many organizations experience *data dispersal*, meaning that data tend to be scattered throughout the organization. Older organizations often have many "legacy" systems that may communicate relatively poorly, causing coordination problems. Thus, it is often desirable to centralize data storage, but this is not necessarily always the case – it might be better to leave departments or working groups "in charge" of the data they use the most, because they are the most motivated to ensure that it is up to date, complete, and accurate. It is also costly, risky, and disruptive to replace older "legacy" information subsystems that are working smoothly. Replacing multiple smaller systems with one larger one can often be very complicated and costly. Sometimes it may be better to create "federated" data sources that dynamically combine information from constituent systems.

Whether or not it takes the form of a federated system, most organizations find it necessary to have some *data fusion* and *coordination*, in which one combines data from multiple sources, sometimes from outside the organization (either from the public domain or by purchase). It may also be advantageous to share some information with suppliers, vendors, or business partners. For example, sharing information about inventories can reduce inventory fluctuations and costs throughout a supply chain.

Other issues are *data accuracy* and *quality*: many organizations have far more errors in their databases than they are aware of. Two causes of data accuracy problems are unnecessary data redundancy and poor coordination between different systems requiring the same data, but there are also other causes, such as lack of employee incentives to enter data correctly, and inadequate error checking of manually entered information.

Another issue is *data security*, which concerns protecting data from unwanted deletion, corruption, or misuse. Data security threats may be either intentional – for example, from hackers or identity thieves – or unintentional, such as from hardware or software malfunctions.

Data security and quality are more easily jeopardized the larger and more complicated an information system becomes, and the more users it has. Therefore, these concerns also tend to grow with the size of an organization.

Classifying Information Systems Tasks: Transaction and Analytical Processing

Information systems perform processing tasks that can be classified into specific categories.

Transaction processing (often called "TPS") involves keeping track of day-to-day events, such as logging orders or shipments, and posting entries to accounting ledgers. In terms of data tables, transaction processing means an ongoing process of adding rows (for example, to reflect a customer placing a new order), modifying table cells scattered throughout a database (for example, if a customer changes their telephone number), and perhaps deleting rows. Typically, each transaction modifies, adds, or deletes a limited number of rows.

Analytical processing means combining data from many or all table rows in order to obtain "higher-level" information. An example of analytical processing would be computing the number of customer orders and total dollar value of orders for the current month and comparing these amounts to similar figures for the previous month.

Analytical processing can be as simple as sorting, grouping, and summarizing, the types of calculations available in an Access query or report. For example, one might want to provide all product development team managers with summaries of their teams' costs for the month, broken down by cost category. This kind of application may be called "classic" MIS (management information systems).

Analytical processing can also be far more sophisticated than what is available in standard queries and reports. For example, *data mining* refers to using statistical or other mathematical techniques to discover data patterns that might not be apparent in standard reports.

Decision support involves using available data to help firms formulate potentially complicated plans or decisions. An example of such a problem might be planning how to route 400 shipments from 20 warehouses to 100 customers at minimum cost.

Database systems like Access can perform simple analytical processing, such as reports, but do not ordinarily perform data mining or decision support by themselves. For such uses, they usually need to be connected to other software modules or enhanced with custom-written programming.

Sometimes it can be a mistake to perform transaction processing and analytical processing on the same database, especially if the volume of transactions is high and the analytical processing is time consuming or complex. The analytical processing may make the transaction system run slowly, or the transactions may interfere with the analytical processing and make *it* run too slowly. Furthermore, if an analytical processing step takes too long, the data it is using may change in the middle of its calculation, causing inconsistent results or errors. "Locking" data to avoid this problem may in turn block transaction processing.

Rather than running transaction and analytical processing simultaneously on the same system, it may be better to make a copy or "snapshot" of the database used for the transaction system, and perform analytical processing on this copy. Such a copy is often called a *data warehouse*. Using this technique, one can pursue analysis on the data warehouse without disrupting the transaction system, and run numerous transactions without disrupting this data analysis. The data warehouse will not reflect the very latest transactions, but for large-scale aggregate analysis, that is probably not a major problem.

Another reason to create a data warehouse might be to consolidate information from several different transaction systems so they can be analyzed together.

What Is Wrong with Just One Table?

At this point, we begin delving into the details of data management concerning how to organize data in multiple tables. So far, we have considered databases with only one table, but such "flat-file" databases have significant limitations, as we will now see.

Suppose we are operating a database for a bank and have the following single table:

LOAN(LoanID, Date, Amt, Rate, Term, Type, FirstName, LastName, Address,
      City, State, Zip, Phone)

This notation indicates that there is a table called LOAN whose fields are called *LoanID*, *Date*, and so forth, through *Phone* (datatypes are not specified in this "outline" shorthand notation, which we will continue using frequently throughout this book). For example, if you were keeping data in an Excel spreadsheet, you would be essentially forced to adopt this "flat-file" strategy.

Now suppose that a customer has two different loans. The Loan IDs for the two loans will be different, so information about the loans will be stored on different rows of the table. At least some of the dates, amounts, rates, terms, and types will probably be different, but the customer name and address information should be exactly the same. However, you must store this information twice, and therefore it has the potential to get "out of sync." This situation creates three classic problems:

- If the customer changes their address, you risk having the database store two different addresses. For example, if the customer calls in reference to loan *A* and gives you the new address, loan *B* might still have the old address.

To avoid such errors, you would need to search the database for all occurrences of the same customer, and change their addresses as well. This kind of problem is known as an *update anomaly*.

- Suppose you would like to record information – such as an address and phone number – pertaining to a customer who does not yet have a loan (for example, because the loan application/approval process for their first loan is incomplete). Unfortunately, there is no natural place in the database to store this information. You must create a "dummy" loan (for example, with a special "type" indicating it is not a real loan) in order to be able to store such data. This kind of problem is called an *insertion anomaly*.

- Suppose a customer pays off their last outstanding loan and is consequently deleted from the loan table. As a result, you lose all record of the customer's address, and you are now unable to contact them in future. This kind of problem is called a *deletion anomaly*.

Anomalies like these can clearly create serious difficulties for transaction processing. For analytical processing performed on data warehouses, some anomalies might not be problematic because we do not perform individual transaction operations on the data warehouse itself. Instead, we periodically reload the warehouse data from the transaction system. We now focus on how to combat anomalies in a transaction processing setting.

Repeating Groups

One "old-fashioned" approach to removing anomalies is called *repeating groups*. To illustrate this approach, suppose that we know that no customer can have more than three loans. Then we could define a wider table like this:

LOAN(FirstName, LastName, Address, City, State, Zip, Phone, LoanID1, Date1, Amt1, Rate1, Term1, Type1, LoanID2, Date2, Amt2, Rate2, Term2, Type2, LoanID3, Date3, Amt3, Rate3, Term3, Type3)

This table has 25 columns: the first 7 describe the customer, the next 6 describe the customer's first loan, the following 6 describe the customer's second loan, and the last 6 describe the customer's third loan. For customers with fewer than three loans, the unused *LoanIDn,...,Typen* fields can contain special codes, such as spaces or zeroes, to indicate that they are not "real." The fields (*LoanID, Date, Amt, Rate, Term, Type*) are called a *repeating group* because essentially the same fields repeat some number of times (in this case, three times). This approach might also be called a "nested table" or "subtable" approach because each record of the main table may be considered to have a subsidiary table containing the six fields *LoanIDn,...,Typen*.

While this approach usually avoids simple anomalies, it has some drawbacks. Depending on exactly how it is implemented, we may have to estimate beforehand the maximum number of times the group can repeat (in this case, three). If we exceed the limit, for example, because a customer has four loans, anomalies once again become a problem.

We can avoid this possibility by choosing a very large number of repeats, but that might be very wasteful of storage space, depending on the exact way the data are stored, and most of the table will likely go unused. It can be difficult to decide on the proper maximum number of repeats.

We may think of repeating groups as being like an "outline" or hierarchical data format. We can visualize each row in the above table in the following outline form:

- Information about a particular customer
  - Information about the customer's first loan
  - Information about the customer's second loan
  - Information about the customer's third loan

The philosophy of relational databases (including Access) is that while this outline form may be a very appropriate way to *present* an organization's data to human beings, it is not the ideal way to store it inside a computer. The preferred approach instead is to use multiple tables and *foreign keys*.

An Illustration of Multiple Tables and Foreign Keys

We now illustrate how the multiple-table/foreign-key approach applies to our loan example. Soon, we will explore the theoretical underpinnings of this approach and consider numerous other business examples. For now, we give a simple overview by means of the loans example we have already presented.

We also introduce the notion of *entity-relationship* (ER) *modeling*. From this perspective, the problem with the one-table approach to our loan database is that we were trying to use a single table to store information pertaining to two different *entities*, that is, two different categories of things, people, or events. In this case, there are two entities, namely, customers and loans, which we may depict as in Figure 3.1.

Figure 3.1 The CUSTOMER and LOAN entities.

If we think about one customer, how many loans could they be associated with? Potentially, a customer may have "many" loans: in principle, a customer may have any nonnegative whole number of loans. On the other hand, if we consider a single loan, how many customers should it be associated with? A loan is taken out by just one customer. Therefore, we say customers and loans are in a *one-to-many relationship*, with the customer entity being the "one" and the loan entity being the "many." This situation is depicted in Figure 3.2.

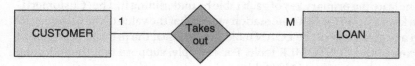

Figure 3.2 Completed ER diagram for customers and loans.

This kind of picture is called an *entity-relationship diagram*, or simply an *ER diagram*. The diamond containing "takes out" is just a "comment" relating the abstract form of the diagram to the original business situation and is not a critical structural part of the diagram.

To translate an ER diagram into a database, the key principle is that *each entity corresponds to its own table*. Each table contains fields for the attributes or properties of the corresponding kind of entity. In this case, for example, we should have two tables:

1) A table for customers storing the properties of customers, such as first name, last name, address, and so forth.
2) A table for loans storing properties of loans, such as the starting date, amount, rate, term, and loan type.

However, we must be careful to make the right connections between the tables: for example, we need to be able to tell which customer owns a particular loan. To make the correct connections, it is helpful if each table has a *primary key*, that is, a field that uniquely identifies each row.

The loan table has an obvious primary key, namely, the loan's ID, as no two loans can have the same ID number.

For customers, let us create a similar key and call it (for example) *CustomerID*. The primary key is necessary because there needs to be an unambiguous way to identify each customer, and a customer's name is not sufficient because two customers could share a name, especially if it is common (such as "John Smith").

For each loan, we store not only the *LoanID*, date, amount, rate, term, and type information, but also a *CustomerID*; the purpose of the *CustomerID* in each record of the LOAN table is to indicate which customer is associated with the loan. We may then describe the structure of the database with the following outline notation:

CUSTOMER(<u>CustomerID</u>, FirstName, LastName, Address, City, State,
      Zip, Phone)

LOAN(<u>LoanID</u>, Date, Amt, Rate, Term, Type, CustomerID)
    CustomerID foreign key to CUSTOMER

We indicate the primary key of each table by underlining it. The "CustomerID foreign key to CUSTOMER" annotation means that the value of the *CustomerID* field in any given row of the LOAN table should equal the primary key value of some row of the CUSTOMER table. For example, suppose that the following row is somewhere in the LOAN table:

(L7838, 2/1/2010, $250,000, 4.3%, 10, "Home Equity", C231)

This row indicates that the loan whose ID is L7838 started on February 1, 2010, with a principal amount of $250,000, a 4.3% interest rate, and a term of 10 years. Furthermore, it is a home equity loan and was taken out by the customer whose *CustomerID* is C231. For more information about that customer, we would first refer to the CUSTOMER table and find the row with primary key C231. From that record, we can determine more information about that customer. For example, if we find

(C231, "Joseph", "Blowe", "284 Random Road", "Edison", NJ, 08341, 7323738391)

in the CUSTOMER table, we can then infer that the first name of the customer who took out loan L7838 is "Joseph." This kind of tracing of a foreign key in one table to the primary key in another is called a *join* operation. We could use repeated operations of this kind, for example, to reconstruct the previous one-table form of the database, if we wanted to view the data in that way. But the multi-table approach is a much better way to store the underlying information, because we avoid the anomalies we discussed earlier.

Specifically, even if a customer has more than one loan, their address is stored in just one place. Changing the address information in the CUSTOMER table effectively changes the address for all of the customer's loans. Thus, there is no danger of update anomalies.

We can store information about a customer who does not have any loans without having to employ any special codes or "tricks." We simply enter the customer data into a row of the CUSTOMER table, and as soon as the customer does indeed have a loan, we start to create matching records in the LOAN table. As a result, there are no insertion anomalies.

Deleting a customer's last remaining loan does not delete their record in the CUSTOMER table, so it does not cause us to lose the customer's address data. Therefore, we do not encounter deletion anomalies.

Primary Keys and Composite Keys

A *primary key* is an attribute or a collection of attributes whose value(s) uniquely and concisely identify each row in a table.

If we suppose that the YWCA allows a member to participate in only one activity at a time, then the only possible primary key for the table above is *MemberID*. That is because each YWCA member can appear at most once in the table, and the value of *MemberID* uniquely identifies any given member. Therefore, each value of *MemberID* can occur once in the table, and it can be used as a primary key.

The *Activity* and *Fee* fields lack this uniqueness property. Any given value, such as "Zumba" for *Activity* or $150 for *Fee*, might occur more than once.

Realistically, your local YWCA would probably not restrict most members from participating in as many activities as they might want. So, let us change our assumptions and suppose that we allow members to participate in more than one activity. This situation might result in a larger version of the ACTIVITY table, as shown in Table 4.2.

Table 4.2 Sample table of YWCA activities, multiple activities permitted per member.

MemberID	Activity	Fee
121	Ceramics	$145
121	Swimming	$200
202	Zumba	$150
202	Vegetarian Cooking	$125
175	Mommy & Me Cooking	$125
199	Zumba	$150
175	Poetry Workshop	$125
215	Tennis	$200
215	Sculpture	$150

As you can see, the *MemberID* field by itself is no longer sufficient to uniquely identify a row of the table. For example, member 121 has two records that respectively list ceramics and swimming as activities. So how can we uniquely identify rows in the table?

The answer is to use what is called a *composite key* or *concatenated key*, consisting of the two columns (*MemberID*, *Activity*). *Concatenation* means appending two or more pieces of information to one another. For example, the concatenation of the strings "fox" and "trot" is "foxtrot." Using a composite key consisting of several fields means that you can use their concatenated, combined value to uniquely identify a record in the table. In the preceding example, there is no point in the same member simultaneously signing up more than once for the same activity, so a single combined value such as (121, "Ceramics") for (*MemberID, Activity*) should only occur in a single row of the table. Therefore, it is possible to use (*MemberID, Activity*) as a composite primary key, and in fact there is no other reasonable choice.

It must be emphasized that **a table can have only one primary key,** but sometimes the primary key may consist of several fields, in which case it is called a composite primary key, as mentioned above. When only a single field makes up the primary key, it is called a *simple* primary key. Sometimes, although not in either version of the YWCA example above, there is more than one possible primary key. In this situation, each possible choice is called a *candidate key*.

As another example, consider the car data shown in Table 4.3.

Table 4.3 Sample table of car data.

LicensePlate	State	Make	Model	Year
DFP120	NJ	Honda	Fit	2012
QYR30Y	NJ	Toyota	Corolla	2009
HZN32P	MA	Ford	Taurus	2002
JWK669	OH	Toyota	Prius	2014
DFP120	TN	Honda	Odyssey	2004
278WXV	MI	Chevrolet	Cruze	2014

LicensePlate cannot be the primary key for this table because it is possible that two cars from different states can have the same license plate number (in this table, DFP120 is an example). However, if we concatenate *LicensePlate* and *State*, the resulting value, such as (DFP120, NJ) or (DFP120, TN), must be unique. Thus, (*LicensePlate, State*) is a candidate key. In fact, it is the only candidate key in this particular table, and thus the only choice of primary key, unless we were to introduce some new field.

Another rule of relational databases is that **primary keys should be minimal**. A composite key is *minimal* if every attribute in it is necessary to uniquely identify a record in the table. That is, a combination of fields is minimal if eliminating any of its attribute makes it unusable as a primary key. For example, the combination (*LicensePlate, State, Make*) in the cars table above is not minimal because we could eliminate *Make* and still have a combination (*LicensePlate, State*) that uniquely identifies each row of the table. On the other hand, (*LicensePlate, State*) is minimal because eliminating *LicensePlate* leaves us with only *State*, which is not a possible primary key, and eliminating *State* leaves only *LicensePlate*, which is also not a possible primary key. The requirement that primary keys be minimal is the reason for the word "concisely" in our definition of a primary key as a collection of attributes that uniquely and concisely identifies each table row.

There are situations in which you may want to create an additional single attribute to serve as a primary key. Such a "made-up" key is called a *synthetic key*. The possible reasons for creating synthetic keys are as follows:

• No suitable primary key is available.
• There is at least one possible composite primary key, but it is excessively complex.
• Some organizations prefer to avoid composite keys whenever possible.

We will see examples of synthetic keys later on. In MS Access, "Autonumber" fields are a common means of creating synthetic keys. Autonumber fields contain values that are automatically filled in by Access and are guaranteed to be unique in each record.

It is customary to list the primary key fields first in our outline notation, but it is not required. Since column order is unimportant in relational databases, the order in which we write down a table's fields is actually irrelevant. The only critical information is the names of fields and which ones are underlined; those that are underlined are part of the primary key.

Foreign Keys and Outline Notation

A *foreign key* is an attribute or a collection of attributes with a value that matches the primary key of a related record, usually in a different table. Consider the STATE and CITY tables shown in Table 4.4.

Under the reasonable assumption that the country would never allow two states to have the same name, there are two candidate keys for the STATE relation, *StateAbbrev* and *StateName*. Each value of these attributes can occur only once in the table, since each row describes a single state. *StateFlower* is not a candidate key, because two states could reasonably choose the same flower, and *StatePopulation* is also not a possible primary key because it is possible (although very unlikely) that two states could have exactly the same population. The combination (*StateFlower*, *StatePopulation*) is also not guaranteed to be unique since it is conceivable (but exceedingly unlikely) that two states could have the same flower and population. Any composite key including either *StateAbbrev* or *StateName* would not be minimal and so would not be an allowable choice either. Thus, we could use either *StateAbbrev* or *StateName*, but as a general rule, succinct, compact

Table 4.4 Sample data for states and cities.

StateAbbrev	StateName	StateFlower	StatePopulation
CT	Connecticut	Mountain Laurel	3,287,116
MI	Michigan	Apple Blossom	9,295,297
SD	South Dakota	Pasque	696,004
TN	Tennessee	Iris	4,877,185
TX	Texas	Bluebonnet	16,989,510

StateAbbrev	CityName	CityPopulation
CT	Hartford	139,739
CT	Madison	14,031
CT	New Haven	156,213
SD	Madison	6,257
SD	Pierre	12,906

primary keys are preferable. Therefore, most database designers would choose *StateAbbrev* as the primary key.

The CITY table presents a different situation. Neither *StateAbbrev* nor *CityName* has a unique value, because the table contains information about multiple cities in the same state, and two cities in different states can have the same name. However, assume for our purposes that the combination (*StateAbbrev, CityName*) is unique and therefore can serve as a primary key. *CityPopulation* is not guaranteed to be unique, either by itself or in combination with other fields, so (*StateAbbrev, CityName*) is the only possible choice unless we were to create a synthetic key or include a zip code field.

Note that it is also inadvisable for a primary key to include fields whose values are likely to change frequently, such as populations. Therefore, experienced database designers would never consider fields like *StatePopulation* or *CityPopulation* for inclusion in primary keys.

In the two tables above, we would naturally expect that any value of *StateAbbrev* occurring in the CITY table should match the value of *StateAbbrev* in the STATE table. For example, if there is no state with the abbreviation "ZX" in the STATE table, we should not be able to enter "ZX" as a value for *StateAbbrev* in the CITY table. In this situation, we say that *StateAbbrev* in CITY is a *foreign key* to the STATE table.

Outline notation is the standard format for expressing database designs that we will use throughout this book. For the CITY-STATE example above, it takes the following form:

STATE(<u>StateAbbrev</u>, StateName, UnionOrder, StateBird, StatePopulation)

CITY(<u>StateAbbrev</u>, <u>CityName</u>, CityPopulation)
   StateAbbrev foreign key to STATE

In this notation, note that you must underline all parts of each primary key and describe foreign keys through the annotation "*FieldName* foreign key to *TableName*" immediately below the table containing the foreign key. In the above example, "StateAbbrev foreign key to STATE" means that the value of the *StateAbbrev* attribute in the CITY table must match the value of the primary key of some record in the STATE table.

When setting up a database, the foreign key will *always* be in the "many" entity or table; otherwise your key would not be atomic as defined earlier in this chapter. For example, if we tried to link STATE and CITY with a foreign key in the "one" end of the relationship, its value would have to be a list of associated cities in the CITY table. This situation would violate the rule that fields should be atomic, that is, that each cell in a table should contain a single value, not a list or subtable.

Creating Entity-Relationship (ER) Diagrams

ER diagrams visually describe the relationships between tables within a database. For instance, in the CITY-STATE example in the previous section, the corresponding ER diagram takes the form shown in Figure 4.1.

Figure 4.1 ER diagram for states and cities.

Each box in the diagram symbolizes a single entity, which is a single category of things, people, or events. Since every table in a database is supposed to store information about instances of a single entity, each entity in the diagram corresponds to a table in the database. The lines and associated "1" and "M" markings in the diagram illustrate specific relationships between tables, which the database implements with foreign keys. For instance, the above diagram illustrates a specific relationship between the STATE table and the CITY table.

In this case, the relationship is called a *one-to-many relationship*. The reason is that if we choose a particular state (that is, one row of the state table), it may be associated with any number of cities (that is, rows of the city table). As an example, the STATE record for Massachusetts might be associated with many records in the CITY database (Boston, Worcester, Lowell, and so on). On the other hand, if we choose a particular city, it is only associated with one state. Thus, the STATE entity is the "one," and the CITY entity is the "many." Therefore, "1" appears at the STATE end of line connecting the two tables, with "M" appearing at the CITY end.

The spatial layout of an ER diagram is not important. For example, in the diagram above, it does not matter whether STATE is to the left or right of CITY, so long as "M" appears next to CITY and "1" next to STATE. The diagram could also be vertical, with STATE either above or below CITY, or even diagonal, and diagram would have exactly the same meaning. What is important is the logical pattern in which the entities are connected, and the position of the "1" and "M" markings next to the relevant entities for each relationship. The diamonds in the middle of the relationship lines – in the case above, the diamond containing "is in" – are also not a critical part of the diagram. They function as comments or annotation that should ideally make the diagram easier to relate to the real-world situation, but they do not contain structural information about the database.

Functional Dependency

Suppose that all rows of a table with the same value for attribute A must also have the same value for B. In this situation, attribute B is called *functionally dependent* on attribute A, meaning that the value of A determines the value of B. For example, consider Table 4.5, which we saw earlier.

Table 4.5 YWCA activity data again, multiple activities per member.

MemberID	Activity	Fee
121	Ceramics	$145
121	Swimming	$200
202	Zumba	$150
202	Vegetarian Cooking	$125
175	Mommy & Me Cooking	$125
199	Zumba	$150
175	Poetry Workshop	$100
215	Tennis	$200
215	Sculpture	$150

Any two rows that have the same value of *Activity*, for example, "Zumba," must have the same value of *Fee*, in this case $150, because the Zumba activity always costs $150 no matter who is participating in it. In this case, *Fee* is functionally dependent on *Activity*, which reflects the real-world situation where the activity completely determines the fee charged. When an attribute *B* is functionally dependent on *A*, we also say that *A* is a *determinant* of *B* and *A determines B*.

Since the value of the primary key uniquely identifies each record in a table, specifying the value of the primary key narrows down every other attribute in the table to one possible value. In other words, every attribute in a table must be functionally dependent on the primary key, otherwise the choice of primary key could not be valid. The same is true of any candidate key, since being a candidate key means precisely that a field is a possible choice of the primary key. Conversely, if an attribute *A* determines every other attribute in the table, it determines the entire contents of a table row, and thus uniquely identifies a row of the table, because no two rows of relational database table can be identical. Thus, the candidate keys for a table are precisely the attributes (or combinations of attributes) that determine every other attribute.

For example, in the STATE relation presented above, *StateAbbrev* is a determinant of all other attributes. The *StateName* attribute is also a determinant of other attributes. Therefore, *StateAbbrev* and *StateName* are both candidate keys for STATE.

In the CITY relation also presented above, the attributes (*StateAbbrev*, *CityName*) together are a determinant of the *CityPopulation* attribute. In other words, once we know the combined values of both *StateAbbrev* and *CityName*, we know the values of all other attributes, and thus (*StateAbbrev*, *CityName*) is a candidate key. However, the attribute *CityName* by itself is not a determinant of the *CityPopulation* attribute because two cities from different states can have the same name and therefore could have different *CityPopulation* values (for example, "Fairview" is a common city name present in many states).

Dependency Diagrams

A *dependency diagram* or *bubble diagram* is a visual representation of functional dependencies. It should not be confused with an ER diagram. A dependency diagram depicts relationships between attributes and is therefore at a lower level and more detailed than an ER diagram, which depicts relationships between entire tables (entities).

In a dependency diagram, each attribute is represented by an oval, and you draw an arrow from oval *A* to oval *B* when attribute *A* is a determinant of attribute *B*. Optionally, the primary key or attributes that are part of the primary key may be indicated by ovals with a heavier border.

For example, when YWCA members were allowed only one activity at a time, the outline notation of the ACTIVITY table reads:

ACTIVITY(<u>MemberID</u>, Activity, Fee)

and its dependency diagram looks like Figure 4.2.

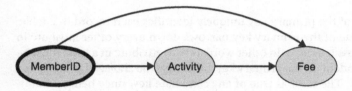

Figure 4.2 Dependency diagram for activity table, one activity per member.

However, when YWCA members can have multiple activities, we instead have Figure 4.3.

ACTIVITY(<u>MemberID</u>, <u>Activity</u>, Fee)

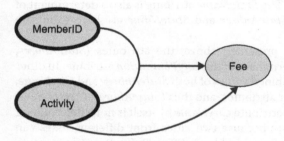

Figure 4.3 Outline description and dependency diagram for activity table, multiple activities per member.

Note that when the determinant is a composite, concatenated attribute, we represent the dependency using a multiple-tailed arrow, as in Figure 4.3.

Partial Dependency

Operational problems with databases can be caused by tables containing improper dependency patterns. One of these patterns, called a *partial dependency*, is a functional dependency within a table whose determinant is part of the primary key but not all of it.

In the example ACTIVITY(<u>MemberID</u>, <u>Activity</u>, Fee), the attribute *Activity*, which is part of the composite primary key but not all of it, determines the value of *Fee*. Therefore, there is a partial dependency between *Activity* and *Fee*. The thick arrow in Figure 4.4 highlights this situation.

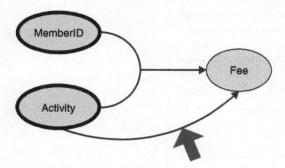

Figure 4.4 A partial dependency.

Note that partial dependencies can occur only in tables with composite primary keys. With a simple primary key, we could not have a determinant that is part but not all of the primary key.

Transitive Dependency

Another improper pattern, called a *transitive dependency*, is a functional dependency between attributes within the same table whose determinant is **not** the primary key, part of the primary key, or a candidate key.

For example, in the table ACTIVITY(MemberID, Activity, Fee), for the situation that each member can sign up for only one activity, *Activity* is not a possible primary key and is not part of the primary key, but determines *Fee*. Therefore, there is a transitive dependency between *Activity* and *Fee*. The transitive dependency is marked with a thick arrow in Figure 4.5.

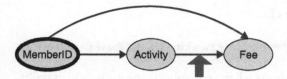

Figure 4.5 A transitive dependency.

Database Anomalies

Database anomalies are operational problems caused by poor database design. We have discussed such issues before, but we review them here. Consider the same table we presented at the beginning of the chapter (for the case of one activity per member; Table 4.6).

Table 4.6 Activities table again, one activity per member.

MemberID	Activity	Fee
121	Ceramics	$145
202	Zumba	$150
175	Mommy & Me Cooking	$125
199	Zumba	$150
215	Tennis	$200

An *insertion anomaly* occurs when you cannot add a row to a relation because you do not have other data that you store with it, or you have to invent "dummy" data for some attributes in order to store the values of other attributes. For example, you want the database to store that Zumba costs $150, but in the table design you do not have anywhere to store this information until a member signs up for Zumba, unless you create a fake member for this purpose.

A *deletion anomaly* occurs when deleting data from a relation causes other critical data to be lost, even though you would have preferred to keep them in the database. For example, if member 215 decides to drop out of the tennis class, and you delete his or her records, your database runs the risk of forgetting that Tennis costs $200.

An *update anomaly* occurs when you must change the contents of more than one cell to reflect the modification of a single datum. For example, if the cost of Zumba changes from $150 to $175, you must change all the records that reference Zumba.

What Causes Anomalies?

Anomalies occur because of the following two kinds of database design errors:

1) *Data redundancy*, which occurs when you replicate the same field in multiple tables, other than to set up foreign keys.
2) You create a database that includes functional dependencies whose determinants are not candidate keys, including partial dependencies and transitive dependencies. For example, in the table ACTIVITY(MemberID, Activity, Fee), *Activity* by itself is not a candidate key but it determines *Fee*, so there is a partial dependency and therefore the potential for anomalies (Figure 4.6).

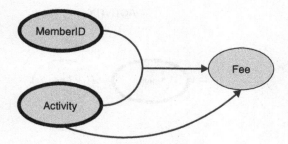

Figure 4.6 Dependency diagram with a partial dependency.

How to Fix Anomalies

The way to fix anomalies is to "normalize" your database design. In this process, you break up tables or create new tables so that all the dependencies within each table have determinants that are primary or candidate keys.

Consider the table ACTIVITY(MemberID, Activity, Fee), for the case in which a member can sign up for only one activity, and which we have already seen to contain a transitive dependency. *Activity* determines *Fee*, so in order for all dependencies to be on a primary key, *Fee* must be in a table whose primary key is *Activity*. Therefore, we create a new table which contains just *Activity* and *Fee*, with *Activity* being the primary key. We remove *Fee* from the original table, leaving just the *MemberID* and *Activity* fields. We use the name ACTIVITY for the table with just the *Activity* and *Fee* fields, and to avoid a duplicate table name, we change the name of the original table to PARTICIPATING. Note that MEMBER would also be a reasonable name for this table, since its primary key is *MemberID*. The database now appears as follows:

PARTICIPATING(MemberID, Activity)
    Activity foreign key to ACTIVITY

ACTIVITY(Activity, Fee)

PARTICPATING		ACTIVITY	
MemberID	**Activity**	**Activity**	**Fee**
121	Ceramics	Ceramics	$145
202	Zumba	Zumba	$150
175	Mommy & Me Cooking	Mommy & Me Cooking	$125
215	Tennis	Tennis	$200

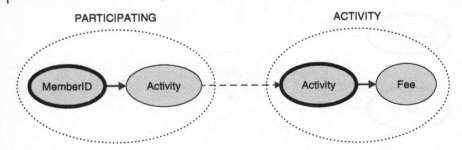

Figure 4.7 Dependency diagram for normalized activity database, one activity per member.

Observe that *Activity* in the PARTICIPATING table is described as a foreign key to ACTIVITY, meaning that any activity present in PARTICIPATING must exist in the ACTIVITY table. For example, we cannot enter "Judo" in the Activity field of the PARTICIPATING table without first creating a "Judo" record in the ACTIVITY table, and setting a fee for that activity. The dependency diagram depicts this foreign key relationship with a dashed line connecting the *Activity* fields in the two tables. Note that it is not considered redundant to have *Activity* in two different tables, because it is functioning as a foreign key. If, for example, we want to find out the fee being paid by member number 175, we look up that primary key in the PARTICIPATING table, find that the corresponding activity is "Mommy & Me Cooking," then locate the record with primary key "Mommy & Me Cooking" in the ACTIVITY table, and finally find that the fee is $125. As mentioned in the previous chapter, this kind of cross-referencing operation between tables is called a "join."

This normalized design (Figure 4.7) does not have the potential for any of the anomalies we discussed earlier. For example, "Tennis" can exist in the ACTIVITY relation with a specified fee, even before any member is enrolled in it. Furthermore, if the person with *MemberID* 215 drops out of the organization, there is no risk of losing the information that tennis costs $200, because we delete only the member's record in PARTICIPATING, not the "Tennis" record in ACTIVITY. Finally, if the cost of Zumba changes, we need to change the cost in just one place in the ACTIVITY table.

Good Database Design Principles

Adhering to the following design principles should help you practice good database design:

- **No redundancy**: You should store a field in only one table, unless it is being used as a foreign key. You may replicate foreign keys because they allow tables to be properly joined together.

- **No "bad" dependencies**: In the dependency diagram of any relation in the database, every determinant should be the whole primary key or a candidate key. Violations of this rule include (but are not limited to) partial dependencies and transitive dependencies.

Normalization, as mentioned earlier, is the process of eliminating "bad" dependencies by splitting up tables and linking them through foreign keys.

Normalization and Zip Codes

We have already seen a number of tables similar to the following:

PERSON(<u>ID</u>, FirstName, LastName, Address, City, State, Zip)

Assume that the zip code consists of just an initial five digits and does not include the "plus 4" segment. Let us make a dependency diagram for this table. Note that somebody's zip code should determine their city and state, so we obtain the situation depicted in Figure 4.8.

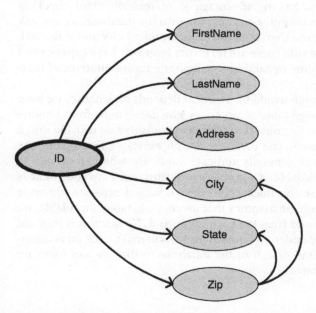

Figure 4.8 Dependency diagram for a table with zip codes.

This diagram contains two transitive dependencies, so technically the design of the table is poor. In practice, this particular situation is usually not disastrous, because the relationships between zip codes and cities and states rarely change. The most common change is that new zip codes are added, but even that is not an everyday occurrence, at least for the five-digit portion of the zip code that determines the city and state.

To be truly in compliance with good database design procedures, however, we should "normalize" the above design by separating the relationship between zip codes, cities, and states into a separate table. We still store zip codes in the PERSON table, but the city name and state now reside in a newly created ZIPCODE table instead of in the PERSON table:

PERSON(<u>ID</u>, FirstName, LastName, Address, Zip)
   Zip foreign key to ZIPCODE

ZIPCODE(<u>Zip</u>, City, State)

Thus, we maintain a "master" zip code table called ZIPCODE containing all zip codes that we might possibly use. For each person, we need only enter their zip code into the PERSON table, and we will automatically link to the ZIPCODE table to obtain their city and state information. This setup saves a bit of storage space and has the advantage of intrinsically error-checking the entry of zip codes: as we enter each person into the database, we can ask them for their zip code, and then read the corresponding city and state back to them in order to make sure there are no errors (you may have experienced such a process either online or talking to telephone representatives of various organizations).

Whether the above design would be practical depends on whether we have access to a sufficiently large table of zip codes (the data can be found online fairly easily, but needs to be converted from a spreadsheet or text file into a relational database format). The database design exercises throughout the rest of this textbook will generally indicate explicitly whether or not to assume such a table is available. If a problem indicates that a zip code table is available, you should use the normalized design with a separate zip code table. However, if the problem assumes that no zip code table is available, we "bend the rules" slightly and treat the *City*, *State*, and *Zip* fields as if they did not have a functional dependency. Sometimes we will make such an assumption to simplify the overall design of the database so that we can focus on some other topic or feature.

Expanding the Customer Loans Database

Let us expand upon the customer loans example from the previous chapter. In that example, we had a CUSTOMER table and a LOAN table, with a one-to-many relationship between a customer and their loans (Figure 4.9).

Figure 4.9 ER diagram for the loans and customers database.

CUSTOMER(<u>CustomerID</u>, FirstName, LastName, Address, City, State,
        Zip, Phone)

LOAN(<u>LoanID</u>, Date, Amt, Rate, Term, Type, CustomerID)
    CustomerID foreign key to CUSTOMER

Suppose that we also want to keep track of loan payments. Each payment is made on a specific loan and has a date and amount.

We cannot store payments in either of the existing tables, since loans have multiple payments, and thus customers also have multiple payments. If we tried to store payment information in either of the existing tables, it would be non-atomic (that is, a list or subtable within a field). Therefore, we need a new table.

Since each payment corresponds to a specific loan, the payment table should be related to the loan table. If we consider one loan, it should in general have many payments, but if we consider one payment, it corresponds to just one loan. Therefore, we have a one-to-many relationship of the form shown in Figure 4.10.

Figure 4.10 One-to-many relationship between loans and payments.

Putting both relationships together, we get the complete ER diagram in Figure 4.11.

Figure 4.11 ER diagram of completed loan database with payments.

Now consider the exact form of the PAYMENT table. We know it should contain the field *LoanID*, which will serve as a foreign key to LOAN and implement the one-to-many relationship (remember, the foreign key is always in the table on the "many" side of the relationship). It will also contain a date and amount.

What primary key should we use for the new PAYMENT table? One possibility is to simply number the payments on each loan as they are received, with the first one being payment number 1, the second being number 2, and so forth. If we record this information as an additional attribute *PaymentNumber*, we can then use (*LoanID*, *PaymentNumber*) as a composite primary key, since no two payments in the system should simultaneously have the same *LoanID* and the same *PaymentNumber*.

We then arrive at the following database outline notation:

CUSTOMER(<u>CustomerID</u>, FirstName, LastName, Address, City, State,
        Zip, Phone)

LOAN(<u>LoanID</u>, Date, Amt, Rate, Term, Type, CustomerID)
    CustomerID foreign key to CUSTOMER

PAYMENT(<u>LoanID</u>, <u>PaymentNumber</u>, DatePaid, Amount)
    LoanID foreign key to LOAN

Note that PAYMENT contains a foreign key as part of its primary key. Records in this table might look like:

(L7838, 1, 2/26/2010, $2557.05)	First payment on loan L7838
(L7838, 2, 4/1/2010, $2557.05)	Second payment on loan L7838
(L7840, 1, 4/25/2010, $875.29)	First payment on a different loan, L7840
(L7838, 3, 4/30/2010, $2557.05)	Third payment on loan L7838

Neither *LoanID* nor *PaymentNumber* is sufficient to uniquely identify a record but their combined, concatenated value is.

Another possibility would be to create a synthetic key *PaymentID* for each payment. In this case, the description of the PAYMENT table would instead be as follows:

PAYMENT(<u>PaymentID</u>, DatePaid, Amount, LoanID)
    LoanID foreign key to LOAN

Although the outline-notation form of the database is slightly different with this approach, there would be no change to the ER diagram, because LOAN and PAYMENT are still in a one-to-many relationship. In this scheme, every time we receive a payment, we assign some unique (and possibly quite long) *PaymentID* number to it. These numbers would be akin to the long, unique transaction numbers you may see assigned to credit card transactions or orders on e-commerce websites.

In either approach to the design, there is no need for a direct relationship between CUSTOMER and PAYMENT. If we want to find out information about the customer making a specific payment, we first trace the *LoanID* foreign key back to corresponding record in LOAN, and then follow the *CustomerID* value we find there back to the appropriate record in CUSTOMER.

DVD Lending Library Example without Loan History

Here is our first business database design exercise:

Northshore Community Center operates a DVD lending library and wants to use one of its PCs for electronic instead of manual record-keeping for the DVD lending operation. Some of the stock of DVDs has been donated by various patrons, and the rest was purchased out of the community center's general fund.

The DVD library has a large number of movies, some of which have the same title (often because of "remakes"). For each movie, you want to keep track of its name, the date it was first released, its primary language, and its category (such as "Comedy," "Action," "Documentary," etc.).

In addition to DVDs, the lending library also lends movies in the Blu-ray format. Sometimes there are multiple copies of the same movie in the same format (for very popular films). The center identifies each copy by a unique barcode number (which it can easily read by attaching an inexpensive USB barcode scanner to the PC). For each copy, the database should keep track of its format (DVD or Blu-ray), the date the community center acquired the copy, whether it was obtained used or new, and whether it was donated or purchased.

Each client of the community center has a membership card with a unique account number. Suppose you want to store each client's first name, last name, date of birth, address information, and phone number. Suppose that you have access to a table giving the city name and state for every zip code in the community center's service area.

Part 1. Initially, suppose we are not interested in tracking our clients' past DVD borrowing history; we simply wish to know which DVDs are currently in stock, which ones are currently on loan, when they were loaned, and who has each loaned DVD. Design a database using only one-to-many relationships.

Note that the problem says that we *do* have access to a zip code table, so we will want to produce a design normalized with respect to zip codes.

People new to the database design process often have difficulty distinguishing between entities and attributes. Recall that *entities* are general categories of things we want to store information about, such as movies, copies of video discs, or clients of the community center. *Attributes* are specific properties of things such as names or addresses. If one is new to the process, one possible way of navigating this distinction is to start by using one large dependency diagram to write down all the fields (attributes) we would like to store. Before we get started, note that to distinguish between different movies with the same name (*The Pink Panther*, for example), we will need a *MovieID* attribute. Writing down all the attributes and dependencies, we arrive at the Figure 4.12.

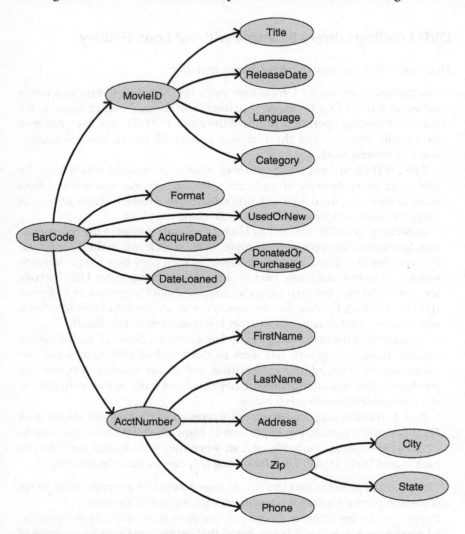

Figure 4.12 Dependency diagram for entire DVD library database without loan histories.

Some points about this diagram:

- It does not show transitively implied dependencies. Such dependencies get their name from the transitive property of common mathematical relationships, for example, that if a, b, and c are numbers and both $a > b$ and $b > c$, then we must also have $a > c$. Similarly, *BarCode* determines *MovieID*, which we may write as *BarCode → MovieID*, and *MovieID* determines *Title*, which we may write as *MovieID → Title*, so it follows that *BarCode* determines Title, that is, *BarCode → Title*. However, we do not show *BarCode → Title* in this version of the diagram precisely because it is transitively implied by *BarCode → MovieID* and *MovieID → Title*. In practice, you may find yourself including some transitively implied dependencies. If so, you may simply erase them as you finish your diagram.

- The reason for the dependencies of *AcctNumber* and *DateLoaned* on *BarCode* may not be obvious yet. It is possible that when you first create a diagram of this kind, a few such key dependencies may be missing.

- After erasing any transitive dependencies, we can now translate the dependency diagram into a database design and an ER diagram. Essentially, every attribute that is at the start of some arrow is the primary key for a table and uniquely identifies an entity; otherwise we will introduce anomalies. For example, *MovieID* is clearly the primary key for an entity that we can call MOVIE, with *Title*, *ReleaseDate*, *Language*, and *Category* as attributes in this table. *BarCode* is the primary key for some entity we may call COPY, which also contains *Format* and *AcquireDate* (as well as some other fields). Similarly, we have an entity/table whose primary key is *AcctNumber*, so we can call this table CLIENT. Finally, we will also have a table whose primary key is *Zip*, so we call this table ZIPCODE.

  Note that while it is often valid to make the head of every arrow the primary key of some table/entity, this rule is in general an oversimplification, because things may become a bit more complicated when there are composite primary keys or multiple candidate keys for the same entity.

- Any attribute that appears at the end of one arrow and the beginning of another arrow is a foreign key and should be present in at least two tables: for example, *MovieID* is the primary key of MOVIE, but should also be present in COPY, to tell us what movie the DVD (or VHS tape or Blu-ray) identified by the given barcode contains.

Here is a partial outline of our database so far:

MOVIE(MovieID, Title, ReleaseDate, Language, Category)

COPY(BarCode, Format, AcquireDate, UsedOrNew, DonatedOrPurchased, ... ,
    MovieID)
    MovieID foreign key to MOVIE

CLIENT(AcctNumber, FirstName, LastName, Address, Zip, Phone)
    Zip foreign key to ZIPCODE

ZIPCODE(Zip, City, State)

Here, *UsedOrNew* could be a simple one-character code such as "U" for used and "N" for new, and *DonatedOrPurchased* could be a similar code such as "D" for donated and "P" for purchased. Alternatively, one could use a yes/no field for each purpose, with field names such as *Used* or *Donated*. For example, if the value of *Used* is "no," we may infer that the DVD was obtained new.

Now let us consider how to keep track of where our stock of DVDs is at any given moment. At any particular time, each copy may either be in stock or in the possession of one of our clients. If we do not want to keep track of past loan history, it is sufficient to keep track of each copy:

- Which client has it, by recording an *AcctNumber* in COPY
- When he or she borrowed it, by recording *DateLoaned* in COPY

If a copy is in the library, we may leave its *AcctNumber* field blank, or use a special client code like "InLibrary." This approach to tracking copies explains the dependency of *AcctNumber* and *DateLoaned* on *BarCode*. We thus arrive at the following database outline:

MOVIE(MovieID, Title, ReleaseDate, Language, Category)

COPY(BarCode, Format, AcquireDate, , UsedOrNew, DonatedOrPurchased,
    AcctNumber, DateLoaned, MovieID)
    MovieID foreign key to MOVIE
    AcctNumber foreign key to CLIENT

CLIENT(AcctNumber, FirstName, LastName, Address, Zip, Phone)
    Zip foreign key to ZIPCODE

ZIPCODE(Zip, City, State)

The accompanying ER diagram appears as in Figure 4.13.

Figure 4.13 ER diagram for DVD library database without loan histories.

Notice that COPY is the "many" of two different relationships and therefore contains two different foreign keys. Note also that the database has the fairly common feature that we need entities (or equivalently tables) for both things and for types of things – in this case, for copies of DVDs and for movies, respectively.

As you become more accustomed to the database design process (or perhaps already), you will probably become able to identify entities and relationships without first drawing an attribute dependency diagram, instead proceeding directly to the ER diagram and then to the database outline.

One enhancement we can make to the design is to have a preapproved list of categories, perhaps something like:

MOVIE(<u>MovieID</u>, Title, ReleaseDate, Language, Category)
    Category foreign key to CATEGORY

CATEGORY(<u>Category</u>)

(The remaining tables are identical)

Such a design would facilitate, for example, having an on-screen pull-down list of categories from which to select when you enter information about a movie. Note that there is no problem with having a table like CATEGORY whose only attribute is its primary key. The resulting ER diagram is as shown in Figure 4.14.

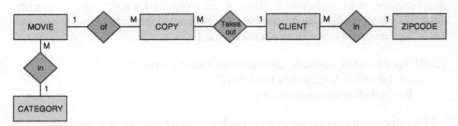

Figure 4.14 ER diagram for DVD library database with a categories table but no loan histories.

Note that this change essentially promotes *Category* from just an attribute to also being an entity. This kind of approach can make sense for attributes that have a relatively limited or proscribed range of values. For instance, we could do much the same thing with *Format* or *Language*.

If we wanted to be able to place a movie in multiple categories (for example, both "Comedy" and "Science Fiction" for *Spaceballs*), we would need a more complicated setup, which we will cover later in the textbook when we introduce many-to-many relationships.

The DVD Lending Library Example with Loan History

Now consider the following more realistic variation on the previous problem:

Part 2. Suppose we change our minds and want to keep track of past history, including when DVDs were loaned and when they were returned. We would like the database to be able to tell us all the past loans on any movie copy, and all the past loans of any client. How would we change the design of the database?

One way of thinking about this change is that we need to store not just one *AcctNumber* and *DateLoaned* for each copy but a list or subtable of multiple *AcctNumber* and *DateLoaned* attributes that convey the copy's entire loan history. However, this approach is prohibited in a relational database setting because we cannot have repeating groups or non-atomic fields. We should not store multiple *AcctNumber* fields in one record of COPY.

Since no table currently in the database can be used to store the new information we want without breaking the rule against non-atomic fields, we must redesign the database to include at least one new table. The key to redesigning this particular database is to realize that some of our entities may need to correspond to *events* rather than to physical objects. The event in question is a "loan," which involves a single client borrowing a single copy of a movie. Let us call the corresponding entity and table LOAN. It will need to contain an *AcctNumber*, to identify which client is involved, and a *BarCode*, to identify which physical media was rented. We can also easily include *DateLoaned* and *DateReturned* fields. We thus obtain the table:

LOAN(AcctNumber, BarCode, DateLoaned, DateReturned)
    AcctNumber foreign key to CLIENT
    BarCode foreign key to COPY

Note that we have not yet determined a primary key for this new table. We will return to that topic shortly. For loans that are not yet complete, we can leave the *DateReturned* field blank (in Access, for example, each field has a yes/no "Required" property; if this property is "no," we may leave the field blank). We should now also remove the *DateLoaned* and *AcctNumber* fields from COPY, since in our new setting (including past history as well as the present moment), they are no longer functionally dependent on *BarCode*. The new ER diagram (including the optional CATEGORY entity) is shown in Figure 4.15.

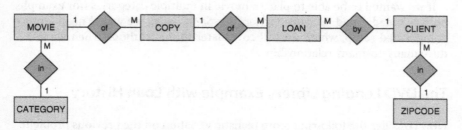

Figure 4.15 ER diagram for DVD library database with a category table and loan histories.

Which primary key do we use for LOAN? It is clear that no single attribute in LOAN can serve as the primary key, as none of their individual values can be guaranteed to be unique. One obvious choice might seem to be the composite key (*AcctNumber, BarCode*), but that would mean that once a particular client has borrowed a given copy of a movie, they may never do so again. Other choices for composite keys might be (*AcctNumber, DateLoaned*), but this choice would prevent a client from borrowing or returning more than one movie at a time. It might be practical, however, if we store *DateLoaned* using the Access Date/Time datatype (or something similar if we are using other software), allowing the times of loan and return to be stored with the accuracy of one second.

With this kind of precise representation of event times, perhaps the best composite choice of primary key would be (*BarCode, DateLoaned*), since a given copy of a movie can be rented only once at any given time. If *DateLoaned* is stored only at the precision of one day, however, this choice would prevent a given DVD from being loaned more than once in a day, a possibly unwelcome operational restriction. *DateReturned* could be used in composite keys much like *DateLoaned* but has the disadvantage that the return date would not be known while a loan is in progress.

Given these difficulties, perhaps the most natural choice for the primary key of LOAN is a synthetic key, for example *LoanID*. With this choice, here is the full database outline:

MOVIE(<u>MovieID</u>, Title, ReleaseDate, Language, Category)
    Category foreign key to CATEGORY

CATEGORY(<u>Category</u>)

COPY(<u>BarCode</u>, Format, AcquireDate, MovieID)
    MovieID foreign key to MOVIE

LOAN(<u>LoanID</u>, AcctNumber, BarCode, DateLoaned, DateReturned)
    AcctNumber foreign key to CLIENT
    BarCode foreign key to COPY

CLIENT(<u>AcctNumber</u>, FirstName, LastName, Address, Zip, Phone)
    Zip foreign key to ZIPCODE

ZIPCODE(<u>Zip</u>, City, State)

However, we should keep in mind that if *DateLoaned* is stored with the precision of minutes or seconds, then (*BarCode, DateLoaned*) would be a possible primary key for LOAN, and we could dispense with the *LoanID* field if we so desired.

Finally, if we consider the way that COPY and CLIENT are indirectly related through the LOAN table, we see that for each client there may be many associated copies of movies, and for each copy of a movie there may over time be many associated clients. Thus, COPY and CLIENT are in a *many-to-many* relationship mediated by the intervening entity LOAN. This setup provides a clue as to how to implement many-to-many relationships, a topic we will cover later in this book.

Subtypes

Subtypes are special relationships used to designate a subgroup within an entity that has special attributes that do not apply to the entity as a whole. This kind of situation is best clarified by an example. Let us consider the following situation:

> For most record-keeping, the Economics department of Enormous State University (ESU) can rely on ESU's central information systems. However, the department has had to keep paper records of special information pertaining to economics majors, especially honors program economics majors. The department would like to develop its own auxiliary computer information system to keep track of such data.
>
> For each student majoring in economics, the department would like to store a first name, middle name/initial, last name, e-mail address, expected graduation date, and actual graduation date (for those who have graduated). Every economics major also has a single departmental academic advisor, who is a member of the economics faculty. The system should be able to remember each student's advisor. For each faculty member, the system should store a first name, middle name/initial, last name, office room number, telephone extension, and e-mail address.
>
> About 4% of economics majors are enrolled in the department's honors program, which requires them to write a senior thesis. The department wants to be able to keep track of which students are in the honors program. For honors students, the department also wants to store the title of the thesis (up to 200 characters text), and the date the thesis was accepted by the department (blank for students who have not finished their theses yet).
>
> 1) Design a database to hold this information, using only one-to-many relationships.
> 2) Create a design that does not waste storage for the thesis title of each non-honors student. This design introduces a new kind of relationship called a subtype (sometimes called a one-to-one relationship, but that is a somewhat misleading tern).
> 3) Now assume that each honor student has a senior thesis supervisor, who may not be the same as the student's departmental academic advisor. Incorporate this information into the database.

First, in response to part (1), let us design a database for this situation, using standard one-to-many relationships. We obtain the ER diagram shown in Figure 4.16 and the following database outline:

Figure 4.16 ER diagram for economics department database, first version.

FACULTY(<u>EmployeeID</u>, FName, MName, LName, Office, Extension, Email)

STUDENT(<u>StudentID</u>, FName, MName, LName, Email, ExpectedGradDate,
ActualGradDate, EmployeeID, HonorsYesNo, ThesisTitle,
ThesisAcceptDate)
EmployeeID foreign key to FACULTY

For students who have not graduated yet, *ActualGradDate* is blank. For non-honors students, *ThesisTitle* and *ThesisAcceptDate* are also blank. For honors students, *HonorsYesNo* has the value "Yes", and it contains "No" for other students.

Now consider part (2) of the problem: one criticism of our initial design is that it wastes a lot of space. If *ThesisTitle* is 200 characters, and we use a standard 8-byte date/time format for *ThesisAcceptDate*, 96% of the records in the STUDENT table could contain 208 unused bytes, roughly doubling the size of the database.[1] This kind of waste of space can be a serious problem in some databases, although in this case, given how cheap and plentiful storage space has become, the database is unlikely to be big enough for such waste to be a major issue.

An alternative is to split STUDENT into two tables, one containing only those fields that are used for most students, and the other containing the fields that apply only to honors students. Both have a primary key of *StudentID*. With this design, we have the following:

FACULTY(<u>EmployeeID</u>, FName, MName, LName, Office, Extension, Email)

STUDENT(<u>StudentID</u>, FName, MName, LName, Email, ExpectedGradDate,
ActualGradDate, EmployeeID)
EmployeeID foreign key to FACULTY

HONORSTUDENT(<u>StudentID</u>, ThesisTitle, ThesisAcceptDate)
StudentID foreign key to STUDENT

---

1 In MS Access, a text field may use less storage space than its field size, and only one byte if it is empty. But in other database systems, a 200-character text field might consume 200 or 201 bytes per record regardless of how much of it is used.

There is no longer any need for the *HonorsYesNo* field, because we know whether or not a student is an honors student by whether or not there is a record with their ID in HONORSTUDENT. Note that *StudentID* in HONORSTUDENT is declared as a foreign key to STUDENT, because someone cannot be an honors student unless they are already a student. The converse does not hold: you can certainly have a student who is not an honors student.

We no longer waste large amounts of space because STUDENT no longer has to have *ThesisTitle* and *ThesisAcceptDate*, fields that are blank for most students. On the other hand, *StudentID* (which should be on the order of 10 bytes) has to be stored twice for 4% of the students, but that consumes far less storage than wasting 208 or more bytes for 96% of students, and storing an additional 1-byte yes/no field for all students. If we want information about an honors student other than their thesis title or thesis acceptance date, we refer to the STUDENT table, following the foreign key *StudentID*.

Suppose we enforce the constraint that any value appearing in a foreign key field must match the primary key value of some record in the table to which it refers (this restriction is called *referential integrity* – see the next chapter for a more complete discussion). With such a constraint, STUDENT and HONORSTUDENT are in an unusual kind of one-to-many relationship, with HONORSTUDENT as the "many" because it holds the foreign key. However, here the "many" is not fully "many," because *StudentID* serves as both the entire primary key of HONORSTUDENT and as a foreign key. For a given Student ID found in the STUDENT table, for example, 347-34-7738, there might not be any corresponding record in HONORSTUDENT (if that student is not in the honors program), or there might be one such record (if the student is enrolled in the honors program). There cannot be more than one corresponding record because *StudentID* is also the primary key of HONORSTUDENT, and therefore HONORSTUDENT can contain at most one record with *StudentID* 347-34-7738. Thus, the "many" in this case is constrained to be either zero or one. As a consequence, the possible primary key values occurring in the HONORSTUDENT table must be a subset of those occurring in the STUDENT table. For this reason, the relationship between STUDENT and HONORSTUDENT is often called a *subtype* relationship. On an ER diagram, such a relationship is depicted in Figure 4.17.

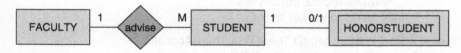

Figure 4.17 ER diagram for economics department database with a subtype.

Note that for each student, there are either zero or one honors students, but for each honors student, there is exactly one student. Subtypes are sometimes also called "one-to-one" relationships, although this terminology is misleading.

They are more accurately described as one-to-many relationships in which "many" is restricted to be zero or one.

In general, one can always use subtypes to avoid having to store blank fields in a database. However, one should consider whether the amount of storage saved is worth the extra structural complexity introduced by creating a subtype. If the number of the bytes per record of blanks avoided is small or if non-blank values are stored in a significant fraction of the records, then a subtype may not save enough space to make it worth introducing an entire extra table, and may use more storage than the original design.

For example, in the designs above, the *ActualGradDate* field is blank for students who have not graduated yet. We could avoid storing such blank fields by having an ALUMNUS entity that is a subtype of STUDENT. However, we would only save the amount of space necessary to store the graduation date, which in Access would be 8 bytes. Over time, furthermore, alumni will far outnumber current students, so the majority of students in the database will be alumni. If the *StudentID* field is stored as a 9-digit text field, for example, then the subtype strategy would be to store an extra 10 bytes for the large majority of students (the alumni) in order to save 8 bytes for a small minority of students (those not yet graduated), clearly a losing proposition.

Now consider part (3) of the problem. Here we suppose that each student has a senior thesis advisor, who might not be the same person as their regular academic advisor. To track this information, we need only add an *EmployeeID* foreign key to HONORSTUDENT (Figure 4.18):

FACULTY(EmployeeID, FName, MName, LName, Office, Extension, Email)

STUDENT(StudentID, FName, MName, LName, Email, ExpectedGradDate,
      ActualGradDate, EmployeeID)
    EmployeeID foreign key to EMPLOYEE

HONORSTUDENT(StudentID, ThesisTitle, ThesisAcceptDate, EmployeeID)
    StudentID foreign key to STUDENT
    EmployeeID foreign key to FACULTY

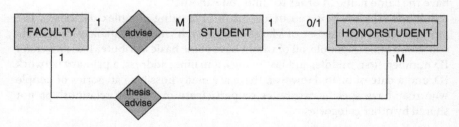

Figure 4.18 ER diagram for economics department database with a subtype and two advisor relationships.

The multiple relationships between HONORSTUDENT and FACULTY are useful and non-redundant because an honor student's general advisor and thesis advisor could be different people. If the thesis and general advisors were restricted to be the same, then the proper design of the database would include only two relationships: the one-to-many relationship between FACULTY and STUDENT, and the subtype relationship between HONORSTUDENT and STUDENT.

Note that the database outline would be more understandable and easier to relate to the real-life situation if we gave more illuminating names than *EmployeeID* to the foreign keys. For example, we could change the name of the foreign key in STUDENT to *RegularAdvisorID*, and the name of the foreign key in HONORSTUDENT to *ThesisAdvisorID*. These names make it reasonably clear how these foreign keys should be interpreted. The outline would then look like this:

FACULTY(<u>EmployeeID</u>, FName, MName, LName, Office, Extension, Email)

STUDENT(<u>StudentID</u>, FName, MName, LName, Email, ExpectedGradDate,
    ActualGradDate, RegularAdvisorID)
    RegularAdvisorID foreign key to FACULTY

HONORSTUDENT(<u>StudentID</u>, ThesisTitle, ThesisAcceptDate, ThesisAdvisorID)
    StudentID foreign key to STUDENT
    ThesisAdvisorID foreign key to FACULTY

Note that the *names* of a foreign key and the corresponding primary key do not have to match, only their datatypes must match. The annotation "*x* foreign key to *Y*" should in fact be interpreted as follows:

> The value of attribute *x* in each record of this table should match the value of the primary key of some record in table *Y*.

Since a table can have only one choice of primary key, the above statement has an unambiguous meaning that does not depend on the name of *Y*'s primary key. It is therefore not necessary for the foreign and primary key attributes to have the same name in order to "find" one another.

Subtype relationships can be useful in organizing complex databases. For example, consider the case of a large university. Its master database most likely contains a table of people, all of whom have some basic attributes like university ID number, first, middle, and last names, a mailing address, a primary network ID, and a date of birth. However, there are many possible categories of people who may have specific attributes or participate in specific relationships not shared by other categories.

For example, students are a particular category, having attributes like a graduation date, and may participate in relationships describing majors, course registrations, and grades. Employees are another class of people who have specific attributes that may not apply to most students, such as a date of hire and an annual salary. Within employees, there is a subset consisting of faculty, who may have specific attributes, such as the date they were granted tenure, that do not apply to other kinds of employees. We can model these overlapping groups of people as a "family tree" of subtypes, as in Figure 4.19.

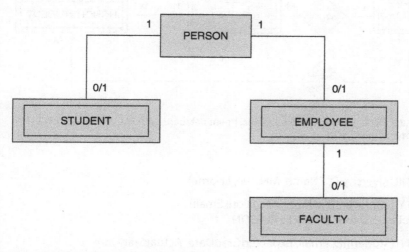

Figure 4.19 Example of a tree of subtypes.

This kind of approach avoids both of two undesirable alternatives: either the PERSON table could have a huge number of attributes (perhaps hundreds) to accommodate every possible subclass of person, most of which would probably be blank in any given record, or we could treat students, employees, faculty, and so forth, as completely different entities. In that case, we might have to duplicate certain attributes, such as name and address information, between multiple tables. For example, if somebody were both a student and an employee, then their address information would have to be stored twice, raising the possibility of update anomalies.

We could apply this principle to the database we just designed, under the assumption that *EmployeeID* and *StudentID* are in fact university IDs and are unique to each person – that is, it is impossible for a faculty member and a student to have the same ID number, say, 233-896-9076, unless they are actually the same person. Under this assumption, we could restructure the database as shown in Figure 4.20.

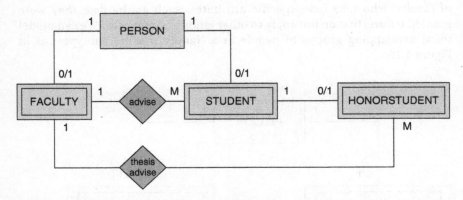

Figure 4.20 ER diagram of economics department database, with FACULTY and STUDENT both subtypes of PERSON.

PERSON(UniversityID, FName, MName, LName)

FACULTY(EmployeeID, Office, Extension, Email)
    EmployeeID foreign key to PERSON

STUDENT(StudentID, Email, ExpectedGradDate, ActualGradDate,
        RegularAdvisorID)
    StudentID foreign key to PERSON
    RegularAdvisorID foreign key to FACULTY

HONORSTUDENT(StudentID, ThesisTitle, ThesisAcceptDate, ThesisAdvisorID)
    StudentID foreign key to STUDENT
    ThesisAdvisorID foreign key to FACULTY

If a faculty member takes a class and thus becomes a student, or a graduate student is hired to teach an undergraduate class, this design avoids the situation of having to store their name information twice. Note that it does not matter to the structure or function of this database that the FACULTY and STUDENT subtypes have a different primary key name than their "parent" entity PERSON: what makes a table a subtype is not the name of its primary key but the fact that its entire primary key is also a foreign key.

Exercises

For each of the following problems, design an appropriate database, drawing an ER diagram and writing a database design outline.

In each question below, assume that any "address information" specified is in US format, consisting of fields for street address, city, two-letter state code, and zip code. Unless stated otherwise in an individual problem, assume that you do *not* have the master zip code table in your databases, so that city, state, and zip code may be treated as independent.

When the problems specify that you should store a "date/time," assume that you will store dates and times together in MS-Access-style "date/time" fields, which are able to store a date and time together in a single attribute.

4.1 **Employee parking permissions:** Your firm maintains gated parking lots, each with its own code ("Lot 23A," for example), number of spaces, and description (example: "behind main manufacturing facility"). Each employee has regular permission to park in exactly one lot. For each employee, you want to store a first name, middle name/initial, last name, home address information, date hired, office phone number, cell phone number, and e-mail address. Each employee may own one or more vehicles and has permission to park any of these vehicles in his or her designated lot. For each vehicle, you want to store the license plate number, the state in which vehicle is registered (using standard two-letter codes), the make, model, year, and color.

4.2 **Restaurant review website:** You operate a community website where registered users may post ratings and reviews of area restaurants. Each registered user has a unique screen name, along with a first name, last name, address information, e-mail address, and phone number; however, your public website displays only the screen name. For each restaurant, you want to store a name, address information, phone number, website URL, category ("steakhouse," "Chinese," etc.). Each review consists of a single registered user's opinion of a single restaurant and consists of a food quality rating on a scale of 1 to 5, dinner cost paid per person, and comments (like a "long text" field in Access 2013 or later, or a "memo" field in earlier Access versions). Each registered user may review many restaurants but is allowed to only have one review per restaurant.

4.3 **PC service records:** You operate the PC support group for a medium-sized company. You wish to keep records of the time your group spends servicing various PCs within the firm. Each company-owned PC is identified by a unique property tag number; in addition, you want to record the PC's make and model, the room number where it is located, and the date it was acquired. Each computer "belongs" to a department of the company, identified by a department code. Each department also has a name. Some departments have only a few computers, but some have as many as a hundred. Every time one of your technicians services a computer, you want to record which computer was serviced, which technician performed the service, the date/time the service started, the date/time it ended, and a description of the work performed. Each technician is identified by an employee ID number; for each technician, you also want to store their first name, middle name/initial, last name, and date hired.

4.4 Restaurant Franchises: You operate a franchise restaurant operation, with a variety of partnerships and smaller companies operating restaurants using your national brand name. For each of these franchisees, you want to keep their name, address information, tax ID (which is unique), and phone number. Each franchisee can have one or more contracts with you; for each contract, you want to store its start date, end date, and monthly payment. Each contract covers one or more restaurants; for each restaurant, you want to track its address, date opened, date of last inspection, and seating capacity.

4.5 Tutoring service: You run a coaching/tutoring service to help high school students prepare for the SAT exam. You have a staff of tutors, each of which has an employee ID, an hourly rate (such as $20 per hour), and personal information consisting of their first name, last name, middle name/initial, address information, phone number, mobile phone number, and e-mail address. For each high school student, you want to keep similar personal information and a student ID number, date of birth, and expected date of graduation from high school. Tutoring takes place in sessions, to each of which you assign a unique ID number. Each session consists of one tutor and one student. In addition to being able to identify the tutor and student involved in each session, you want to store its start date/time and end date/time.

4.6 Musical instrument lending program: You work for a program that makes musical instruments available to underprivileged children. For each general type of instrument, you want to store a name (such as "flute" or "trombone") and the minimum student age for which the type of instrument is suitable. Each particular instrument is identified by a property tag carrying a unique number. For each individual instrument, you want to store its type, manufacturer, model name, date manufactured, and notes. For each child, you want to store the first name, middle name/initial, last name, date of birth, gender, address information, and phone number. You also want to keep track of loans of instruments to children, each of which involves one instrument and one child. For each loan, you want to keep track of the date the loan started and (if applicable) the date the loan ended. Assume that you *do* have access to a master zip code table specifying the city and state for each zip code in the program's service area.

4.7 **Swim club membership records:** Widevale swim club has been keeping its membership records in a spreadsheet, but this year the swim club board has decided to use a true database instead. Each membership consists of one or more people living at the same address. For each membership you need to record a membership "type code" (such as "regular," "senior," and "military discount") reflecting discounts for certain employers, senior citizens, and so forth. The annual fee for the membership is determined by the type code. For each membership, you also want to store the date payment was received and address information. Each membership applies to all people residing at the registered address, and for each person covered by a membership, you wish to store a first name, middle name/initial, last name, gender, date of birth, phone number, and e-mail address.

4.8 **One-person consulting business:** You are a freelance consultant, working alone, and want to keep detailed records of the time you spend working for your clients. For each client, you want to store an ID number, name, address information, phone number, and e-mail address. Each client may have one or more jobs, each of which has a unique job ticket number, a description, an agreed hourly rate, and a yes/no field indicating whether the job has been completed. You work on a particular job in one or more "work sessions": for each work session, you want to store the date/time you started working, the date/time you stopped working, and a brief description of what you accomplished during that session. Some jobs may be completed in a single session, but others may require a large number of sessions spread out over a number of months.

4.9 **Electric guitar repair:** You operate a small business repairing electric guitars. For each of your customers, you want to store a first name, last name, phone number, and address information. A customer may have more than one instrument, but each instrument has just one owner. For each instrument, you want to store the maker, model, color, year made, and some comments. For each instrument, there may be one or more repair jobs. For each repair job, you want to store a description of work wanted, hours spent, dollars charged, the date/time the instrument was dropped off, the date/time you started work, the date/time you completed work, description of work actually done, and the date/time the instrument was picked up. Even if a customer drops off or picks up several instruments at once, they are considered different repair jobs.

4.10 Human resources: You are designing a database for your company's human resources department. For each employee, you want to keep an employee ID number, first name, middle initial, last name, birth date, hire date, home phone, and home address information. You also need to be able to reach employees at work, so you need to store each employee's office address, office phone number, e-mail address, and office fax number. Each employee is assigned to exactly one branch office, and each branch office has address information and a name. All employees assigned to a given branch office have the same office address information, but possibly differing office phone and office fax numbers (for each attribute, think carefully about which table it belongs in). Each employee must choose exactly one of the available health plans. For each health plan, you must store its name, monthly premium, deductible, and payment percentage.

4.11 Piano lessons: You operate a music school that specializes in piano lessons. You have a staff of piano teachers, for each of whom you want to store a first name, middle initial, last name, street address, city, state, zip, date hired, and hourly lesson rate (for example, $50 per hour). Your clients consist of households, each of which may have multiple students. For each student, you want to store a first name, middle initial, last name, date of birth, and current proficiency level (for example, beginner, intermediate, or advanced). All students from the same household have the same street address, city, state, zip, and credit card information consisting of a card number, expiration date, and security code. Lessons are given at your school in private rooms, each with its own piano. For each room, you want to store the room number, the type of piano (upright, grand, baby grand, and so on), the piano manufacturer, and the year the piano was made. Each lesson involves one student and one teacher meeting in one room; in addition to recording the student, teacher, and room, you also want to store the starting date/time and ending date/time of each lesson. Assume that you *do* have access to a suitable zip code table.

4.12 Career placement office: You need to set up a database for your college's career placement office. For each student, you want to store the student ID number, first name, middle name/initial, last name, address information, cell phone number, e-mail, and expected graduation date. You also want to keep information on employers, including employer name, address information, and main phone number. Each employer has one or more recruiters; each recruiter only works for only one employer. For each recruiter, you want to store a first name, middle name/initial, last name, address information, office phone number, cell phone number, and e-mail. Your office has a facility in which recruiters and students can meet for preliminary job interviews, and you want your system to keep track of the schedule for these interviews. Each interview consists of a single recruiter meeting a single student. For each interview, you want to store the date/time scheduled to start, date/time actually started (blank for interviews in the future), date/time scheduled to end, date/time actually ended (blank for interviews that have not been held yet), room number, and comments.

4.13 Plumbing dispatcher: Your firm dispatches plumbers to perform repairs in customers' homes. For each plumber, you want to store a (unique) tax ID number, first name, last name, address information, regular phone number, mobile phone number, date of last certification, and date hired. For each customer, you want to store first name, last name, address information, and phone number. You also want to schedule and keep track of visits by plumbers to customers. Each visit involves one plumber visiting one customer. You should store the scheduled date/time of the visit, actual date/time the visit started, and the actual date/time it ended, along with a (text) description of work done and the amount charged. Assume that you *do* have access to a master zip code table.

4.14 Selling a single product: Your firm has a single product, and gives each salesperson exclusive rights to a specific set of customers — that is, each customer always deals with the same salesperson. For salespeople, you need to keep track of their first name, last name, and office phone number. Customers have a name, address information, phone number, and fax number. For orders, you need to know the date placed, number of units ordered, total price, and date shipped. Total price is subject to negotiation, and is thus not completely determined by the number of units ordered. As time goes by, each customer places multiple orders.

4.15 Corporate PC Repair: You work in the IT support division of a large firm and are responsible for keeping track of PC repairs and service throughout the organization. Each computer in the organization is identified by a unique property tag number and is for the use of a single employee; your database needs to remember to which employee each computer is assigned. An employee can have more than one computer — for example, a desktop and a laptop. For each computer, you also want to store its date of purchase and its configuration. Each configuration represents a type of computer that the company has purchased; for each configuration, you want to store the manufacturer name, model name, hard disk size, memory size, processor name, and screen size.

Typically, you order computers in large batches, so many computers share the same configuration.

Each employee is identified by an employee ID number. For each employee, you want to record their first name, middle initials, last name, phone number, e-mail address, office room number, and date hired. The database should also remember at which location each employee is stationed. Each employee is assigned to a single company location (such as "headquarters," "West Coast sales," etc.), each of which is identified by a four-letter location code. In addition to this code, you want to store each location's name and address information. Assume you do have access to a master zip code table.

Your database should also keep track of every service event. For each service event, your database needs to remember which computer was serviced, the date/time the service started, the date/time it ended, a text description of the work performed, and who performed it. Dates and times should be stored together in MS-Access-style "Date/Time" fields. The technicians servicing the computers are all employees of your firm, and information about them is stored in the same table as all other employees.

You may create synthetic keys as necessary or convenient.

4.16 Charity walkathon: You work for a charity that holds "walkathon" fundraisers around the country. Each walkathon has a name, date, and location. For each walkathon, there are a number of teams, each of which has a name and a fundraising goal. Each team has one or more walkers, for which you store first name, last name, address information, email address, phone number, and personal fundraising goal. A walker can be on only one team per walkathon but over time may be on multiple teams in different walkathons.

For each walker, there are multiple donations, for which you store the first name, last name, and e-mail of the donor, address information, date donated, and dollar amount. Assume you do have access to a zip code table with city, state, and zip code information for all relevant zip codes.

4.17 Student case competitions: Your company sponsors case competitions between teams of college business students. You plan to hold dozens of different regional competitions at various dates and at various locations around the country. For each competition, you want to store a name, the planned date of the competition, the name of the venue, and the address of the venue. For each participating college, you want to store the college name, a contact phone number, and a contact address. Each team can participate in only a single competition, but each college is allowed to send more than one team to a competition. Each team is assigned a number, which is unique within the competition in which it is competing, but not among all teams: for example, two different teams could both have team number 3 if they are in different competitions. Each team also gives itself a name; you want your database to store both the team name and number. Finally, each team consists of more than one student; for each student, you want to store a first name, last name, middle name/initial, date of birth, major, and expected graduation date. All students on a given team must come from the same college, and each student can be on only one team.

4.18 Musical Instrument Dealer: You operate a business that buys, sells, and repairs bowed musical instruments such as violins, violas, cellos, and acoustic basses. You consider anybody who either sells an instrument from you or buys one from you to be a "customer." Most of the stock you deal in are mass-produced models, but a few are extremely expensive antique instruments. Due to your volume of business, you are moving from paper record-keeping to a relational database.

For each customer, you want the new system to store a customer title (Dr., Prof., Mr., Ms., etc.), first name, middle name/initial, last name, address information, phone number, and e-mail address.

For each instrument you deal with, you want to store its type (violin, cello, etc.), manufacturer, year of manufacture, model (if any), and serial number (if any). Most modern producers of instruments assign a model name and serial number to each instrument they make, but some small artisanal and older classic instrument producers do not. Of the thousands of instruments that pass through your business each year, a small percentage are classic instruments that have "provenance" information describing their history. When an instrument has such information, you want the database to store a provenance summary that you will enter in a 255-character text field.

You also want to track transactions involving each instrument. It is common for you to sell an instrument (for example, to a student) and then buy it back again. For each transaction, you need to record a code indicating whether it was a purchase or a sale, which instrument was involved, which customer was involved, the date, and the price.

Sometimes, you perform minor repair work on instruments using your own in-house staff. For each repair, you want to record which instrument was involved, the date, and a description of the repair.

Design a database to hold all this information. You may create synthetic keys as necessary or convenient. If possible, avoid having blank provenance fields for instruments not needing provenance information.

4.19 Youth Baseball League: You want to keep records for your local area youth baseball league, as follows:

- Each player can only be on one team. For each player, you want to keep first name, last name, home address, and phone number.
- Each team has a name, a mascot, and a shirt color.
- Teams may have more than one coach, but each coach works only for one team. You want to store each coach's first name, last name, home address, phone number, and mobile phone number.
- Each team has a home field where it holds practice sessions and home games. Each field has a name and address information. Several teams can have the same home field.
- In addition to knowing each team's home field, you need to store all necessary information to identify each team's players and coaches.
- Assume that you do have the master zip code table available.
- A small minority of the players have medical conditions and play under a doctor's supervision. For such players, we want to store a 256-character text description of the condition, the doctor's name, and the doctor's phone number.

Design the database so that you do not need to rely on blank fields to indicate that a player does not have medical supervision — that is, keep medical data in a separate table, only for players who need it.

4.20 County real estate records: You are creating an electronic version of the records of your county's register of deeds. The county has a number of municipalities (towns, villages, cities, etc.), and for each one you want to store a name, a type (city, township, borough, etc.), and date of incorporation. Each municipality has numerous buildings, each of which is identified by a block number and lot number (each building within a given municipality has a unique combination of block number and lot number). For each building, you want to store a street address, zip code, and the year in which it was constructed. Note that zip codes do not correspond perfectly to municipalities: some municipalities have multiple zip codes, and the boundaries of zip codes and municipalities are not perfectly aligned. Each building may have been sold many times; for each sale, you want to record its price, date, and the name of the person or company the building was sold to (you record owners' names using a single, long "name" field because some owners are corporations).

Finally, a small percentage of buildings in the county are in the national register of historic places; for these buildings, you want to record a 255-character description of the unique features of the building, the date it was inducted into the historic register, and the ID number the register assigned to it. Assume that you have access to a data table that includes the zip code and corresponding post office name for each zip code that intersects the county; include this table in your database (all these zip codes are in the same state as your county, so the state need not be stored). Set up your database so that the records for non-historic buildings do not have to store empty fields for historic-register-related data.

4.21 Restaurant Health Inspection Office: Your office oversees restaurant health inspections for Somerton County. You have a staff of inspectors, for each of whom you want to store a first name, last name, date hired, office phone number, and mobile phone number. For each restaurant in the county, you want to store a name, address information, phone number, and date opened. You also want your system to remember who owns each restaurant. Each restaurant has one owner, but an owner may have many restaurants. For each owner, you want to store a name, address information, phone number, and e-mail address.

An inspection involves a single inspector visiting a single restaurant. For each inspection, you also want to store the date/time that the inspection started. Historically, about 98% of inspections are "pass" inspections, meaning that no health violations were found. The remaining 2% are "fail" inspections. For each fail inspection, you want to store a 255-character description of the health violations found.

Design a database to store this information, taking care not to waste storage to describe violations for "pass" inspections. Draw an ER diagram and write a database design outline.

4.22 Campus buses: You are in charge of maintenance records for the bus fleet operated by Gigantic State University (GSU). You operate a number of different kinds of bus, for example "General Motors EX250" or "Flxible R-5000." For each kind of bus, you want to keep track of the manufacturer, model "number" (which may contain letters), recommended maintenance interval in both miles and days of operation, grade of oil recommended, and engine oil capacity.

For each bus in your fleet, you want to be able to retrieve records of all maintenance operations performed on it. For each maintenance operation, you want to be able to retrieve the time the maintenance began, the bus's odometer mileage, and text (up to 255 characters) indicating what maintenance was performed.

The event of a bus leaving the depot is called a *dispatch*. For each bus, you want to be able to retrieve information regarding all its dispatches. This information should include date/time and odometer mileage when leaving the depot, date/time and mileage of return to the depot, which driver, and 255 characters worth of text for driver comments (such as "bus seemed louder than usual" or "brakes were grabbing"). Each driver has a unique driver's license number, along with a first name, last name, middle name/initial, date of birth, cell phone number, home phone number, and date of last safety training. By law, your drivers cannot use out-of-state licenses, so all driver's licenses are from the same state.

A Design a database to store all this information. Draw an ER diagram, and write a database design outline.

B Now suppose that only 5% of dispatches result in driver comments, while 95% result in no driver comments. Add a table to your database so that driver comments are stored in a separate table, but each comment can still be associated with a particular dispatch event. Draw a new ER diagram, and rewrite the database design outline.

5

Multiple Tables in Access

Access provides straightforward methods for creating and visualizing the relationships between tables, as well as for querying data stored in multiple tables. In this chapter, we will cover setting up table links in the Relationships window, understanding referential integrity, cascading updates and deletions, creating nested table views and nested forms, and querying multiple tables.

The Relationships Window and Referential Integrity

Consider the database shown in Figure 5.1, which we encountered when we first introduced multi-table databases.

CUSTOMER(CustomerID, FirstName, LastName, Address, City, State, Zip, Phone)

LOAN(LoanID, Date, Amt, Rate, Term, Type, CustomerID)
   CustomerID foreign key to CUSTOMER

PAYMENT(LoanID, PaymentNumber, Date, Amount)
   LoanID foreign key to LOAN.

Here, we have adopted the approach in which PAYMENT has a composite key consisting of the *LoanID* and a *PaymentNumber* within each loan. How would such a database work in MS Access?

First, we save and open the file loans-3tables-clean.mdb from the book website entry for this chapter. Remember that you must first save the file and then open it. Do not try to directly open the file from your browser, or you might not be able to make changes. This Access file contains the three tables described above, including some sample data. The file type .mdb is for Access 2000 and 2003 databases, but Access versions 2007 and later are also able to open and manipulate files in this format.

Introductory Relational Database Design for Business, with Microsoft Access, First Edition. Jonathan Eckstein and Bonnie R. Schultz.
© 2018 John Wiley & Sons Ltd. Published 2018 by John Wiley & Sons Ltd.

Figure 5.1 ER diagram for loan database with payments.

To enable editing once you have opened the file, you might have to press the "Enable" or "Enable Content" button in a yellow banner at the top of the screen.

The loans-3tables-clean.mdb file contains the tables in the database outlined above, but it does not yet contain the necessary relationship definitions. To tell Access about the relationships, we proceed as follows: click the "Database Tools" tab, and then click the "Relationships" icon. Then drag each of the tables from the left of the screen into the Relationships window (Figure 5.2).

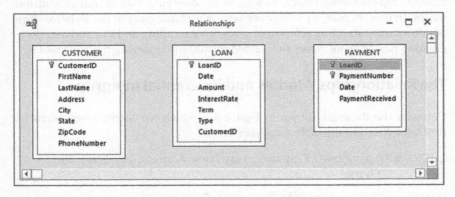

Figure 5.2 Relationships Window before creating relationships.

Next, click on a foreign key and drag it over the primary key it is supposed to match – for example, drag *CustomerID* in the LOAN table over *CustomerID* in the CUSTOMER table. A small window pops up showing the intended key match between the tables (Figure 5.3). You should check "Enforce Referential Integrity" and then "Create."

Referential integrity means that the value in a foreign key attribute must match the primary key of some record in the related table. For example, we cannot have "C0005" as the value of *CustomerID* in the LOAN table unless there actually is some record in the CUSTOMER table whose primary key is C0005. Referential integrity maintains the conditions necessary for a valid foreign key.

After we click "Create," Access creates the intended relationship (Figure 5.4). Note that the "∞" next to the line connecting between the tables stands for "many." If we had not clicked "Enforce referential integrity," the "1" and "∞" would not show up next to the relationship line, although in principle one

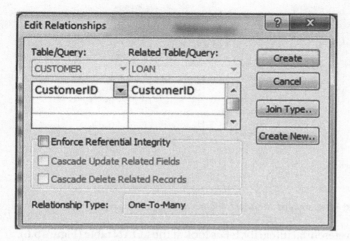

Figure 5.3 The Edit Relationship dialog box.

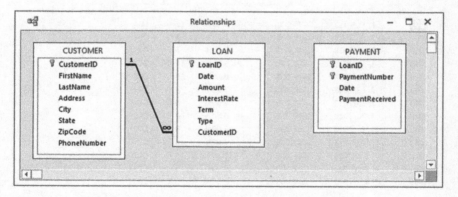

Figure 5.4 Relationships Window with CUSTOMER-LOAN relationship.

could deduce the one-to-many nature of the relationship because *CustomerID* is the primary key of the CUSTOMER table.

We repeat the procedure between the *LoanID* field of the PAYMENT table and the *LoanID* field of the LOAN table, and obtain our complete relationship setup (Figure 5.5).

The Relationships window contains a graphical form of the same information in our database outline notation: the name of each table, the names of all the attributes, an indication of each table's primary key, and all foreign key relationships. Make sure to press the Save button at the top left of the Access window, and then close the Relationships window. Access should now be aware of the relationships between the database tables.

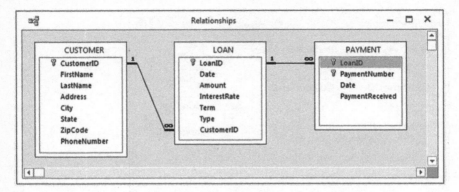

Figure 5.5 Completed Relationships Window for loans database with payments.

To demonstrate referential integrity, let us look at the LOAN table (Figure 5.6).

LoanID	Date	Amount	InterestRate	Ter	Ty	CustomerID	Click to Add
L001	1/15/2013	$475,000	6.90%	15	M	C04	
L004	1/23/2013	$35,000	7.20%	5	C	C04	
L010	1/25/2013	$10,000	5.50%	3	C	C05	
L014	1/31/2013	$12,000	9.50%	10	O	C04	
L020	2/8/2013	$525,000	6.50%	30	M	C06	
L022	2/12/2013	$10,500	7.50%	5	O	C99	
L026	2/15/2013	$35,000	6.50%	5	O	C10	
L028	2/20/2013	$250,000	8.80%	30	M	C08	
L030	2/21/2013	$5,000	10.00%	3	O	C08	
L031	2/28/2013	$200,000	7.00%	15	M	C01	
L032	3/1/2013	$25,000	10.00%	3	C	C02	
L033	3/1/2013	$20,000	9.50%	5	O	C05	
L039	3/3/2013	$56,000	7.50%	5	C	C09	

Figure 5.6 Access displays the LOAN table.

Suppose we try to enter a new loan with *CustomerID* "C53" (Figure 5.7).

L100	5/1/2012	$150,000	6.00%	15	M	C03	
L109	5/3/2012	$350,000	8.20%	30	M	C04	
L120	5/8/2012	$275,000	9.20%	15	M	C07	
L200	2/7/2011	$200,000	4.20%	10	C	C53	
*							

Figure 5.7 Trying to enter a nonexistent customer in the LOAN table.

If we try to save this record (for example, by hitting "Enter"), we receive an error message that a "related record" is required in the CUSTOMER table.

The meaning of this message is that since customer C53 does not exist, "C53" is not an acceptable value for the *CustomerID* foreign key. Instead, before trying to enter this value in a record in the LOAN table, we must *first* create customer C53 (Figure 5.8).

Customer	First Name	Last Name	Address	City	St	Zip Cod	Phone Numbe
⊞ C01	Eileen	Faulkner	7245 NW 8 Street	Minneapolis	MN	55346	(612) 894-1511
⊞ C02	Scott	Wit	5660 NW 175 Terr.	Baltimore	MD	21224	(410) 753-0345
⊞ C03	Benjamin	Grauer	10000 Sample Roa	Coral Springs	FL	33073	(305) 444-5555
⊞ C05	Alex	Rey	3456 Main Highwa	Denver	CO	80228	(303) 555-6666
⊞ C06	Ted	Myerson	6545 Stone Street	Chapel Hill	NC	27515	(919) 942-7654
⊞ C08	Michelle	Zacco	488 Gold Street	Gainesville	FL	32601	(904) 374-5660
⊞ C09	David	Powell	5070 Battle Road	Decatur	GA	30034	(301) 345-6556
⊞ C10	Matt	Hirsch	777 NW 67 Avenu	Fort Lee	NJ	07624	(201) 664-3211
⊞ C53	Joseph	Blowe	222 Easton Street	Somerset	NJ	08821	(732) 838-2929

Figure 5.8 Access displays the CUSTOMER table.

After such a customer exists in the CUSTOMER table, we can save a loan record matching it.

Access uses a pencil icon on the left side of the table window to indicate that a record is in the process of being modified or inserted and has not been saved yet. When the pencil disappears, then (if you do not receive an error message) the record is now saved within the database. Remember that, unlike other Office programs, you do not save the entire file in one operation but instead continually save individual objects or records within a database file.

Note that in this database, customer IDs start with "C," loan IDs start with "L," and so forth. In this case, these conventions are enforced by *validation rules* we can see in the Design View of the table, as shown in Figure 5.9.

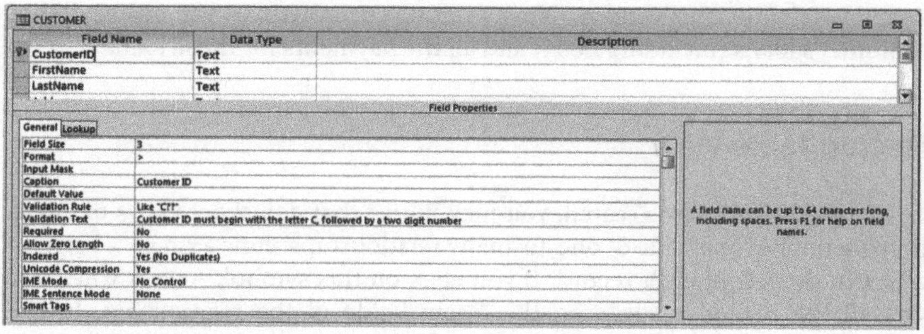

Figure 5.9 Table Design View, showing a validation rule.

Here, the "C" is actually part of the customer ID. By using an input mask instead of a validation rule, Access can also be set up so that the "C" characters appear when the IDs are displayed, but they are not actually stored in the database.

Cascading updates. Now consider what happens if we try to change customer C07's ID to "C99" in the CUSTOMER table. Access prevents us from making the change because there are loans with *CustomerID* C07 in the LOAN table, so changing the customer's ID would break referential integrity: the loans with C07 as their *CustomerID* would no longer be referring to a valid customer record. However, we can tell Access to make "cascading" changes to maintain referential integrity:

1) Close all open table windows.
2) Reopen the Relationships window.
3) Double-click the relationship line between CUSTOMER and LOAN.
4) Check "Cascade update related fields" and click "OK."

Now, we are allowed to change "C07" to "C99" in the CUSTOMER table: Access simply updates any foreign keys that matched customer "C07" to instead match customer "C99," so that the connection pattern between records remains unchanged. If you look at the LOAN table after making the change, you will see that all the loans that used to have "C07" as their *CustomerID* have had it changed to "C99." This process can "chain" across multiple relationships, so long as they all have cascading updates enabled.

Cascading deletes. Next, try to delete the LOAN record for loan L001: select the whole record by clicking to the left of it, and then hit the "Delete" key. Again, we get an error message because there are payments that have a *LoanID* of L001, meaning that deletion of the loan would violate referential integrity. We could instead proceed by first deleting all these payment records and then deleting the loan. Enabling the *cascading deletes* property of the relationship causes this process to happen automatically. Like cascading updates, it also will "chain" across multiple relationships that have the cascading property enabled. As an example, for each relationship in the relationship window, double-click check "Cascade delete related records," and then close the dialog box. Next, save the Relationships window. Now, deleting customer C04 will delete all that customer's loans (including L001) and all the payments for those loans.

Nested Table View

Once relationships are created, you may notice that datasheet views of tables that are on the "one" side of one-to-many relationships show a small "+" sign in a box to the left of each record. If you click on this symbol, Access will show you all the related records on the "many" side of the relationship. In the CUSTOMER table, for example, clicking the "+" next to customer "C01" causes Access to display a subtable of all the customer's loans (Figure 5.10).

This feature gives the database the *appearance* of having repeating groups and is useful for exploring the data. However, the actual data are stored in tables using the relational structure that we have specified.

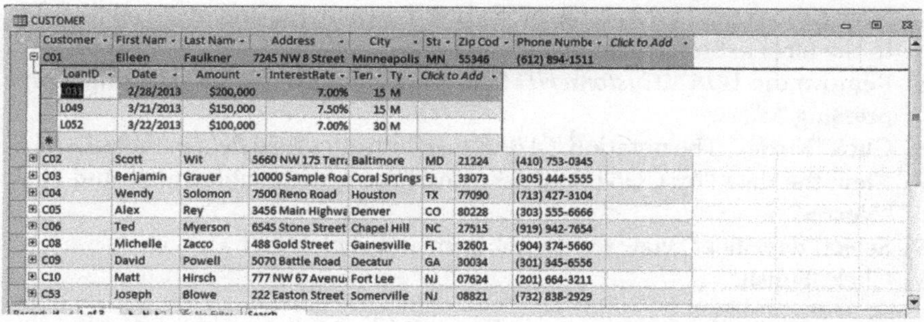

Figure 5.10 Example of nested table view.

Access' nested table display feature works on multiple levels. For example, click on the "+" next to L049 in the subtable, and a sub-subtable of that loan's payments appears (Figure 5.11).

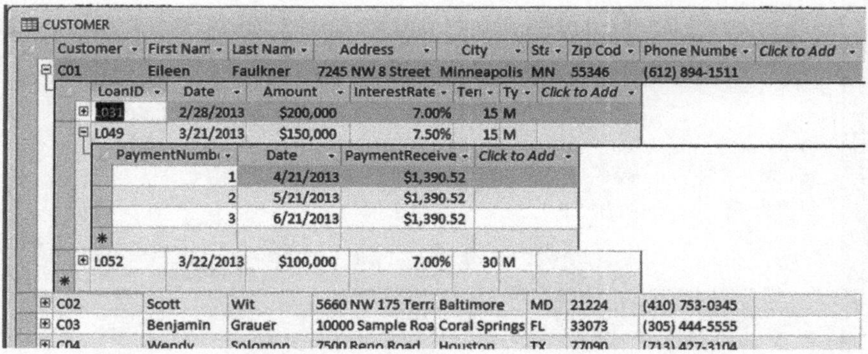

Figure 5.11 Using nested table view with multiple levels of nesting.

Nested Forms

The nested table view feature can be handy, but is not very user-friendly. Its main utility is for relatively sophisticated users. Fortunately, Access allows you to create forms that have similar functionality but are more accessible. Suppose we want a form that shows all the information about a customer and information about each of their loans:

1) Select the "Create" tab in the ribbon.
2) Press the "Form Wizard" button.
3) Choose the CUSTOMER table in the pull-down menu, and move all its fields to the form list with ">>".

4) Now choose the LOAN table in the pull-down menu, and move all its fields to the form list too (again using ">>").
5) Remove the *LOAN.CustomerID* field from the form list by selecting it and pressing "<".
6) Click "Next >". The notation *TABLE.field* indicates field *field* in table *TABLE*.
7) View the data "by CUSTOMER" using "Form with subform(s)" and click "Next >".
8) Select "datasheet" view for the subform and click "Next >".
9) Click "Finish."

Access creates the form shown in Figure 5.12.

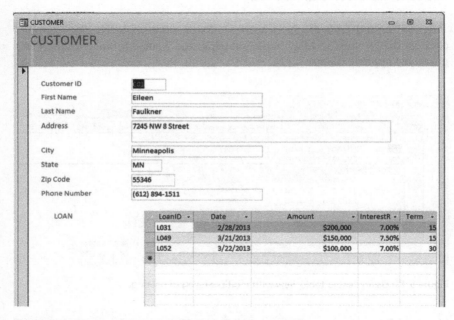

Figure 5.12 Access creates a nested form for customers and loans.

Together with the information for a given customer, we see a table describing all of that customer's loans. This kind of hierarchical data view can be very helpful to people using a database, even if it does not exactly reflect the way the data are actually stored.

Here, Access is actually using *two* form objects, which we may call "outer" and "inner," with a special linkage. The outer form is a form object called "CUSTOMER," and the inner one is a form object called "LOAN Subform." This situation is useful to keep in mind when editing the forms. To populate the data in the form, Access takes guidance from the relationship window information, and implicitly performs a "join" of the two tables, so that the inner form only displays loan records whose *CustomerID* matches the *CustomerID* of the record currently being shown in the outer form. When you display such a nested form in Form View, both its inner and outer parts are "live," letting you make data changes, additions, and deletions.

Using Design View, we make some minor adjustments in to the appearance of the two forms, obtaining something a bit more visually appealing (Figure 5.13).

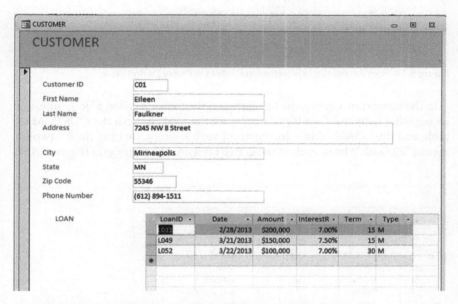

Figure 5.13 Fine-tuning the design of the nested customer-loan form.

Note that adjustments to the column widths of the subform may be made directly in Form View. Save the form design and close it.

Queries with Multiple Tables

Next, we will see how to perform queries on multiple-table databases. In the "Create" panel of the ribbon, we click "Query Design" and are presented with the "Add Tables" dialog box. We add the CUSTOMER and LOAN tables to the query and then click "Close." Because of the relationships we have already defined, Access assumes that the tables will be related in the same way in our query (Figure 5.14).

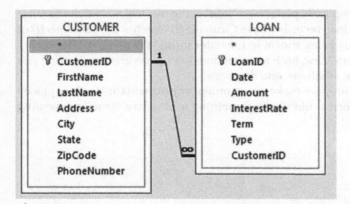

Figure 5.14 How Access displays two related tables in Query Design View.

In the context of a query, the line between the tables is called a "join" line. Let us see what happens if we try to display all the fields in both the CUSTOMER table and the LOAN table – to construct such a query, we drag the "*" (which means "all fields") from each of those two tables to the query grid (Figure 5.15).

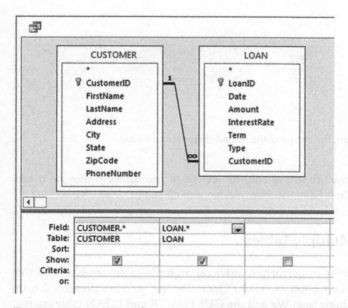

Figure 5.15 Design View of a query joining the CUSTOMER and LOAN tables.

If we hit the "!Run" (exclamation mark) icon in the ribbon, we see information on all loans, with the corresponding customer information appended to the front of each one. This is essentially the same "flat file" presentation we had when we first considered this example, except that it is the output of a query, not the way the data are actually stored in the database.

Here, Access is computing the *inner join* of the two tables. Each row of this table looks like a row of CUSTOMER next to a row of LOAN. However, Access does not juxtapose all possible rows of CUSTOMER with all possible rows of LOAN but only those rows that "make sense" according to the defined relationships, in this case those that have matching *CustomerID* fields.

Using the same upper-left-hand button that selects between Datasheet View and Design View, open the "SQL View" of the query. We then see the following expression of the query in SQL, which stands for *Structured Query Language* (often pronounced "sequel"):

```
SELECT CUSTOMER.*, LOAN.*
FROM CUSTOMER INNER JOIN LOAN
     ON CUSTOMER.CustomerID = LOAN.CustomerID;
```

This statement instructs the query to show all fields from CUSTOMER and all fields from LOAN, based on the rows in the table obtained by joining LOAN and CUSTOMER with matching *CustomerID values*. That is, CUSTOMER INNER JOIN LOAN ON CUSTOMER.CustomerID = LOAN.CustomerID means the (temporary) table one obtains by taking each combination of a row from LOAN concatenated with a row from CUSTOMER, subject to the restriction that their *CustomerID* fields have to match. From this temporarily constructed table, we show all possible fields. Although Access' graphical view may be more intuitive to work with, it is very useful to become familiar with SQL representations of queries, because every relational database system provides some form of SQL (subject to some minor variations in dialect), whereas the Access Query Design View is unique to Access. Access is not powerful enough to store the kinds of huge, many-user corporate databases that you might eventually have to query, so knowing SQL might well be useful.

Suppose we create a new customer who has no loans, say customer C54. After creating such a customer, note that their information will not appear in the query output, even if we rerun the query. The reason is that, since there are no loan records with customer ID C54, there are no combinations of matching customer-loan records in which this value of *CustomerID* is represented, so the join operation does not produce any rows that have customer C54 in them.

Access, like most relational database software, can perform several kinds of joins between tables. One kind is called an *outer join*, which may be either a *left join* or *right join*, depending on which table is mentioned first in the SQL expression of the query. To see what an outer join looks like, return to Design View and double-click the join line between CUSTOMER and LOAN (or right-click it and select "Join Properties"). Then click the button that says "Include ALL records from 'CUSTOMER' and only those records from 'LOAN' where the joined fields are equal" (Figure 5.16).

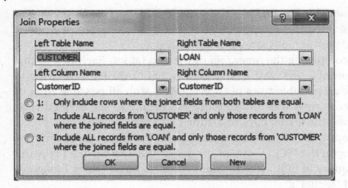

Figure 5.16 Manipulating join properties in Query Design View.

After clicking "OK," you should see a small arrow appear on the join line between the tables, indicating that the query uses an outer join (Figure 5.17).

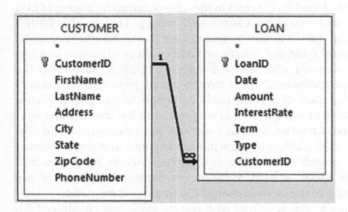

Figure 5.17 How Access displays an outer join.

If you run the query now, one line will appear for each customer who has no loans, but the loan fields will be blank. If we select "SQL View" again under the View button, we see a slightly different query command:

```
SELECT CUSTOMER.*, LOAN.*
FROM CUSTOMER LEFT JOIN LOAN ON CUSTOMER.CustomerID=
                        LOAN.CustomerID;
```

The INNER JOIN clause from the previous version of the query has now become a LEFT JOIN, indicating that at least one representative of the table on the left must be included even if there is no matching record on the right. The RIGHT JOIN clause in SQL works similarly, but forces inclusion of the table on the right (depending on the exact sequence of operations you followed to create this query, you may find that "left" and "right" are reversed in your version).

Modifying or deleting the relationships/joins in the Query Design window affects only the particular query you are currently working on. Such changes do not change or remove the "master" relationships defined in the Relationships window, which holds the overall "schema" of the database.

Let us try a few more multi-table queries:

1) Create a new query, and add the CUSTOMER and LOAN tables to it.
2) From CUSTOMER, drag *CustomerID*, *FirstName*, *LastName*, *City*, *State*, and *ZipCode* to the query grid.
3) From LOAN, drag *LoanID*, *Date*, *Amount*, and *Term* to the grid.

Conceptually, Access processes such a query in two steps. First, it creates the same kind of inner join that we created for the previous query: a table whose records consist of all matching pairs of records from the constituent tables. Then it simply deletes the columns that we did not request in the output. We can also instruct the query to drop *rows* from the result by entering criteria much as in our earlier, simpler queries. Suppose we try the criteria shown in Figure 5.18:

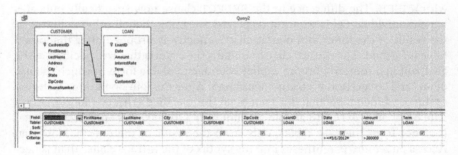

Figure 5.18 A multi-table query with record selection criteria.

1) In the Criteria line, put ">200000" in the *Amount* column.
2) On the same line, put "> = #3/1/2012#" in the *Date* column (recall that Access uses "#" to signify the start and end of a date).

Remember that Access combines multiple criteria specified on the same row of the grid with an "and" logical operation. Therefore, if we run the query, we obtain all loans made on or after March 1, 2013, whose amount was at more than $200,000 (Table 5.1).

Table 5.1 Output of the multi-table query with record selection criteria.

Customer ID	First Name	Last Name	City	State	Zip Code	Loan ID	Date	Amount	Term
C10	Matt	Hirsch	Fort Lee	NJ	07624	L062	4/22/2013	$350,000.00	15
C99	Lori	Sangas-tiano	Santa Rosa	CA	95403	L120	5/8/2013	$275,000.00	15

Let us examine the SQL form of this query:

```
SELECT  CUSTOMER.CustomerID, CUSTOMER.FirstName,
        CUSTOMER.LastName, CUSTOMER.City,
        CUSTOMER.State, CUSTOMER.ZipCode, LOAN.LoanID,
        LOAN.Date, LOAN.Amount, LOAN.Term
FROM    CUSTOMER INNER JOIN LOAN
        ON CUSTOMER.CustomerID = LOAN.CustomerID
WHERE   (((LOAN.Date)>=#3/1/2012#) AND
        ((LOAN.Amount)>200000));
```

The FROM clause here is identical to the original form of the previous query. However, the SELECT clause is different, and there is a new clause starting with WHERE. The difference in the SELECT clause now specifically indicates which individual fields we want displayed, meaning that all other columns in the result of the inner join operation are effectively dropped after the joined table is formed. The WHERE clause contains the criteria that we specified in the grid, but in a somewhat more explicitly understandable form in which the use of an "and" operation is clearly mentioned. After the join operation, each row of the combined table that does not meet the specified criteria – in this case, a date on or after 3/1/2013 and an amount over $200,000 – is effectively deleted (but not from the base tables, only from the result of the query). Note that Access puts more parentheses into the syntax of the WHERE clause than is necessary, and that you should not use a $ sign or quotes when entering currency amounts into SQL.

Multiple Joins and Aggregation

Next we will introduce the concept of queries with *aggregation* operations, which combine blocks of data into a single element; we have already used aggregation operations when constructing simple reports. Let us create a new query, and add *all three* tables to it (Figure 5.19).

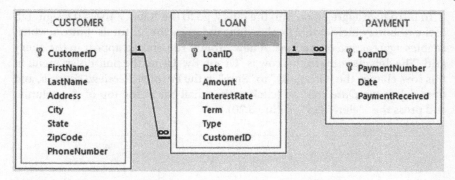

Figure 5.19 How Access displays three related tables in Query Design View.

We then drag the following attributes to the query grid:

- *CustomerID* (from CUSTOMER)
- *FirstName* (from CUSTOMER)
- *LastName* (from CUSTOMER)
- *LoanID* (from LOAN)
- *Date* (from PAYMENT)
- *PaymentReceived* (from PAYMENT)

Running this query produces a large amount of data. Essentially, it shows the date and amount of every payment received in the database, prefixed with the ID and name of the customer making the payment and the ID of the loan the payment was made on. We can think of Access as executing this query by first performing a three-way join that constructs a large table whose rows consist of a row from CUSTOMER, a row from LOAN, and a row from PAYMENT, but only those combinations that have matching keys according to the relationships we have defined. If you look at the SQL view, you will see this join is expressed as a composition of two two-way inner joins, like this:

```
FROM (CUSTOMER INNER JOIN LOAN
      ON CUSTOMER.CustomerID = LOAN.CustomerID)
    INNER JOIN PAYMENT ON LOAN.LoanID = PAYMENT.LoanID;
```

This expression joins the first two tables just as we did in the previous two queries and then joins the resulting temporary table to the PAYMENT table by matching the *LoanID* fields. The result essentially consists of every row of PAYMENT, prefixed with the corresponding rows of CUSTOMER and LOAN. In the next step of processing the query, Access drops the columns we did not request in the output.

To introduce aggregation into the query, go to the "Query Tools /Design" tab of the ribbon (which should be showing) and press the "Σ Totals" button, which enables aggregation operations. A new "Total:" row should appear in the query grid. The default entry in this row is "Group By." Using the pull-down menu in this row, change the "Group By" to "Sum" in the *PaymentReceived* column, and then delete the *Date* column (click at the small bar at the top of the column, and press the "delete" key) (Figure 5.20).

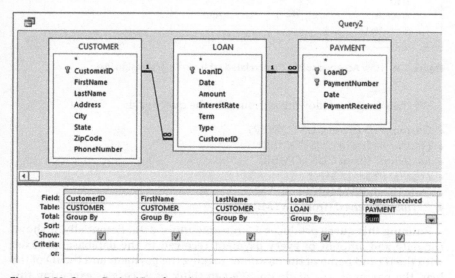

Figure 5.20 Query Design View for a three-table query.

Running the query now results the total amount received on each loan, along with its ID and the corresponding customer's name and ID (Table 5.2). Conceptually, Access performs this query as follows:

- After performing the three-table join described above, Access divides the columns into groups. The groups are defined as follows: if two records are identical in *every* "group by" column, they are in the same group; otherwise, the records are in different groups.
- Each group becomes one row in the query output.
- For each group, Access displays the common value of the "group by" columns. By definition, their values are all identical, so this display only requires one row per group.
- For the remaining columns, Access combines the values within each group as specified by the "Totals:" row – in this case, using the Sum operation.

The effect here is to group the records by *LoanID*: two records having the same *LoanID* in the result of the join implies that their *CustomerID*, *FirstName*,

Table 5.2 Output of the three-table query.

Customer ID	First Name	Last Name	Loan ID	Sum of Payment Received
C01	Eileen	Faulkner	L031	$7,190.64
C01	Eileen	Faulkner	L049	$4,171.56
C01	Eileen	Faulkner	L052	$1,995.90
C02	Scott	Wit	L032	$2,420.04
C02	Scott	Wit	L054	$405.52
C03	Benjamin	Grauer	L047	$5,477.19
C03	Benjamin	Grauer	L053	$1,379.22
C03	Benjamin	Grauer	L057	$1,232.42
C03	Benjamin	Grauer	L100	$1,265.79
C05	Alex	Rey	L010	$1,518.84
C05	Alex	Rey	L033	$1,260.12
C06	Ted	Myerson	L020	$13,273.44
C08	Michelle	Zacco	L028	$7,802.76
C08	Michelle	Zacco	L030	$645.36
C08	Michelle	Zacco	L060	$2,075.80
C10	Matt	Hirsch	L026	$2,739.28
C10	Matt	Hirsch	L040	$3,810.93
C10	Matt	Hirsch	L062	$6,498.98
C99	Lori	Sangastiano	L022	$841.60
C99	Lori	Sangastiano	L120	$2,822.05

and *LastName* must be equal, so the specified grouping on these additional columns has no practical effect. Within each group, specifying the Sum operation in the *PaymentReceived* column causes the query to add up the payments. If we also wanted a count of payments, we could add another column from PAYMENT (say, *PaymentReceived* again), and aggregate it by the Count operation (Figure 5.21 and Table 5.3).

We can easily add criteria to the query. For example, we could add "> = 4" in the Count column and "<= 3000" in the Sum column (on the same line), to only show loans with at least four payments totaling no more than $3000 (Figure 5.22). If we run this query, we now see only a few customers (Table 5.4).

By default, criteria entered into the Access Query Design View grid are applied at the end of the query, after aggregation. Later in this book, we will see how to specify criteria to be applied *before* aggregation. Note that for

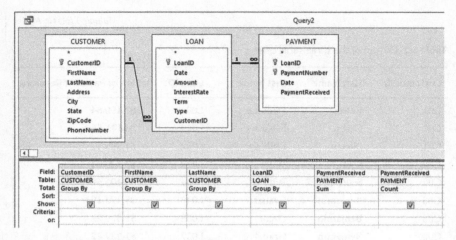

Figure 5.21 Three-table query with aggregation.

Table 5.3 Result of three-table query with aggregation.

Customer ID	First Name	Last Name	Loan ID	Sum of Payment Received	Count of Payment Received
C01	Eileen	Faulkner	L031	$7,190.64	4
C01	Eileen	Faulkner	L049	$4,171.56	3
C01	Eileen	Faulkner	L052	$1,995.90	3
C02	Scott	Wit	L032	$2,420.04	3
C02	Scott	Wit	L054	$405.52	2
C03	Benjamin	Grauer	L047	$5,477.19	3
C03	Benjamin	Grauer	L053	$1,379.22	3
C03	Benjamin	Grauer	L057	$1,232.42	2
C03	Benjamin	Grauer	L100	$1,265.79	1
C05	Alex	Rey	L010	$1,518.84	5
C05	Alex	Rey	L033	$1,260.12	3
C06	Ted	Myerson	L020	$13,273.44	4
C08	Michelle	Zacco	L028	$7,802.76	4
C08	Michelle	Zacco	L030	$645.36	4
C08	Michelle	Zacco	L060	$2,075.80	2
C10	Matt	Hirsch	L026	$2,739.28	4
C10	Matt	Hirsch	L040	$3,810.93	3
C10	Matt	Hirsch	L062	$6,498.98	2
C99	Lori	Sangastiano	L022	$841.60	4
C99	Lori	Sangastiano	L120	$2,822.05	1

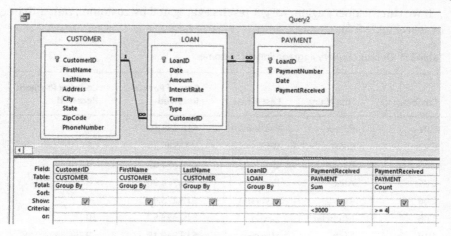

Figure 5.22 Adding criteria to the query with aggregation.

Table 5.4 Result of aggregation query with criteria.

Customer ID	First Name	Last Name	Loan ID	Sum of Payment Received	Count of Payment Received
C05	Alex	Rey	L010	$1,518.84	5
C08	Michelle	Zacco	L030	$645.36	4
C10	Matt	Hirsch	L026	$2,739.28	4
C99	Lori	Sangastiano	L022	$841.60	4

"Group By" columns there is no distinction between applying conditions before or after aggregation: for example, it would not matter whether we were to delete all rows having the first name "Eileen" before forming groups, or later delete all groups with the first name "Eileen."

Now, delete the criteria you placed in the grid. Next, delete the *LoanID* column from the grid (to accomplish this, click the top of the column so the entire column is selected and then press the "delete" key; see Figure 5.23).

Field:	CustomerID	FirstName	LastName	PaymentReceived	PaymentReceived
Table:	CUSTOMER	CUSTOMER	CUSTOMER	PAYMENT	PAYMENT
Total:	Group By	Group By	Group By	Sum	Count
Sort:					
Show:	☑	☑	☑	☑	☑
Criteria:					
or:					

Figure 5.23 Aggregating by customer instead of by order.

113

114 *Introductory Relational Database Design for Business, with Microsoft Access*
If we run the query again, we get results aggregated by customer, rather than by loan (Table 5.5).

Table 5.5 Output of query aggregating by customer.

Customer ID	First Name	Last Name	Sum of Payment Received	Count of Payment Received
C01	Eileen	Faulkner	$13,358.10	10
C02	Scott	Wit	$2,825.56	5
C03	Benjamin	Grauer	$9,354.62	9
C05	Alex	Rey	$2,778.96	8
C06	Ted	Myerson	$13,273.44	4
C08	Michelle	Zacco	$10,523.92	10
C10	Matt	Hirsch	$13,049.19	9
C99	Lori	Sangastiano	$3,663.65	5

Customers with multiple loans now have the payments from all their loans lumped together, because we are no longer grouping by *LoanID*.

Note that even though we are no longer asking for any output fields from LOAN, the relationships we have defined still instruct Access to compute the results of the query by performing a three-way join of CUSTOMER, LOAN, and PAYMENT. After the join, but before aggregation, all columns from LOAN are deleted.

Suppose that we do not want to see *CustomerID*s in the query output, but we still want to group by customer. It might seem natural to just delete the *CustomerID* column from the query grid, but that might have undesirable consequences – if we have two customers with the same name (for example, "Jane Chen"), their records would get lumped together, because all the "group by" fields are equal. To avoid this misleading behavior, we simply uncheck the "show" box under *CustomerID* (Figure 5.24).

Field:	CustomerID	FirstName	LastName	PaymentReceived	PaymentReceived
Table:	CUSTOMER	CUSTOMER	CUSTOMER	PAYMENT	PAYMENT
Total:	Group By	Group By	Group By	Sum	Count
Sort:					
Show:	☐	☑	☑	☑	☑
Criteria:					
or:					

Figure 5.24 Grouping by customer IDs without displaying them.

The result will be that we still group by the *CustomerID* attribute, so two customers with the same name will appear on different output lines. The output now looks like Table 5.6.

Table 5.6 Output of query grouping by customer IDs but not displaying them.

First Name	Last Name	Sum of Payment Received	Count of Payment Received
Eileen	Faulkner	$13,358.10	10
Scott	Wit	$2,825.56	5
Benjamin	Grauer	$9,354.62	9
Alex	Rey	$2,778.96	8
Ted	Myerson	$13,273.44	4
Michelle	Zacco	$10,523.92	10
Matt	Hirsch	$13,049.19	9
Lori	Sangastiano	$3,663.65	5

Personnel: Database Design with Multiple Paths between Tables

Consider the following business situation:

You are keeping personnel records on employees. For each employee, you want the database to store the first name, last name, home address information, home phone number, office address information, and work phone number/extension. Each employee works at a single branch office. Everybody in a branch office has the same office address information and work phone number, except for a phone extension of up to four digits. You also want to store the names of the branch offices.

Each employee is assigned to one health plan. For each health plan, you want to store its name and a monthly premium. Each health plan is offered by a health plan provider, which has a name, address information, and a phone number. Some providers offer more than one plan. For example, Blue Cross offers a traditional plan, a PPO plan, and an HMO plan.

Assume that you have a national zip code data table available.

Design a normalized database to store all this information.

Since we assume that we have a master zip code table available, all the address information in the database should consist of just a street address and a zip code. We refer to the zip code table to determine the city name and state. For simplicity, we will use a single street address field. In reality, one might want to have two fields, one for the first address line, and one for an optional second line.

The entities/tables we need for this database are as follows:

- EMPLOYEE – to hold information pertaining to employees, such as their names, home addresses, and phone numbers
- HEALTHPLAN – to hold information pertaining to health plans, such as their names and premiums
- PROVIDER – to hold information pertaining to health plan providers
- BRANCHOFFICE – to hold information pertaining to branch offices, such as their names and addresses
- ZIPCODE – to hold information pertaining to zip codes, namely, the city/town name and state

Let us set aside zip codes for the moment, and consider the other entities:

- We will need a relationship between EMPLOYEE and HEALTHPLAN to indicate which health plan each employee has. Here, EMPLOYEE is clearly the "many" and HEALTHPLAN is the "one": one employee has one health plan, but one health plan potentially has many employees. This arrangement makes sense: we should have a foreign key in each EMPLOYEE record (EMPLOYEE is "the many") indicating which health plan the employee has.
- We will need a relationship between HEALTHPLAN and PROVIDER to indicate which provider offers each health plan. Here, HEALTHPLAN is the "many" and PROVIDER is the "one," because each health plan is offered by just one provider, but some providers may offer several plans.
- We need a relationship between EMPLOYEE and BRANCHOFFICE to indicate where the employees are assigned. Here, EMPLOYEE is the "many" because each employee is assigned to just one office, but a branch office may obviously have multiple employees.

We obtain the partial ER diagram shown in Figure 5.25.

Figure 5.25 ER diagram for the personnel database, before including zip codes.

Now let us consider zip codes. The following entities have address information:

- PROVIDER, which indicates where the health care provider is located
- EMPLOYEE, which indicates where the employee lives
- BRANCHOFFICE, which indicates where the branch office is located (and thus where the employees assigned to it work)

Thus, each of the tables PROVIDER, EMPLOYEE, and BRANCHOFFICE will need a foreign key to the ZIPCODE table so that we can find the requisite city and state information. Note that the three kinds of address information in the database are *semantically different*; that is, that they give us information about different things.

We create a ZIPCODE entity, and place it in a one-to-many relationship between each of the entities PROVIDER, EMPLOYEE, and BRANCHOFFICE. In each case, the zip code is the "one," because each provider, employee, and branch office is in only one zip code. We certainly can have more than one employee live in a given zip code, and while it is somewhat unlikely there would be more than one health care provider or branch office in a zip code, we do not want to preclude that possibility. In any event, it would make very little sense to put foreign keys indicating health care providers and branch offices in the ZIPCODE table, so ZIPCODE must be the "one" of the relationships.

We now have the complete ER diagram (Figure 5.26).

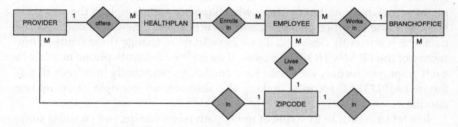

Figure 5.26 ER diagram for personnel database with zip codes.

This is our first example of what may be called a *multi-path* pattern of relationships, that is, a design having multiple distinct ways to relate records in different tables. For example, there are several different ways to move from EMPLOYEE to ZIPCODE by following the relationship connections in the diagram. These multiple paths are justified because they are semantically different – they mean different things. We will return to this notion in more detail after we write the database outline:

EMPLOYEE(<u>EmployeeID</u>, FName, LName, Address, Zip, Phone,
        PlanID, BranchID, Extension)
   PlanID foreign key to HEALTHPLAN
   BranchID foreign key to BRANCHOFFICE
   Zip foreign key to ZIPCODE

HEALTHPLAN(<u>PlanID</u>, Name, Premium, ProviderID)
   ProviderID foreign key to PROVIDER

PROVIDER(<u>ProviderID</u>, Name, Address, Zip, Phone)
   Zip foreign key to ZIPCODE

BRANCHOFFICE(<u>BranchID</u>, Name, Address, Zip, Phone)
   Zip foreign key to ZIPCODE

ZIPCODE(<u>Zip</u>, City, State)

Here, we are using synthetic keys for all the tables, except for ZIPCODE, which has the obvious primary key of *Zip*.

Note that EMPLOYEE is on the "many" side of three relationships and consequently contains three different foreign keys.

An employee's home phone number is stored in their EMPLOYEE record. However, we do not store the entire work phone number in EMPLOYEE, but only the extension. That is because an employee's work phone number, other than the extension, is determined by their branch office, and is therefore stored in BRANCHOFFICE. To determine an employee's full work phone number, we would use their *BranchID* to find their branch's main phone number, and then append the employee's extension from the EMPLOYEE table. This process might seem laborious, but consider what happens, for example, if the area code holding a branch office gets split, and the office gets a new area code. As the database is currently designed, all we have to do is change three digits in one record of the BRANCHOFFICE table. If we had the full work phone number in each employee record, we would have to change potentially hundreds of different EMPLOYEE records, making the situation an example of an update anomaly.

Now let us return to the issue of multi-path relationships and consider some examples of relating a record in EMPLOYEE with one in ZIPCODE. Recall that the notation *TABLE.field* refers to field *field* in table *TABLE*. Suppose we start with a record in EMPLOYEE:

- If we simply use *EMPLOYEE.Zip* to find a record in ZIPCODE, we are finding the town in which the employee lives.
- If we follow *EMPLOYEE.BranchID* to a record of BRANCHOFFICE, and then follow *BRANCHOFFICE.Zip* to a record in ZIPCODE, we are finding the town in which the employee works.
- If we follow *EMPLOYEE.PlanID* to a record in HEALTHPLAN, then *HEALTHPLAN.ProviderID* to a record in PROVIDER, and then *PROVIDER. Zip* to a record of ZIPCODE, we are finding the town where the employee would send correspondence about his or her health plan.

Note that all of these associations between a record in EMPLOYEE and a record in ZIPCODE have different meanings, so the existence of such multiple paths is justified. *Unless* there are such differences in meaning, multiple relationship paths between the same pair of tables are redundant and should be avoided. For example, we do not need a relationship between EMPLOYEE and PROVIDER, and thus a *ProviderID* field in EMPLOYEE, since the only sensible association – the provider who administers the employee's health plan – is already available by tracing *PlanID* to HEALTHPLAN, and finding *ProviderID* there.

Creating the Database in Access using Autonumber Keys

Let us create this database in Access. In Access, primary key fields are designated by right-clicking in the rectangle to the left of the field name and selecting "primary key."

In general, the datatype and field size of a foreign key must be exactly the same as the datatype and field size of the primary key it is supposed to match. For the purposes of this rule, "Autonumber" and "Number" are really the same datatype, the only difference being that Autonumber fields are automatically filled in by Access as you create records.

We will use "Autonumber" for the synthetic keys in our database, so that Access creates their values for us. All such Autonumber fields default to the "Long integer" field size, which means a 32-bit whole number value (depending on your version of Access, the only other choice may be "replication ID," a kind of 128-bit value for which Access is phasing out support). We match a primary key of type "Autonumber(Long integer)" with a foreign key that is "Number(Long integer)" – that is, the same kind of number, just not automatically filled in. In the properties pane, Autonumber fields can be designated as either "increment" (1, 2, 3, etc.) or "random," in case you want to conceal the order in which records are created.

Using the Create/Table button, we create the following tables:

- ZIPCODE: Primary key ZIP, with datatype Text(5) – we use this shorthand to denote a (short) text field with a maximum size of five characters. Set the input mask to "00000". This input mask allows only numeric digits and forces all five characters to be entered.
- BRANCHOFFICE: Primary key *BranchID*, with datatype Autonumber(Long integer) and format "\B00". Although the branch office ID is stored as a long integer, allowing potentially billions of branch offices, the format "\B00" displays it as "B" followed by two digits. However, changing the convention for displaying branch office IDs is as simple as changing this one format specifier. To match the ZIPCODE table, *Zip* in BRANCHOFFICE should also be Text(5) with an input mask of "00000".
- PROVIDER: Primary key *ProviderID*, AutoNumber(Long integer), format "\P00".
- HEALTHPLAN: Primary key *PlanID*, AutoNumber(Long integer), format "\H000". As discussed above, ProviderID in this table should be a Number(Long integer), with a matching format "\P00".
- EMPLOYEE: Primary key *EmployeeID*, AutoNumber(Long integer), format "\E00000". We should match the datatype (except for Autonumber versus Number), field length, input mask, and format of all the foreign keys in this table with their corresponding primary keys in other tables.

Next, we define relationships between the tables using the Database Tools/ Relationships window (Figure 5.27).

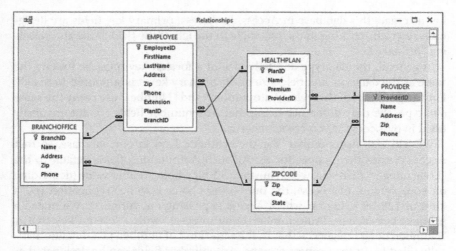

Figure 5.27 Completed Relationships Window for personnel database.

We should enable referential integrity when we define each relationship, and press the Save button to save the contents of the Relationships window.

Next, enter some (fabricated) sample data in the following order:

- Zip codes
- Branch Offices
- Providers
- Health Plans
- Employees

Note that while a few other orders are possible, the order in which we may enter records is tightly constrained by referential integrity – essentially, in any one-to-many relationship, information in the "one" table must be entered first, and only then may matching information be inserted into the "many" table, or it is impossible to maintain referential integrity. Here, this principle implies that zip code information has to be created first, employee data last, and provider data must be entered before health plan data.

A Simple Query and a Different Way to Express Joins in SQL

Suppose we want a query that returns the following for each employee:

- Employee ID
- First name

- Last name
- Branch office name
- Office phone number, consistent with the branch office phone number plus extension

To accomplish this:

1) We select the "Create" tab.
2) Select "Query Design."
3) Add the EMPLOYEE and BRANCHOFFICE tables to the query.
4) Drag the following fields to the grid:
   - *EmployeeID* from EMPLOYEE
   - *FirstName* from EMPLOYEE
   - *LastName* from EMPLOYEE
   - *Name* (or whatever we called the branch office name field) from BRANCHOFICE
   - *Phone* from BRANCHOFFICE
   - *Extension* from EMPLOYEE
5) We press "Run" to execute the query.

We obtain something like Table 5.7, depending on the sample data that we entered into the tables.

Table 5.7 Output of personnel database query.

Employee ID	First Name	Last Name	Name	Phone	Extension
E0001	Jonathan	Eckstein	Central NJ	(732) 764-5768	8903
E0002	Erving	Snodgrass	Southern California	(890) 234-9803	2309
E0003	Joanne	Poole	Southern California	(890) 234-9803	2278

If we switch to SQL view, we see the following:

```
SELECT EMPLOYEE.EmployeeID, EMPLOYEE.FirstName, EMPLOYEE.
      LastName,BRANCHOFFICE.Name, BRANCHOFFICE.Phone,
      EMPLOYEE.Extension
FROM EMPLOYEE INNER JOIN BRANCHOFFICE
      ON EMPLOYEE.BranchID=BRANCHOFFICE.BranchID;
```

This statement specifies that we join the EMPLOYEE and BRANCHOFFICE tables in the usual way, based on matching the *BranchID* field, and then display the requested fields.

When the SQL language was first created, the INNER JOIN syntax (which is now part of the SQL standard) did not exist. Instead, one would specify this query as follows:

```
SELECT  EMPLOYEE.EmployeeID, EMPLOYEE.FirstName,
        EMPLOYEE.LastName, BRANCHOFFICE.Name,
        BRANCHOFFICE.Phone, EMPLOYEE.Extension
FROM    EMPLOYEE, BRANCHOFFICE
WHERE   EMPLOYEE.BranchID = BRANCHOFFICE.BranchID;
```

This means essentially the same thing as the previous SQL command: the expression EMPLOYEE, BRANCHOFFICE refers to the table created by taking all combinations of a row from EMPLOYEE and a row from BRANCHOFFICE. This table is called the "Cartesian join" (after the French philosopher and mathematician René Descartes) or "cross join." Most of the rows of this table are in this case meaningless, since they match an employee with an unrelated branch office. The clause WHERE EMPLOYEE.BranchID = BRANCHOFFICE.BranchID, however, immediately discards all such meaningless combinations, retaining only those combinations with matching *BranchID* fields. The resulting table is exactly the same as the result of the inner join, from which we then display the desired fields.

Before executing the above query, most relational database systems perform an analysis called *query optimization*, in which they would detect that the above query is equivalent to an inner join. They would then know not to explicitly form the potentially huge Cartesian join table, an operation that could make the query run slowly. The result of the query would be exactly the same in any case. We cover this topic because the original WHERE syntax can be much easier to read when more than two tables are involved. Simple SQL queries of this form have the following syntax:

```
SELECT  Table1.Field1, Table2.Field2, … , TableN.FieldN
FROM    Table1, Table2, … , TableM
WHERE   Conditions for filtering records ;
```

Conceptually, statements of this type instruct the database system to form the potentially gigantic table formed from all combinations of a record from *Table1*, a record from *Table2*, and so forth through *TableM*, then discard all records that do not meet the conditions in the WHERE clause, and from this result display the fields referred to in the SELECT clause.

Often, as in the simple query of the EMPLOYEE and BRANCHOFFICE tables, the only filter conditions in the WHERE clause specify how to match records from the various tables, but it is also possible to include additional conditions.

Exercises

Some of the following exercises ask for an Access "Documenter" report. The procedure to create such reports is as follows:

- In the ribbon, choose the "Database Tools" pane.
- Click the "Database Documenter" button.
- Make sure you are looking at the "Tables" tab, and click the "Select All" button.
- Click the "Options" button. Under the "Print Table Definition" box that appears:
  - Check *only* "relationships" under "Include for table." Uncheck the other two boxes for this heading.
  - Choose "Names, data types and sizes" under "Include for fields."
  - Choose "Nothing" under "Include for indexes."
  - Click the "OK" button in the "Print Table Definition" box.

  Click the "OK" button in the "Documenter" box. Print the resulting report by pressing the "Print..." button.

5.1 **Portfolio tracking:** You have a large investment portfolio, and want to set up a database to keep track of your holdings. You do businesses with multiple brokerage firms, and you have more than one account with some of these firms (for example, one for your IRA and another for day trading). For each brokerage firm, you want to store a name, description, address, city, state, zip code, and phone number. For this problem, assume that you do not have access to a zip code table. For each account, you want to keep track of its account number, date opened, cash balance, and type (for example, "401(k)" or "regular"). In addition to cash, each account may contain one or more holdings of securities: for example, 1000 shares of IBM and 500 shares of Ford Motor Company. For each holding, you want to store the number of shares, the ticker symbol of the security, the date you acquired the shares, and their cost basis. Shares in some securities (such as mutual funds) may be fractional. Securities are identified by a ticker symbols consisting of up to eight characters (for example, CSCO for Cisco Systems or VZ for Verizon). Assume you have access to a master table giving a name and description for each ticker symbol that appears in your portfolio. You may hold the same security in different accounts, and have multiple holdings of the same security (acquired at different times) in the same account.

A Design a database to hold all this information. You may create synthetic keys as necessary or convenient. Create a database design outline and an ER diagram.

B In Access, create all the necessary tables for this database, and choose a reasonable datatype for each attribute. Assume phone numbers are in standard US format. Create all necessary relationships between the tables and enforce referential integrity. You do *not* have to enter any data or create any forms. Create a "Documenter" report for the database.

5.2 Stockbroker's office: You are setting up a system to track trades and portfolios for a small stockbroker's office. For each broker in the office, you want to store a first name, middle name/initial, last name, phone extension number, cell phone number, e-mail address, and date hired. For each of the firm's clients, you want to store a first name, middle name/initial, last name, address information, home phone number, work phone number, cell phone number, and e-mail address. Each client is assigned to a single stockbroker, and the database should remember which one. You also have a master list of securities which your firm is licensed to trade. For each security, you want to store a ticker symbol and a description. No two securities may have the same ticker symbol. Finally, you want to keep track of each client's transactions. For each transaction, you want to store the date/time it occurred, a transaction type ("Buy," "Sell," "Dividend," etc.), which security was involved, the net number of shares, and the net cash. For example, (ignoring commissions) buying 100 shares of IBM at $98.55 per share would mean a transaction type of "Buy," net number of shares = +100, and net cash = –$9,855.00; while selling 10 shares of Cisco Systems (ticker symbol CSCO) at $27.21 per share would mean a transaction type of "Sell," net number of shares = –10, and net cash = +$272.10.

A Design a database to hold all this information. You can create synthetic keys as necessary or convenient. Create a database design outline and an ER diagram.

B In Access, create all the necessary tables for this database, and choose a reasonable datatype for each attribute. Assume phone numbers are in standard US format. Create all necessary relationships between the tables and enforce referential integrity. You need not enter any data or create any forms. Create a "Documenter" report for the database.

5.3 Homework assignment website: The Somerton High School PTO is creating a website that will allow students to quickly look up their homework assignments. The database supporting this website will keep track of departments, teachers, classes, and assignments. Each department has a name such as "math," "science," or "English," and each teacher is a member of a single department. For each teacher, the database should store a title ("Mr.", "Ms.", "Dr.", etc.), first name, middle initial, last name, office phone number, and e-mail address. Each class is taught by one teacher; for each class, the database should store a name, description, meeting period (for example, seventh period), and room number. Finally each class has multiple assignments. For each assignment, the database should store the date assigned, the date due, and a text description of the work assigned. Obviously, the database also needs to remember which class each assignment is for, and which teacher teaches each class.

A Design a database to hold all this information. You may create synthetic keys as necessary or convenient. Create a database design outline and an ER diagram.

B In Access, create all the necessary tables for this database, and choose a reasonable datatype for each attribute. Assume phone numbers are in standard US format. If you use any "AutoNumber" synthetic primary keys, note that a matching foreign key should have a datatype of "Number," with a field length of "Long integer." Create all necessary relationships between the tables and enforce referential integrity. You do not have to enter any data or create any forms. Create a "Documenter" report for the database.

5.4 Alumni office: The alumni office of Enormous State University (ESU) wants to keep track of alumni and their charitable gifts to the university. For each alumnus, you want to store a first name, middle name, last name, address information (street address, city, state, and zip code), a home phone number, a mobile phone number, and an e-mail address. Assume that you do have access to a master table of zip codes, cities, and states, which you will include in your database design. Each alumnus may have multiple degrees. Every time a degree is granted, you want to keep track of to whom the degree was awarded, the year the degree was awarded, the type of degree (BA, MBA, PhD, JD, etc.), which school awarded the degree, and the student's major. The database should also contain a table listing all the university's schools (of which there are dozens), including a short name (up to 40 characters) and a full name (up to 100 characters). Each alumnus may make multiple charitable gifts to the university. For each gift, you want to keep track of the date it was made, who made it, and the dollar amount of the gift. Write a database design outline and draw an entity-relationship diagram for a database appropriate for this information.

A Design a database to hold all this information. You can create synthetic keys as necessary or convenient. Create a database design outline and an ER diagram.

B In Access, create all the necessary tables for this database, and choose a reasonable datatype for each attribute. Assume phone numbers are in standard US format. Create all necessary relationships between the tables and enforce referential integrity. You do not have to enter any data or create any forms. Create a "Documenter" report for the database.

5.5 Motorcycle dealership: You want to keep information on past sales at a motorcycle dealership, including information on motorcycles, salespeople, and customers. Assume that the dealership sells only new motorcycles and that all of them come from the same manufacturer.

For each salesperson, you want to store their first name, last name, middle name/initial, employee ID number, and date hired. For each customer, you want to store a customer ID number, first name, last name, middle name/initial, address information (city, state, and zip), phone number, and e-mail address. Assume that you do not have zip code table data available.

Each kind of motorcycle is called a model, and has a unique model number. For each model, you want to store its name, engine size in cubic centimeters (cc) (an integer number), and the date introduced. Each individual motorcycle sold is identified by a unique 16-digit serial "number" (which may also contain letters). For each motorcycle sale, you want to record the serial number, date of sale, and sale price. You also want to know which customer bought the motorcycle, which salesperson made the sale, and what model the motorcycle was.

A Design a database to hold all this information. You can create synthetic keys as necessary or convenient. Create a database design outline and an ER diagram.

B In Access, create all the necessary tables for this database, and choose a reasonable datatype for each attribute. Assume phone numbers are in standard US format. Create all necessary relationships between the tables and enforce referential integrity. You do not have to enter any data or create any forms. Create a "Documenter" report for the database.

5.6 **Law office:** You are trying to automate the records for your uncle's law firm. Multiple attorneys work for the firm, and for each of them you want to store their first name, middle name, last name, date hired, hourly billing rate, and date promoted to partner (blank if the attorney is not a partner). For each client, you want to store a first name, last name, middle name, phone number, address, city, state, and zip code (assume you do not have a zip code table). Each case is identified by a unique "docket number" and has a name and description. A case is always for a single client, but a client may have more than one case. Finally, you want to keep track of attorney billable hours. Each record of billable hours involves one attorney working on one case. For each billable hours record, the database should remember which attorney did the work, which case was involved, the date, the number of hours billed (fractions are allowed), and a description of the work performed.

A Design a database to hold all this information. You can create synthetic keys as necessary or convenient. Use the synthetic keys *ClientID* and *AttorneyID* for clients and attorneys, respectively. Create a database design outline and an ER diagram.

B In Access, create all the necessary tables for this database, and choose a reasonable datatype for each attribute. Assume phone numbers are in standard US format. Create all necessary relationships between the tables and enforce referential integrity. You do not have to enter any data or create any forms. Create a "Documenter" report for the database.

6

More about Forms and Navigation

Forms let you display data in a convenient visual design that is easily understood by people who might not understand the technical aspects of relational databases. Think of forms as attractive "windows" onto the data in your tables. In this chapter, we will explore more features of Access forms, including the "navigation" forms that provide a convenient means of choosing among other forms. If one combines a properly designed database, an appropriate set of forms for viewing its data, and a navigation form for choosing among them, one can produce a fully functional database application without any traditional computer programming.

More Capabilities of Forms

First, open the file `personnel-before-navigation.accdb`, which is similar to the personnel database created earlier in this textbook, except that it includes a full zip code table. For this chapter, it is important to use Access 2010 or later, since the functionality we will be exploring is implemented differently in earlier versions of Access.

If you see a warning banner, press its *Enable...* button to allow the database to fully function.

We will start by creating a form for viewing and modifying the EMPLOYEE table:

1) In the "Create" part of the ribbon, select "Form Wizard" (from the "Forms" area).
2) Choose the EMPLOYEE table from the drop-down list, and move all the fields to the form by pressing ">>".
3) Next, select the ZIPCODE table, and move the *City* and *State* fields to the form using ">". This makes the form implicitly perform a query based on the relationship we already defined between EMPLOYEE and ZIPCODE, retrieving the city and state name corresponding to the employee's zip code. Press "Next >".

Introductory Relational Database Design for Business, with Microsoft Access, First Edition.
Jonathan Eckstein and Bonnie R. Schultz.
© 2018 John Wiley & Sons Ltd. Published 2018 by John Wiley & Sons Ltd.

4) Choose to view the data "by EMPLOYEE." The other option, "by ZIPCODE," would give us a hierarchical form with a description of each zip code and a scrolling list of the employees living in that zip code (it is possible to imagine a situation in which such a form might be useful, but it is not what we want as a primary way of viewing data on employees).
5) Press "Next >" and choose the "columnar" layout. Press "Next >" again.
6) Call the form "Employee Form" and press "Finish."

We obtain a form as shown in Figure 6.1.

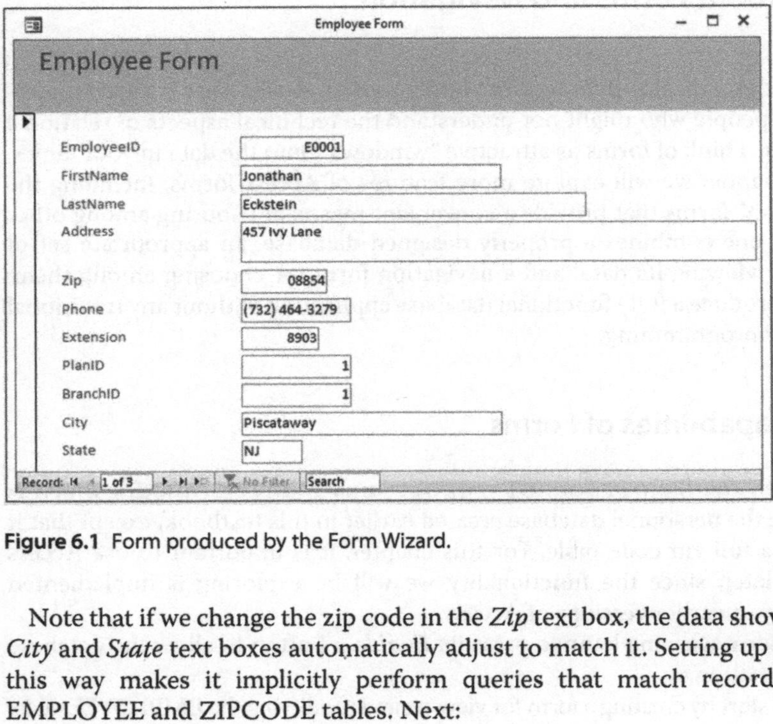

Figure 6.1 Form produced by the Form Wizard.

Note that if we change the zip code in the *Zip* text box, the data shown in the *City* and *State* text boxes automatically adjust to match it. Setting up the form this way makes it implicitly perform queries that match records in the EMPLOYEE and ZIPCODE tables. Next:

1) Switch to the design view of the form.
2) For each of the *City* and *State* text boxes on the form, select the box, go to the properties tab and set the "locked" property to "Yes." If you do not see the properties tab, right-click on either box and choose "Properties." The "locked" property is easy to find under the "Data" sub-tab of the properties box, and setting it to "Yes" prevents the user from changing the data shown in the box. If we did not set the "locked" property and we were to change "Piscataway" to "Edison" in the *City* text box, Access would change the value of the *Name* field of record 08854 in the ZIPCODE table from "Piscataway" to "Edison", invalidating our zip code table. An alternative way to prevent such inadvertent data corruption would be to write-lock the entire ZIPCODE table.

3) Adjust the size of the form header, and change the header text from "Employee Form" to "Employee Information."
4) Still in design view, rearrange the text boxes so that the city and state boxes appear just below the zip code box.
5) Delete the "PlanID" box and its label. We now replace it with a combo box allowing us to pick one of the known health plans, as follows:
   a) On the "Design" tab, click the "Combo box" tool (📇), and use it to draw a box on the form. When you release the mouse, a "wizard" should pop up.
   b) Choose "I want the combo box to look up the values in a table or query" and click "Next >".
   c) Choose "Table: HEALTHPLAN" and click "Next >".
   d) Select the "Name" field to appear in the combo box and click "Next >".
   e) Choose to sort the health plans ascending by name and click "Next >". You will now see a prompt on how wide you would like the columns. In response, just press "Next >" again.
   f) Choose "store that value in this field:" and select "PlanID" in the drop-down menu.
   g) Type "Health Plan" as the label value, and then click "Finish."
6) If you return to form view, we now have a drop-down menu that displays the name of the employee's health plan and allows one to change health plans by simply selecting from a list. This approach is much more intuitive and convenient than just displaying the plan ID. By a similar procedure, replace the "BranchID" box with a combo box for displaying and choosing branch offices by name.

We should now have a finished form that looks like Figure 6.2.

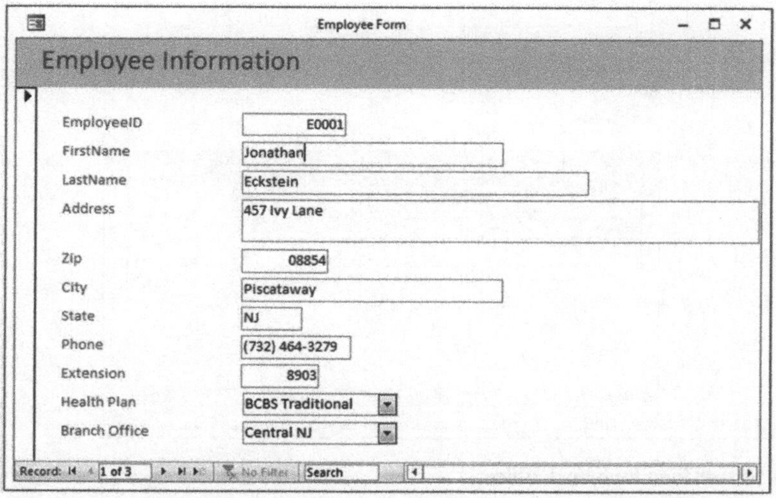

Figure 6.2 Employee form with combo boxes to select health plans and branch offices.

Now let us create a form for viewing branch offices:

- The form will include all information in the BRANCHOFFICE table.
- It will display the office's city and state, determined from the ZIPCODE table.
- It will include a scrolling list of employees in the office, showing their first names, last names, and extensions.

We again use the form wizard, as follows:

1) In the first wizard pane, include all fields from BRANCHOFFICE, *City* and *State* from ZIPCODE, and *FirstName, LastName,* and *Extension* from EMPLOYEE.
2) Select to view the data "by BRANCHOFFICE," with subforms.
3) Select the "tabular" view for the subform.
4) Call the forms "Branch Offices" and "Employee Subform for Branch Offices."
5) As before, do not forget to lock the "City" and "State" boxes to prevent corruption of the ZIPCODE table.
6) Optionally, we can adjust the formatting and layout of the form: we can put city and state right after the zip code, and adjust the headings and column widths in the subform (Figure 6.3). To edit the appearance of the subform, you need to separately open the subform in design view.

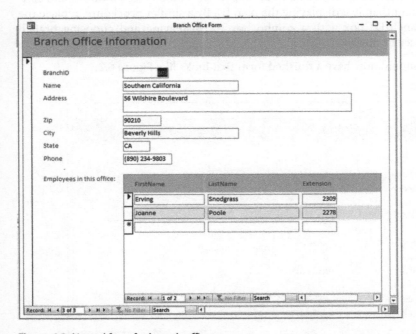

Figure 6.3 Nested form for branch offices.

Now let us create a form for viewing health plans, using a similar procedure. It should include the following:

- All the information in the HEALTHPLAN table
- Instead of the *ProviderID*, the provider name in a combo box
- Provider phone number
- A scrolling list of employees in the plan, showing their first names, last names, and the names of their branch office

Note that in creating the form in the first pane of the form wizard, we need to include the following:

- All fields from the HEALTHPLAN table
- The *Phone* field from the PROVIDER table
- The first and last name fields from the EMPLOYEE table
- The *Name* field from the BRANCHOFFICE table

After some minor adjustments in field names and the like, we obtain the form shown in Figure 6.4.

By default, the branch office name in the subform will display under the confusing heading "Name," because that is the field name in the BRANCHOFFICE table. To achieve the results shown in Figure 6.4, simply change the contents of the

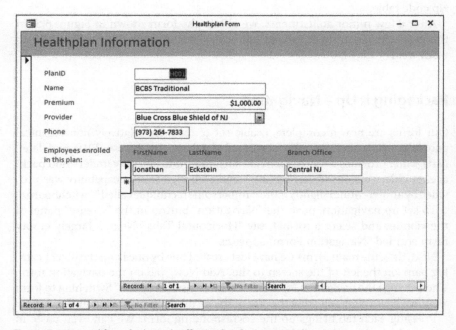

Figure 6.4 Nested form for branch offices, after formatting adjustments.

label box for this column in the header portion of the subform. It is advisable to lock the branch office name box in the detail portion of the subform, because editing values in this box would change the name of a branch office, something that is probably undesirable in this form.

Note that we do not include city and state fields in this form, because Access will become confused about which relationships we wish to use in order to relate health plans to zip codes. This confusion arises because of the multiple paths between HEALTHPLAN and ZIPCODE tables in the database design. If we wanted to include the provider city and state and/or employee city and state, we would first explicitly create a query that retrieves information using the correct pathway, and then base the form on that query (forms may be based on queries as well as directly on tables).

Finally, we create a form for viewing health plan providers. Here, we want the following:

- All the information in the PROVIDER table
- The city and state corresponding to the provider's zip code
- A scrolling list of the provider's health plans, including their name and premium

The procedure for creating this form is similar to the others. Again, remember to lock the *City* and *State* text boxes to prevent accidental corruption of the zip code table.

After a few minor adjustments, we obtain the form shown in Figure 6.5 (in this case with a datasheet view of subform, although a tabular view would also work well).

Packaging it Up – Navigation

Our forms are now a complete, usable set of tools for relatively non-technical people to view and edit the personnel database. In Access 2010 and later, *Navigation* provides a way to combine such tools into an easily understood package. In older versions of Access (2007 and earlier), a similar capability was provided by a different and slightly more cumbersome technique called "Switchboards."

To set up navigation, push the "Navigation" button in the "Create" panel of the ribbon, and select a format, say "Horizontal Tabs." Next, a largely empty form entitled "Navigation Form" appears.

Next, drag the main forms we have just created one by one from the object catalog pane on the left of the screen to the "Add New" tab on the navigation form. Then change the navigation form title to "Employee Database." Switching to form view, we have (after adjusting the size of the form) the form shown in Figure 6.6.

Pressing each tab brings up the corresponding form. We can even paste in clip art from the web into the navigation form header to provide some visual flair (Figure 6.7).

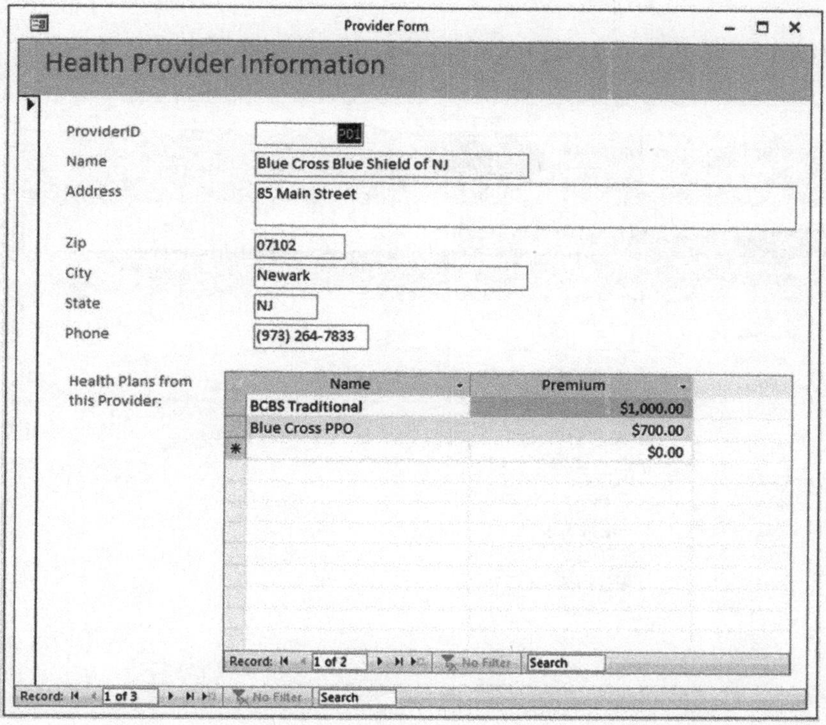

Figure 6.5 Nested form for health providers.

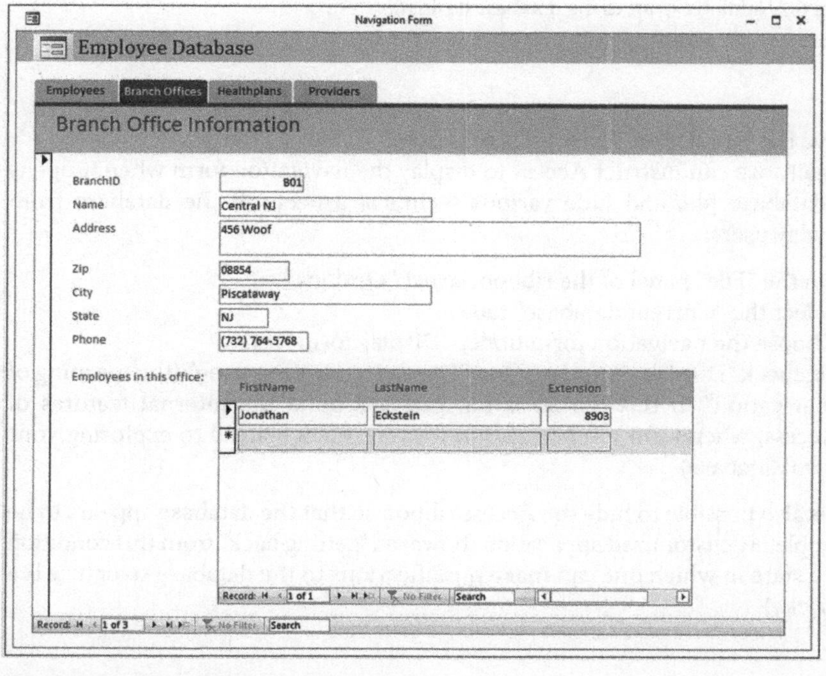

Figure 6.6 Database navigation form.

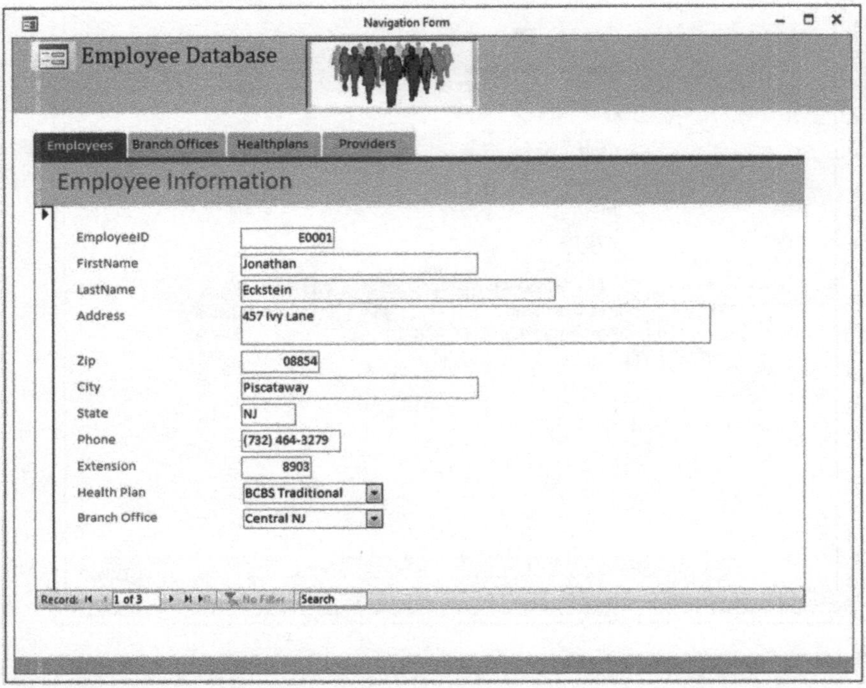

Figure 6.7 Adding clip art to the database navigation form.

Save the Navigation Form as "Navigation."

Finally, we can instruct Access to display the navigation form when it opens the database file, and hide various technical aspects of the database from everyday users:

1) On the "File" panel of the ribbon, select "Options."
2) Select the "Current database" tab.
3) Choose the navigation form under "Display form."
4) Uncheck "Display status bar" and "Display navigation pane" (the meaning of "navigation" in this option is navigating around the internal features of Access, whereas in the Navigation form it refers instead to exploring your own database).

It is also possible to hide the Access ribbon so that the database appears to be a completely customized application (however, "getting back" from this condition into a state in which one can make modifications to the database structure is a bit tricky).

Exercises

6.1 **Alumni office:** The alumni office of Enormous State University (ESU) wants to keep track of alumni and their charitable gifts to the university. For each alumnus, you want to store a first name, middle name, last name, address information (street address, city, state, and zip code), a home phone number, a mobile phone number, and an e-mail address. Assume that you do have access to a master zip code table of zip codes, cities, and states, which you will include in your database design. Each alumnus may have multiple degrees. Every time a degree is granted, you want to keep track of to whom the degree was awarded, the year the degree was awarded, the type of degree (BA, MBA, PhD, JD, etc.), which school awarded the degree, and the student's major. The database should also contain a table listing all the university's schools (of which there are dozens), including a short name (up to 40 characters) and a full name (up to 100 characters). Each alumnus may make multiple charitable gifts to the university. For each gift, you want to keep track of the date it was made, who made it, and the dollar amount of the gift.

A Design a database for this situation, creating a database outline and an ER diagram.

B Use Access to create a database with the structure you have designed, creating all the necessary tables and relationships between them.

C Use the form wizard to create a form for viewing alumni and their gifts. The header should be "Alumni Information with Gifts," and every field of the main table for alumni should be shown. The city and state corresponding to the zip code should also be shown, but should be locked to prevent accidental corruption of the zip code table. There should also be a scrolling list of all the alumnus' gifts, showing the date and amount given.

D Create a similar form for alumni, but with the scrolling subform instead showing all the alumnus' degrees, with the short name of the school, the type of degree, the date, and the major. Within the subform, use a combo box for the short name of school field, so that new information can be entered easily. *Hint:* When using the form wizard, make sure you include the primary key field for schools, and then replace the resulting field in the subform with a combo box that brings up the school's short name.

E Use the form wizard to create a form for viewing schools. All attributes associated with a school should be shown, along with a scrolling subform showing, for each degree award, the first name and last name of the recipient, the degree type, the date, and major.

F Create a navigation form whose tabs bring up each of the three forms you created in parts (c)–(e). Include some clip art from the web in the form header.

Note: With some extra work, the forms in parts (b) and (c) could be combined into single form with two different scrolling subforms. However, we have not covered the necessary techniques in this text.

G Make sure all your forms look reasonably attractive.

H Enter some test data to make sure your database application functions as intended (you do not have to enter very much — just 3–4 records per table).

6.2 **Motorcycle dealership:** You want to keep information on past sales at a motorcycle dealership, including information on motorcycles, salespeople, and customers. Assume that the dealership sells only new motorcycles and all of them come from the same manufacturer.

For each salesperson, you want to store their first name, last name, middle name/initial, employee ID number, and date hired. For each customer, you want to store a customer ID number, first name, last name, middle name/initial, address information, phone number, and e-mail address.

Each kind of motorcycle is called a *model*, and has unique model number. For each model, you want to store its name, engine size in cubic centimeters (CC) (an integer), and the date introduced. Each individual motorcycle sold is identified by a unique 16-digit serial "number" (which may also contain letters). For each motorcycle sale, you want to record the serial number, date of sale, and sale price. You also want to know which customer bought the motorcycle, which salesperson made the sale, and what model the motorcycle was.

A Create a database design outline and an ER diagram for a database appropriate for this application.

B Use Access to create a database with the structure you have designed, creating all the necessary tables and relationships between them.

C Use the form wizard to create a form for viewing and entering motorcycles/sales. The header should be "Motorcycle Sale." The corresponding model name should be included in a combo box. The customer and salesperson involved in the sale should each be displayed in combo boxes showing last names, and not as IDs.

D Use the form wizard to create a nested form for model information (model name, engine size, etc.). The form header should be "Model." The subform should show the dates, sales prices, and customer first and last names for all sales of that model.

E Use the form wizard to create a nested form that shows the information for each salesperson, and a scrolling subform for all their sales. The header should be "Salesperson." The subform should include the date of each sale by that salesperson, the price, the model name, and the customer last name.

F Use the form wizard to create a nested form that shows all the information about a customer, including their city and state, along with a scrolling subform for all their purchases. The header should read "Customers." The subform should include the date of purchase, the model name, the price, and the salesperson last name.

G Create a navigation form whose tabs bring up each of the forms you created in parts (c)–(f). Include some clip art from the web in the form header.

H Make sure all your forms look reasonably attractive.

I Enter some test data to make sure your database application functions as intended (you do not have to enter very much — just 3–4 records per table).

6.3 **Law office:** You are trying to automate the records for your uncle's law firm. Multiple attorneys work for the firm, and for each of them you want to store their first name, middle name, last name, date hired, hourly billing rate, and date promoted to partner (blank if the attorney is not a partner). For each client, you want to store a first name, last name, middle name, phone number, address, city, state, and zip code (assume you do not have a zip code table). Each case is identified by a unique "docket number" and has a name and description. A case is always for a single client, but a client may have more than one case. Finally, you want to keep track of attorney billable hours. Each record of billable hours involves one attorney working on one case. For each billable hours record, the database should remember which attorney did the work, which case was involved, the date, the number of hours billed (fractions are allowed), and a description of the work performed.

A Draw an ER diagram and write a database design outline for this application. Use the synthetic keys "ClientID" and "AttorneyID" for clients and attorneys, respectively.

B Create a database matching your design in Microsoft Access. Create all the necessary tables and relationships between them.

C Use the form wizard to make a form that shows all the information on cases, plus the associated client first and last name. Instead of simple text box for the client ID field, substitute a combo box that also shows the client first and last name when you pull it down (make a combo box that includes the client ID, client first name, and client last name, and does not hide the key field). There should be a scrolling subform showing all the case's billable hours information. The scrolling section should show the date, hours billed, attorney last name, and description.

D Use the form wizard to make a form showing all the data for each attorney, with a scrolling subform showing all his or her hours billed. The subform should show the case name, date, hours spent, and description.

E Use the form wizard to create a form showing each client, with a scrolling subform for all of their cases, showing the docket number and case name.

F Use the form wizard to make a form for entering hours billed. To display the case involved, use a combo box that displays the case name but selects the docket number. For the attorney involved, use a combo box that displays the attorney ID, but also shows attorney first and last names when you select a value – the procedure for doing this is similar to the selection of clients in part (b). There should be simple text boxes for all the remaining fields in the hours billed table.

G Create a navigation form whose tabs bring up each of the forms you created in parts (c)–(f). Include some clip art from the web in the form header.

H Make sure all your forms look reasonably attractive.

I Enter a small amount of made-up data into the database – at least three records for each table.

7

Many-to-Many Relationships

By now you should be adept at recognizing one-to-many relationships and mapping out corresponding entity-relationship (ER) diagrams. However, there are cases in which simple one-to-many relationships are insufficient. One common situation of this kind is when one must keep track of membership in potentially overlapping groups, as in the following example.

Focus Groups Example

Consider the following problem:

> Your firm performs marketing research using focus groups composed of volunteer consumers. You would like to design a database to keep track of these groups and some related information.
>
> For each consumer volunteer, you would like to store name information, address information, phone number, date of birth, gender, marital status, number of children, and approximate annual family income. Assume that you do have access to a complete zip code table.
>
> Each focus group typically consists of 5–20 consumer volunteers, but there is no strict upper limit on the size of a group. Consumer volunteers can sometimes be members of more than one group. In addition to storing which consumers are members of each group, you also want to store each group's name, date formed, and a description.
>
> Each group can have multiple meetings. For each meeting, you want to store its date/time started, its date/time ended, and a brief description of the discussion topic. Each meeting has a single moderator, who is one of your employees and is not considered a member of the group. Different meetings of the same group may have different moderators.

Introductory Relational Database Design for Business, with Microsoft Access, First Edition.
Jonathan Eckstein and Bonnie R. Schultz.
© 2018 John Wiley & Sons Ltd. Published 2018 by John Wiley & Sons Ltd.

For each employee, you want to store name information, home and mobile phone numbers, date of birth, date hired, and gender.

Design a database to store all this information. Further data about your employees is stored in your Human Resource department's database, which we will not consider here. Make sure that the focus group database stores enough information to be able to answer all of the following queries:

- Who are the members of group X?
- Which groups have consumer Y as a member?
- What are the dates of all meetings moderated by employee Z?
- Which groups have ever had meetings moderated by employee W?

We can construct most of the database for this situation using the techniques we have already learned, but we are left with one puzzle (see Figure 7.1).

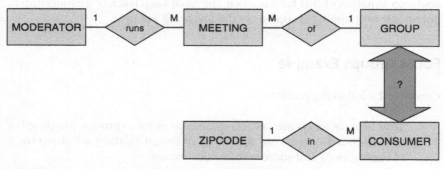

Figure 7.1 Incomplete ER diagram for the focus groups database.

MODERATOR(<u>EmployeeID</u>, FName, MName, LName, Phone, MobilePhone,
      BirthDate, HireDate, Gender)

GROUP(<u>GroupID</u>, Name, DateFormed, Description)

MEETING(<u>GroupID</u>, <u>DateTimeStarted</u>, DateTimeEnded, EmployeeID, Topic)
  GroupID foreign key to GROUP
  EmployeeID foreign key to MODERATOR

CONSUMER(<u>ConsumerID</u>, FName, MName, LName, StreetAddress, Zip,
      BirthDate, Gender, MaritalStatus, Children, Income)
  Zip foreign key to ZIPCODE

ZIPCODE(<u>Zip</u>, City, State)   [Incomplete]

Here, we use a composite primary key for MEETING, namely, (*GroupID*, *DateTimeStarted*). This choice is valid because a single group cannot start more than one meeting at a time. Several other choices of composite primary key are possible for MEETING, or we could just create a synthetic key.

The key issue concerns how to relate GROUP and CONSUMER. Clearly we need to keep track of which consumers are in which groups, but a one-to-many relationship is insufficient. If we put the foreign key in GROUP, it would have to be non-atomic, meaning that the foreign key would have to be a list, because groups contain multiple consumers. But we cannot do the opposite, either, because consumers can be in more than one group: if we put the foreign key in CONSUMER, it would have to be a list of the groups to which the consumer belongs. The relationship between GROUP and CONSUMER is genuinely many-to-many: if we pick one group, it contains many consumers, and if we pick one consumer, he or she may be in many groups.

How can we implement this relationship? The answer may be deduced by considering the implicit relationship that exists between groups and moderators. If we consider a single moderator, he or she can be related to many meetings, with each meeting involving one group. So, each moderator can be indirectly associated with many groups, namely, all the groups for which they have moderated meetings. In turn, if we pick one group, it can also be directly related to many meetings, each of which is related to one moderator. So, each group can be indirectly related to many moderators, namely, those who have moderated its meetings. Taken together, there is an implicit, indirect many-to-many relationship between MODERATOR and GROUP, through the table MEETING (Figure 7.2).

Figure 7.2 How the MODERATOR and GROUP tables are indirectly related through MEETING.

This configuration of tables gives us a clue as to how the foreign keys should be placed between GROUP and CONSUMER. They cannot be placed in either GROUP or CONSUMER, since they would have to be non-atomic, but what if they were placed in a new table "between" GROUP and CONSUMER, the same way MEETING is "between" MODERATOR and GROUP? So, we add a new table to the database, called (for example) ENROLL, as follows:

ENROLL(<u>GroupID</u>, <u>ConsumerID</u>)
   GroupID foreign key to GROUP
   ConsumerID foreign key to CONSUMER

The presence of a record in this table signifies that the indicated group and consumer are related. For example, if ENROLL contains the record (12, 233-23-1873), it indicates that the consumer with ID 233-23-1873 is a member of group 12. We choose the primary key to be (*GroupID*, *ConsumerID*), which in this case happens to be the entire record. We cannot pick just *GroupID* or just *ConsumerID* as the primary key, as that would make ENROLL a subtype of either GROUP or CONSUMER, respectively. We could also create a synthetic key, but in this case the composite key prevents pointless duplications from entering the database: somebody is either a member of a particular group or they are not – there is no reason to record membership more than once for the same consumer in the same group, as would be possible were we to use a synthetic key.

In our ER diagram, we could depict the relationship between GROUP and CONSUMER as two one-to-many relationships, as in Figure 7.3.

Figure 7.3 Introducing a new table to mediate the many-to-many relationship between GROUP and CONSUMER.

The conventions of ER diagrams also allow a kind of "shorthand" to stand in for this common pattern, namely (Figure 7.4):

Figure 7.4 Shorthand depiction of a many-to-many relationship.

This form of the diagram is meant to suggest that the principal reason for the existence of the table ENROLL is to implement a many-to-many relationship between GROUP and CONSUMER. The two diagram fragments above may be considered essentially equivalent and interchangeable; the second one is just a kind of abbreviation or shorthand for the first. Generally speaking, if the intermediary table (in this case ENROLL) contains only the two foreign keys, and these keys jointly form its primary key, then we prefer the second, shorthand form, because the only real reason for the intermediary table to exist is to represent a many-to-many relationship. This is the case in the example of the ENROLL table above.

To summarize, the full ER diagram is as shown in Figure 7.5 and the complete database outline is as follows:

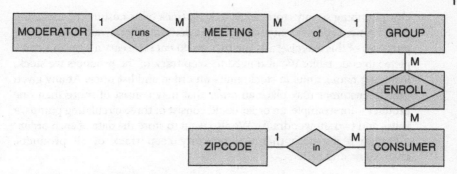

Figure 7.5 Completed ER diagram for the focus groups database.

MODERATOR(<u>EmployeeID</u>, FName, MName, LName, Phone, MobilePhone, BirthDate, HireDate, Gender)

GROUP(<u>GroupID</u>, Name, DateFormed, Description)

MEETING(<u>GroupID</u>, <u>DateTimeStarted</u>, DateTimeEnded, EmployeeID, Topic)
    GroupID foreign key to GROUP
    EmployeeID foreign key to MODERATOR

ENROLL(<u>GroupID</u>, <u>ConsumerID</u>)
    GroupID foreign key to GROUP
    ConsumerID foreign key to CONSUMER

CONSUMER(<u>ConsumerID</u>, FName, MName, LName, StreetAddress, Zip, BirthDate, Gender, MaritalStatus, Children, Income)
    Zip foreign key to ZIPCODE

ZIPCODE(<u>Zip</u>, City, State)

Note that all the queries mentioned in the problem are now possible, although multiple joins may be necessary to implement some of them. For example, to print the names of the members of a group named X, we find the appropriate *GroupID* in GROUP, find all corresponding records in ENROLL, then find all the corresponding records in CONSUMER, and finally print the consumer names.

The Plumbing Store: Many-to-Many with an Additional Quantity Field

We now explore a database design structure common in most kinds of sales operations. Consider the following example:

Our plumbing supply store needs to keep track of its customers, including their names, address, city, state, zip code, and phone number. For the purposes of this exercise, assume that we do *not* have easy access to a complete zip code table. We also need to keep track of the products we stock, including name, units in stock, units on order, and list price. At any given time, a customer may place an *order* that may consist of more than one product – for example, an order could consist of three circulating pumps, a valve, and two shower drains. We also want to store the date of each order.

Design a database that will properly keep track of all products, customers, and orders.

We clearly need entities/tables for customers, products, and orders:

CUSTOMER(CustomerID, FName, LName, Address, City, State, Zip)

ORDERS(OrderID, CustomerID, OrderDate)
    CustomerID foreign key to CUSTOMER

PRODUCT(ProductID, Name, UnitsInStock, UnitPrice, UnitsOnOrder)
                                                        [Incomplete]

Since we are assuming that we do not have a zip code table, we store *City* and *State* for the customer address in the CUSTOMER table. A common alternative name for *ProductID* is "SKU," which stands for "stock-keeping unit" and is sometimes pronounced like "skew." If two items have identical *ProductID*s or SKUs, they should be completely interchangeable: for example, for items such as shirts or shoes, they should be not only the same brand and model, but also the same color and size. This database has a minor departure from our usual naming conventions, in that we call the orders table ORDERS rather than ORDER. The reason is that the word "ORDER" has special meaning in SQL, so using it as the name of a table can cause some confusion when writing SQL code.

Note that here we are not tracking individual packages or items by serial number, the way a car dealership might track individual cars on its sales lot by their VIN (vehicle identification number) identifiers, or a real estate agency might track individual houses or condominiums. The PRODUCT table here could just as well be called KINDOFPRODUCT: if *UnitsInStock* for a given product ID is 23, that means we have 23 completely interchangeable instances of that product in stock. This situation is typical of high-volume sales operations: a large store like Target or Best Buy does not track the serial numbers of individual mice or video games it has in stock, it merely knows the quantity it has in stock.

Clearly CUSTOMER and ORDERS are in a one-to-many relationship, with ORDERS being the "many," as we can tell from the foreign key placement of *CustomerID* in ORDERS. However, a one-to-many relationship will not suffice for ORDERS and PRODUCT, because a single kind of product can be in many orders, and a single order can contain many kinds of product. Thus, we need an additional table to track the correspondence between orders and products. Common names for such a table are "line item" or "order detail." We therefore create an additional table as follows:

ORDERDETAIL(OrderID, ProductID)
    OrderID foreign key to ORDERS
    ProductID foreign key to PRODUCT   [Incomplete]

Adding this table to the design, we discover there is one kind of information that the database still does not contain, namely, order quantities. For example, if an order contains three identical faucets, where does the "three" get stored?

The answer is that it should be stored in ORDERDETAIL, because the amount ordered depends on both the *OrderID* and the *ProductID*. If the amount ordered were in ORDERS, it would have to be the same for all products represented in the order, and if it were in PRODUCT, the quantity of the product would have to be the same in all orders. Neither of these restrictions make sense, so the full form of the ORDERDETAIL table should be as follows:

ORDERDETAIL(OrderID, ProductID, Quantity)
    OrderID foreign key to ORDERS
    ProductID foreign key to PRODUCT

For example, a record of the form (O0001, P0013, 4) in ORDERDETAIL means that order O0001 contains four items of type P0013.

For reference, here is the full database design:

CUSTOMER(CustomerID, FName, LName, Address, City, State, Zip)

ORDERS(OrderID, CustomerID, OrderDate)
    CustomerID foreign key to CUSTOMER

PRODUCT(ProductID, Name, UnitsInStock, UnitPrice)

ORDERDETAIL(OrderID, ProductID, Quantity)
    OrderID foreign key to ORDERS
    ProductID foreign key to PRODUCT

The ER diagram can take either of the two equivalent forms shown in Figures 7.6 and 7.7.

Figure 7.6 Plumbing store database depicted with only one-to-many relationships.

or

Figure 7.7 Plumbing store database depicted as having a many-to-many relationship.

In this case, one might well argue that the first, "expanded" form is preferable, because ORDERDETAIL contains other fields besides just the two foreign keys implementing the many-to-many relationship. Its primary key of (*OrderID*, *ProductID*) is arguably better than a synthetic key, because if two items with the same *ProductID* are really interchangeable, there should be no reason to list them on different lines of the order manifest. To elaborate, imagine the printout or receipt that a customer might receive with their order (see Figure 7.8).

```
CustomerID:      C004        Date:    March 4, 2014
Order Number:    O0023

Joseph Blowe
21 Sycamore Circle
Piscataway, NJ 08854

Description                 Quantity    Price
Undersink Stopcock Valve       2        $  29.99
Retro Nickel Plate Faucet      1        $ 119.99
Drain Set                      1        $  49.00

etc...
```

Figure 7.8 Sample invoice from the plumbing store.

Each record in ORDERDETAIL corresponds to a line somewhere in the bottom section of such a receipt, hence the common alternative name LINEITEM. If there were two lines for completely interchangeable items on the same receipt, there would be no reason not to simply condense them into one line with a larger quantity; hence, the composite primary key (*OrderID*, *ProductID*) makes sense for ORDERDETAIL.

Hands-On Exercise and More About Queries and SQL

From the book website, download and save the database `plumbingstore-clean.mdb`. Now, open the saved database and press "enable content" on the yellow warning banner (if it appears).

The tables in this database are essentially identical to the design we just created. It contains some example data, but it does not yet contain any relationships. As usual, we use the Relationships button in the Database Tools tab

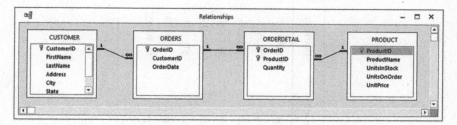

Figure 7.9 Relationship Window for the plumbing store database.

to create the relationships. Dragging each of the tables from the right pane or right-clicking and selecting "Show Table," we place all four tables in the relationship window and draw the necessary relationships, enforcing referential integrity for each of them (Figure 7.9).

Our eventual goal will be to execute a query showing the total price paid for each order. First, let us create a conceptually simple query showing:

- OrderID
- Customer first and last name
- Order date
- Product name
- Quantity
- Unit price

Using the Query Design button, and showing all the tables, we create a query as shown in Figure 7.10.

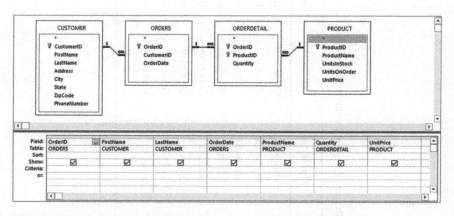

Figure 7.10 Design View for the first query of the plumbing store database.

The output of this query is quite lengthy, and starts as shown in Table 7.1. We essentially get one line of output for every row in the ORDERDETAIL table, joined with appropriate information from other tables. Next, it can be helpful to compute the full price paid on each line, that is, the product of *Quantity*

Table 7.1 Output of the first plumbing store query.

OrderID	First Name	Last Name	Order Date	Product Name	Quantity	UnitPrice
O0001	Margerita	Colon	4/15/2013	Massage Shower System	1.00	$449.95
O0001	Margerita	Colon	4/15/2013	Replacement Valve Units Type A	4.00	$9.99
O0001	Margerita	Colon	4/15/2013	Budget Filter System	1.00	$115.95
O0002	Leonard	Goodman	4/18/2013	Ivory Clawfoot Tub	1.00	$1,899.00
O0002	Leonard	Goodman	4/18/2013	Nickel Deluxe Kitchen Faucet	1.00	$499.00
O0002	Leonard	Goodman	4/18/2013	Chrome Modern Kitchen Faucet	1.00	$189.95
O0002	Leonard	Goodman	4/18/2013	Complete Bathroom Kit	1.00	$1,395.00
O0003	Geoffrey	Hammer	4/18/2013	Infinity Master Tub	1.00	$2,599.00
...	...	...	...	...	...	...

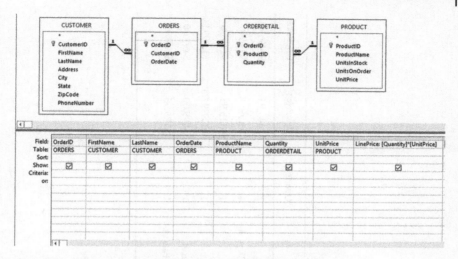

Figure 7.11 Adding a computed field to the plumbing store query.

and *UnitPrice*. We can add this computed field to the query as shown in Figure 7.11, by adding a computed field *LinePrice* equal to [*Quantity*]*[*UnitPrice*]. We now get the output shown in Table 7.2.

Some common but rather cryptic alternative names for *LinePrice* that one sometimes sees on receipts and invoices are "extension" and "extended price." Now let us examine the SQL view of the query in question:

```
SELECT ORDERS.OrderID, CUSTOMER.FirstName,
       CUSTOMER.LastName, ORDERS.OrderDate,
       PRODUCT. ProductName, ORDERDETAIL.Quantity,
       PRODUCT. UnitPrice,
       [Quantity]*[UnitPrice] AS LinePrice
FROM PRODUCT INNER JOIN …;
```

Above, we omit displaying the complicated compound inner join that combines all the tables. If we want to display a computed field in SQL, we just put its formula in the SELECT clause. In this case, the computed field formula is [Quantity] * [UnitPrice]. The additional syntax AS LinePrice indicates that the resulting computed column should have the name LinePrice. Note that Access automatically inserts the [ ] characters here, but they are optional because there are no spaces or other special characters in the field names Quantity and UnitPrice.

To return to our originally stated goal, suppose we want to create a query showing for each order:

- The *OrderID*
- The customer's first and last name
- The order date
- The total dollar amount of the order

Table 7.2 Output of the plumbing store query with a computed field.

OrderID	First Name	Last Name	Order Date	Product Name	Quantity	UnitPrice	LinePrice
O0001	Margerita	Colon	4/15/2013	Massage Shower System	1	$449.95	$449.95
O0001	Margerita	Colon	4/15/2013	Replacement Valve Units Type A	4	$9.99	$39.96
O0001	Margerita	Colon	4/15/2013	Budget Filter System	1	$115.95	$115.95
O0002	Leonard	Goodman	4/18/2013	Ivory Clawfoot Tub	1	$1,899.00	$1,899.00
O0002	Leonard	Goodman	4/18/2013	Nickel Deluxe Kitchen Faucet	1	$499.00	$499.00
O0002	Leonard	Goodman	4/18/2013	Chrome Modern Kitchen Faucet	1	$189.95	$189.95
…	…	…	…	…	…	…	…

The total dollar amount of each order (ignoring taxes for simplicity) is simply the sum of its *LinePrice*s. We press the "Totals" (Σ) button (near the top of the query design window), which causes a new "Totals" row to appear in the grid. We then select "Sum" in the *LinePrice* column of this new row (Figure 7.12).

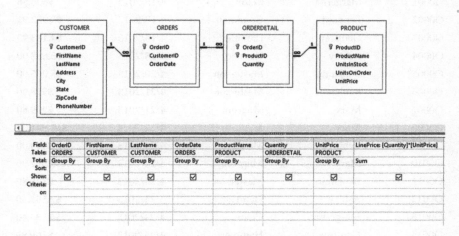

Figure 7.12 Introducing aggregation to the computed field query.

Now we must also delete the *ProductName, Quantity*, and *UnitPrice* columns, since otherwise Access will group by these columns, preventing all the rows originating from a single order from forming a single aggregation group. After this deletion, we arrive at the query design shown in Figure 7.13.

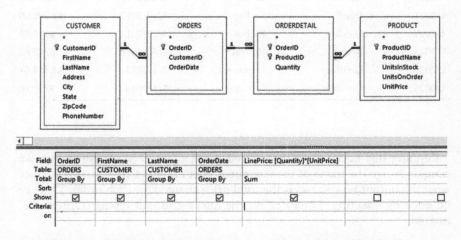

Figure 7.13 Completed plumbing store query showing the total value of each order.

Table 7.3 Completed plumbing store query with total value of each order.

OrderID	First Name	Last Name	Order Date	LinePrice
O0001	Margerita	Colon	4/15/2013	$605.86
O0002	Leonard	Goodman	4/18/2013	$3,982.95
O0003	Geoffrey	Hammer	4/18/2013	$4,183.95
O0004	Ashley	Flannery	4/18/2013	$5,688.00
O0005	Benjamin	Masterson	4/20/2013	$5,055.90
O0006	Benjamin	Masterson	4/21/2013	$998.90
O0007	Mary	Milgrom	4/21/2013	$209.80
O0008	Mary	Milgrom	4/22/2013	$17,931.00
O0009	Benjamin	Masterson	4/22/2013	$499.00
O0010	Mary	Milgrom	4/22/2013	$5,642.95
O0011	Benjamin	Masterson	4/24/2013	$739.80
O0012	Ashley	Flannery	4/24/2013	$2,558.50
O0013	Margerita	Colon	4/24/2013	$4,535.40
O0014	Geoffrey	Hammer	4/25/2013	$109.85
O0015	Xiaoming	Wang	4/25/2013	$249.90
O0016	Geoffrey	Hammer	4/26/2013	$259.90
O0017	Laura	Ng	4/26/2013	$79.90
O0018	Laura	Ng	4/26/2013	$742.80
O0019	Robert	Sloan	4/27/2013	$249.75
O0020	Robert	Sloan	4/28/2013	$569.95
O0021	Derek	Escher	4/29/2013	$2,299.00
O0022	Derek	Escher	4/29/2013	$115.95
O0023	Joseph	Brower	4/30/2013	$225.85
O0024	Geoffrey	Hammer	5/1/2013	$3,358.67
O0025	Geoffrey	Hammer	5/1/2013	$757.90

Running this query gives the desired result (Table 7.3). At this point, we should change the name of the computed field *LinePrice* to *OrderPrice*, since what the output now shows is the total price charged for each order. This can be done by selecting "LinePrice" in the query grid and typing "OrderPrice" instead.

Let us examine the SQL for this query:

```
SELECT    ORDERS.OrderID, CUSTOMER.FirstName,
          CUSTOMER.LastName, ORDERS.OrderDate,
          Sum([Quantity]*[UnitPrice]) AS OrderPrice
FROM      Products INNER JOIN ...
GROUP BY  ORDERS.OrderID, CUSTOMER.FirstName,
          CUSTOMER.LastName, ORDERS.OrderDate;
```

The GROUP BY clause instructs the query to form groups by the indicated fields, and the Sum(...) operation indicates that the sum of the values [Quantity]*[UnitPrice] over each group, rather than just [Quantity]*[UnitPrice], should be displayed. The AS clause now reads AS OrderPrice because we have changed the name of the resulting quantity to OrderPrice.

Here, the *OrderID* field determines the value of all the other "group by" fields. Thus, while we are technically grouping by the fields ORDERS.OrderID, CUSTOMER.FirstName, CUSTOMER.LastName, and ORDERS.OrderDate, we are effectively grouping just by ORDERS.OrderID, because any two records with identical *OrderID* fields will necessarily have their other "group by" fields identical as well. While some database systems might allow us to group only by *OrderID* in this case, Access does not. It requires all fields appearing in the SELECT clause to be within an aggregation function like Sum() or to be a grouped by.

We could make the query more human-readable, but with the same results, by changing it to:

```
SELECT    ORDERS.OrderID, CUSTOMER.FirstName,
          CUSTOMER.LastName, ORDERS.OrderDate,
          Sum([Quantity]*[UnitPrice]) AS OrderPrice
FROM      PRODUCT, CUSTOMER, ORDERS, ORDERDETAIL
WHERE     CUSTOMER.CustomerID=ORDERS.CustomerID AND
          ORDERS.OrderID=ORDERDETAIL.OrderID AND
          PRODUCT.ProductID=ORDERDETAIL.ProductID
GROUP BY  ORDERS.OrderID, CUSTOMER.FirstName,
          CUSTOMER.LastName, ORDERS.OrderDate;
```

Conceptually, this syntax specifies that the query form a table consisting of all combinations of records from the tables PRODUCT, CUSTOMER, ORDERS, and ORDERDETAIL, but then discard all combinations that do not have matching keys. The result is then grouped and processed as before. In some database engines, the INNER JOIN syntax might run faster, but for most commercial database systems, a built-in SQL "query optimization" feature should automatically recognize that the two queries are asking for the same result, and cause the second query to run at essentially the same speed as the first.

Project Teams: Many-to-Many with "Flavors" of Membership

Consider the following problem:

> You are keeping track of employees in your company and their involvement in project teams. For each employee, you want to keep track of a first name, middle initial, last name, address information, home phone number, office extension phone, and e-mail address.
>
> Each employee is a member of a single "department" (such as "R&D" or "Operations"). For each department, you want to store a name, description, and mission statement.
>
> Each employee is also housed at a single location. Each location has name, main phone number, and address information.
>
> Project teams are groups of employees tasked with coordinating certain projects within the company; each one has a name, a description, and a date formed. Each project team may have multiple members, and there is nothing to prevent an employee from being a member of multiple project teams. There are two levels of membership in a project team, "regular" and "principal." "Principal" members are expected to play a leadership role, but many teams have more than one "principal" member. An employee may take a principal role in one team and a regular role on another team.
>
> All address information consists of an address, city, state, and zip code. Assume that you *do* have access to a zip code table.
>
> Draw an ER diagram, and write a design outline of a database that is able to track all this information.

The main entities that we need for this example are as follows:

- Employees
- Departments
- Locations
- Project teams
- Zip codes

Most of the relationships needed are of the simple one-to-many variety, except that we need a many-to-many relationship between employees and project teams. Multiple employees may work on one team, and there is no prohibition regarding an employee being on multiple teams. Thus, we arrive at the ER diagram of Figure 7.14.

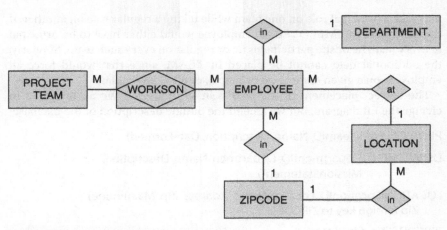

Figure 7.14 ER diagram for project teams database.

Using a "classic" many-to-many pattern between EMPLOYEE and PROJECTTEAM (similarly to the focus groups example), we then obtain the following outline:

PROJECTTEAM(<u>TeamID</u>, Name, Description, DateFormed)

DEPARTMENT(<u>DepartmentID</u>, DepartmentName, Description, MissionStatement)

LOCATION(<u>LocationID</u>, LocationName, Address, Zip, MainPhone)
    Zip foreign key to ZIPCODE

ZIPCODE(<u>Zip</u>, City, State)

EMPLOYEE(<u>EmployeeID</u>, FName, MiddleInit, LName, Address, Zip, HomePhone, OfficeExtension, Email, DepartmentID, LocationID)
    Zip foreign key to ZIPCODE
    DepartmentID foreign key to DEPARTMENT
    LocationID foreign key to LOCATION

WORKSON(<u>EmployeeID</u>, <u>TeamID</u>)
    EmployeeID foreign key to EMPLOYEE   [Incomplete]
    TeamID foreign key to TEAM

The appearance of a specific pair in the WORKSON table indicates that a particular employee works on a particular team.

There is one kind of information that this design does not store: whether an employee works on a particular team on a "principal" or "regular" basis. We may imagine using a code ("P" or "R") or a yes/no field to store this information, but to which table should such an attribute belong? We cannot place this field in EMPLOYEE, since the problem explicitly states that an employee may take a principal role on one team while taking a regular role on another; if this field were in EMPLOYEE, an employee would either have to be principal in every team he or she participates in, or regular on every such team. Similarly, the additional field cannot be placed in TEAM, since that would force all employees on a given team to be principal, or all to be regular.

The correct placement of the field is in WORKSON. We do not need to change the ER diagram, but we amend the outline description of the database:

PROJECTTEAM(<u>TeamID</u>, Name, Description, DateFormed)

DEPARTMENT(<u>DepartmentID</u>, DepartmentName, Description, MissionStatement)

LOCATION(<u>LocationID</u>, LocationName, Address, Zip, MainPhone)
    Zip foreign key to ZIPCODE

ZIPCODE(<u>Zip</u>, City, State)

EMPLOYEE(<u>EmployeeID</u>, FName, MiddleInit, LName, Address, Zip, HomePhone, OfficeExtension, Email, DepartmentID, LocationID)

    Zip foreign key to ZIPCODE
    DepartmentID foreign key to DEPARTMENT
    Location foreign key to LOCATION

WORKSON(<u>EmployeeID</u>, <u>TeamID</u>, Principal)
    EmployeeID foreign key to EMPLOYEE
    TeamID foreign key to TEAM

Here, *Principal* is a yes/no field that contains "yes" for principal assignments and "no" for regular assignments. Instead of a yes/no field, we could also use a short text field containing a code such as "P" for principal or "R" for regular. "ASSIGNMENT" would be another reasonable name for the table WORKSON (other possibilities are TEAMDETAIL and EMPLOYEETEAM). Since WORKSON now contains another attribute in addition to the two foreign keys, one might prefer to use the "expanded" ER diagram (Figure 7.15).

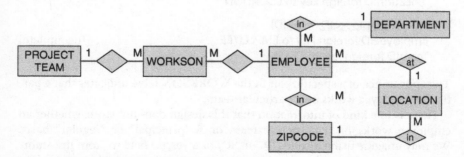

Figure 7.15 ER diagram for project teams database, showing two one-to-many relationships in place of the many-to-many relationship.

An alternative to the design of the WORKSON table above would be to have two intermediary tables, one for principal assignments and one for regular assignments. That is, instead of WORKSON, we would have two tables:

PRINCIPAL(<u>EmployeeID</u>, <u>TeamID</u>)
    EmployeeID foreign key to EMPLOYEE
    TeamID foreign key to TEAM

REGULAR(<u>EmployeeID</u>, <u>TeamID</u>)
    EmployeeID foreign key to EMPLOYEE
    TeamID foreign key to TEAM

We would record principal work assignments in the PRINCIPAL table and regular ones in the REGULAR table. The ER diagram would now look like this Figure 7.16.

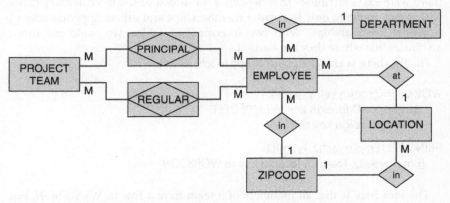

Figure 7.16 ER diagram for project teams database with two parallel many-to-many relationships (not recommended).

There are examples when multiple relationships between the same pair of tables make sense, as we will see in the next chapter, although more often for one-to-many relationships than for many-to-many relationships. Here, however, such an approach is not recommended because it has several significant disadvantages:

- There is no longer an inherent constraint, as we have in the previous design, that a particular employee's work on a particular team is either principal or regular but not both. This constraint is enforced in the previous design by having the composite attribute (*EmployeeID, TeamID*) as the primary key of WORKSON. If we were to record principal and regular assignments in separate tables, this constraint would not be implicit in the design of the database, and enforcing it would require relatively complicated programming. Note that if we really wanted to relax this constraint and allow principal and regular assignments for the same employee-team pair, the one-relationship design could still easily be used: we would just change the primary key of WORKSON to be the larger composite attribute (*EmployeeID, TeamID, Principal*), that is, the entire record.

- Some queries may be much more difficult to express. For example, if we want to list all the employees working on a given team, regardless of whether they are principal or regular, the two-relationship design makes it impossible to formulate a corresponding simple MS Access or SQL "SELECT" query. Instead, we must perform two different queries and combine them (an operation called UNION in Access and SQL). By contrast, queries like the one just described are straightforward in the one-relationship design, yet it is still easy to query just principal or just regular assignments (by placing a selection criterion on the *Principal* field).

One possible advantage to the two-relationship approach above would be if there were extra attributes that needed to be added to the intermediary table, with some applying only to regular memberships and others applying only to principal memberships. With two intermediary tables, we could put those attributes just where they are needed.

Finally, there is another possible approach, as follows:

WORKSON(<u>EmployeeID</u>, <u>TeamID</u>)
    EmployeeID foreign key to EMPLOYEE
    TeamID foreign key to TEAM

PRINCIPAL(<u>EmployeeID</u>, <u>TeamID</u>)
    (EmployeeID, TeamID) foreign key to WORKSON

The idea here is that all members of a team have a row in WORKSON, but principal members also have a matching row in PRINCIPAL. Regular members of a team have just a row in WORKSON but no matching row in PRINCIPAL. The foreign key designation in PRINCIPAL prevents somebody from being a principal member of team without being a member. This design is depicted in Figure 7.17.

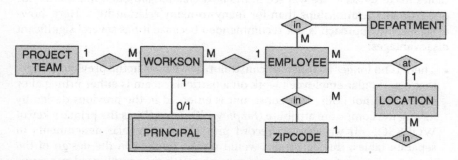

Figure 7.17 A subtype-based approach to multiple "flavors" of membership.

Here, PRINCIPAL is a subtype of WORKSON. This design has the practical advantages of the original design, although it is more complicated. Since putting a yes/no or code variable into WORKSON requires only one byte per record, the complexity of the subtype approach would be justified by the possible savings in storage only if the WORKSON table had a huge number of rows but just a tiny percentage of the group memberships were "principal." If there were some storage-intensive attributes applying only to principal memberships but not to regular memberships, the subtype approach would become more attractive, since we could place these fields in PRINCIPAL and not have to leave them blank for the vast majority of records in WORKSON.

The Library

We will now study progressively more complicated, realistic sample problems. Consider the following situation:

> You have volunteered to design a database for your local library. Each title carried by the library is identified by a unique "ISBN" code. You will also assign a unique code to each author represented in the library's collection (some have similar or identical names). Some "authors" are companies, and some do not have traditional Western names, so you will not divide author names into a "first" and "last" part. Some books have more than one author. Sometimes the order in which authors are listed is important, so that information also needs to be stored in some way. For each author, you want to store the following, when applicable: date of birth, date of death, and the country of birth.
>
> A few of the authors live nearby and occasionally come to the library for readings, book signings, and so forth. For these authors, you keep contact information including postal address, e-mail address, and phone number.
>
> Each book has a single publisher. You assign a unique code to each publisher and want to store the publisher's name and contact information. For each book, you want to store its publication date.
>
> You have more than one copy of some books. Each copy is identified by a unique bar code number. For each copy, you want to store the date it was acquired and whether it was acquired used or new.
>
> You have a large number of borrowers, each identified by a unique library card number. For each borrower, you keep contact information, including their address, phone number, and e-mail address. You want to keep track of all past and present borrowing, including the borrow date and return date (the return date does not apply to books currently on loan), and the number of times the loan has been renewed.
>
> Draw an ER diagram, and write a design outline of the database. Assume you *do* have access to a zip code table.

Here are the entities needed:

- AUTHOR (with subtype LOCALAUTHOR for those few authors for which we have personal contact information)
- BOOK
- PUBLISHER
- COPY
- LOAN
- BORROWER
- ZIPCODE

Note that the total number of authors represented in the library is likely to be large, certainly in the thousands, but we will have personal contact information for only a very small minority. Therefore, it makes some sense to store author contact information in a subtype.

The arrangement of BOOK, COPY, LOAN, and BORROWER is essentially identical to the DVD lending library example we studied earlier, which stands to reason since the business situations are very similar. We have address information for records in LOCALAUTHOR, PUBLISHER, and BORROWER, so those tables should be related to ZIPCODE.

The place where we need a many-to-many relationship is between BOOK and AUTHOR, because some books have multiple authors, and there are also authors with multiple books. The ER diagram should look like Figure 7.18.

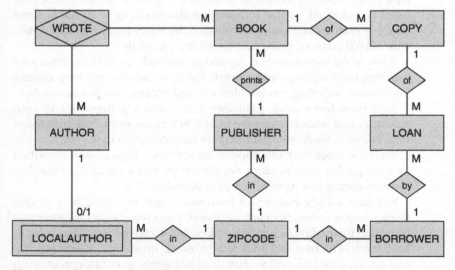

Figure 7.18 ER diagram for the library database.

If we identify authors by a synthetic key *AuthorID*, and books by their ISBN numbers, we might imagine that the WROTE table would have the following structure:

WROTE(AuthorID, ISBN)
    AuthorID foreign key to AUTHOR   [Incomplete]
    ISBN foreign key to BOOK

However, one piece of information is lost this way, namely, the order of authorship, which may be very important for some books. Note that ordered lists are a relatively difficult kind of information to store in relational databases because the order of rows in a table is not considered significant, and in general cannot be controlled. Unfortunately, in this case, we are in the position of having to store an ordered list without disrupting or forgetting its order. The simplest approach here is to add another attribute to WROTE which contains 1 for the first author, 2 for the second author, 3 for the third author, and so forth. If we call this attribute *AuthorOrder*, we obtain:

WROTE(AuthorID, ISBN, AuthorOrder)
    AuthorID foreign key to AUTHOR
    ISBN foreign key to BOOK

By keeping AuthorOrder out of the primary key, we make sure that each author appears at most once for each book. Unfortunately, there are other constraints that we would ideally like to have, but which the design does not automatically enforce, such as that no two authors should have the same *AuthorOrder* value on the same book, and every book having a first author. Some supplementary programming (through, for example, using a VBA module in Access) would be necessary to enforce such constraints. The full database outline looks like this:

ZIPCODE(Zip, City, State)

AUTHOR(AuthorID, Name, BirthDate, DeathDate, BirthNationality)

LOCALAUTHOR(AuthorID, Address, Zip, Phone, EMail)
    AuthorID foreign key to AUTHOR
    Zip foreign key to ZIPCODE

PUBLISHER(PublisherID, Name, Address, Zip, Phone, EMail)
    Zip foreign key to ZIPCODE

BOOK(ISBN, Title, PublisherID, DatePublished)
    PublisherID foreign key to PUBLISHER

WROTE(<u>AuthorID</u>, <u>ISBN</u>, AuthorOrder)
    AuthorID foreign key to AUTHOR
    ISBN foreign key to BOOK

COPY(<u>BarCode</u>, ISBN, AcquireDate, UsedOrNew)
    ISBN foreign key to BOOK

BORROWER(<u>CardNumber</u>, FName, MName, LName, Address, Zip, Phone, EMail)
    Zip foreign key to ZIPCODE

LOAN(CardNumber, <u>BarCode</u>, <u>BorrowDateTime</u>, ReturnDateTime, TimesRenewed)
    CardNumber foreign key to BORROWER
    BarCode foreign key to COPY

Note that we leave *DeathDate* blank for authors who are still alive, and *ReturnDateTime* blank for loans that are still with the borrower. Subtypes are not warranted to save the small amount of storage accounted for in such blank fields, especially considering that completed loans should far outnumber currently active loans unless we purge completed loans from the database very frequently.

This design shows a composite key for LOAN, based on the observation that a particular copy of a book can be borrowed only once at a particular instant. A synthetic key is also possible.

In the ER diagram, we could expand the AUTHOR-WROTE-BOOK many-to-many relationship into two one-to-many relationships. In the diagram, we might also conceivably condense the relationships between COPY, LOAN, and BORROWER to a single many-to-many relationship, but that would probably be confusing due to the large number of fields besides *CardNumber* and *BarCode* in LOAN, and because LOAN's primary key is not (*CardNumber, BarCode*).

This is the most complicated database we have designed so far, containing nine tables. Note that by commercial standards, such a design would still be considered very simple. Commercial ERP systems, which are meant to fill the needs of entire large or midsized corporations, may contain tens of thousands of tables. Functional area systems have a more modest scope and hence need fewer tables, but dozens or hundreds of tables are common. For example, a real library would require more than nine tables, in order to keep track of holds, renewals, and other details we did not consider. For this reason, it may well be better to simply purchase an off-the-shelf product designed specifically for the type of operation or organization at hand, rather than designing something from scratch. Such a product would still at its heart contain a relational database. However, such products may be expensive, and in some cases may be difficult or impossible to adapt to any unique or unusual business practices of a particular organization or to interconnect with other vendors' software, so there may sometimes be countervailing advantages to "growing your own" database design. For standardized businesses such as car repair shops or dental offices, it is highly likely that a suitable off-the-shelf product may be found at reasonable cost. For applications such as payroll, where many complicated accounting and taxation rules are involved, it may also be difficult for an inexperienced person to devise a correct system that would withstand an audit. On the other hand, for simple problems or for unique or new situations, skill at proper "from scratch" design of a customized database can be very valuable.

Exercises

7.1 **Tour operator:** You manage a tour company that operates tours of local historical and natural attractions. You have several dozen different tour packages, each with a name (such as "Exploring Native Ruins" or "Bird-Watching Hike"), a scheduled duration in minutes, a per-guest price, and a maximum number of guests. You also have a staff of dozens of guides, for each of which you want to store a first name, middle initial, last name, and date hired. For each guest who has ever taken or has booked a reservation to take one of your tours, you want to store a first name, middle initial, last name, gender, date of birth, and mobile phone number. You group guests into households, for each of which you want to store address information (street address, city, state, and zip code), and a primary credit card number. Assume that you have access to a national zip code table that you wish to include in your database design, and that each guest can be a member of only one household. A tour consists of one of your guides taking a group of guests on one of the tour packages. For each tour, you want your system to remember what tour package it was, which guide conducted it, and which guests participated. You also want to store a scheduled start date and time, and an actual completion time (blank for tours that are in the future). Over time, guests can participate in more than one tour. Draw an ER diagram, and write a database design outline for a database appropriate for this information.

7.2 **Compatibility of auto parts:** Zip Guys, Inc., runs a large network of auto part stores. Each part they offer for sale is identified by an SKU code assigned by Zip Guys. For each part, they want to store the part manufacturer name, a manufacturer's part number, a unit price, and the associated part type; each part has only one type. Part types are identified by a code, along with a description: for example "FUELFILT" for "fuel filter" or "SIGLAMP" for "signaling lamp." A critical function of Zip Guys' database is to identify the compatibility of each part with each type of vehicle. Each type of vehicle is identified by a specific "vehicle type code" that corresponds to a specific combination of vehicle make, model name, year, and engine description (such as "2.8 liter V6"). Usually, a given part fits more than one vehicle type, and there are, of course, a large variety of parts that can fit any given vehicle. The database needs to be organized so that when a customer has a request such as "I need a tail light bulb for a 2008 Toyota Matrix," the store staff can query the database to find out which appropriate part(s) the store sells will fit the customer's vehicle. Your database should also contain a table of known vehicle makes (but, for simplicity, do not include separate tables for known model names and engine types). Design a database for this information, creating an ER diagram and a database design outline.

7.3 EcoBus Corporation: EcoBus Corporation makes hybrid natural-gas-fueled buses for various clients, including city, state, and county transit authorities. This database is concerned with the ordering of buses. EcoBus currently has dozens of basic bus models, each of which has a unique model number, along with a length, width, height, basic gross weight, and list price. For each of the firm's customers, you want to store a name (for example, "NJ Transit"), address, city, state zip, code, phone number, and contact person name (assume that you do not want to maintain a separate table for zip codes). Over time, customers may place multiple orders; for each order, you want to store the date of the order and the percentage discount negotiated from the list price of the order. Each order consists of one or more "production batches." A production batch consists of a number of buses that are all the same model and have same option packages. Each production batch is identified by the serial number of the first bus in the batch; the remaining buses in the production batch have consecutive serial numbers. Your system needs to know the number of buses in each batch, the model of bus, and which option packages apply to buses in the batch.

Options are sold only in option "packages," each consisting of one or more options. Each option package has a unique catalog number, a name (for example, "cold climate engine kit" or "bicycle storage"), a description, and a list price. Each individual option has a unique option code and description. Some individual options are in more than one option package.

Design a database to store this information.

7.4 People and student clubs at a university: Every person affiliated with Giant State University (GSU), be they a student, faculty member, or staff member, has a university ID card with a unique ID number. For every affiliated person, the university database stores a family name and given name, the person's gender, a postal address consisting of a street address, city, state and zip code, and a primary e-mail address. Assume that GSU has access to a zip code table.

For specific categories of people, the university stores additional information: for students, the university stores the date of admission and expected graduation date. For administrative staff, the university stores the date of hire and administrative job classification code. For faculty, they store the name of the institution at which the faculty member earned their doctoral degree, the year of the degree, and the field it was obtained in.

Note that the categories of faculty, administrative staff, and students can overlap. For example, an administrative staff member might take a course for credit and thus also be a student, or an administrator might also be a faculty member.

GSU also has a large number of student clubs. For each club, the university wants to store a name, a description, and a date formed. Each club also has a single faculty advisor, who must be a member of GSU's faculty; the database should remember the identity of the faculty advisor for each club. Although it is uncommon, it is possible for a faculty member to be the advisor for more than one club.

Finally, the database should remember which students are members of each club. All club members must be students; a student can be a member of as many clubs as they wish, and there is no limit on the number of members of a given club.

Design the portion of the university's database needed to store all the information mentioned above, drawing an ER diagram and writing a database design outline. You may add "ID" fields wherever necessary. Assume that the university has access to a national zip code table, and try to avoid storing blank fields for attributes that do not apply to a particular class of person: for example, you should not have to store a blank administrative job classification field for students or faculty who are not also administrative staff.

7.5 Central Jersey Adult Education: Central Jersey Adult Education (CJAE) runs a variety of night and weekend classes in cooking, exercise, stress management, gardening, art, and other popular topics at various locations throughout central New Jersey. Each course CJAE offers is identified by a course code and has a name, description, tuition fee, and number of course meetings (some courses consist of just one meeting; others may consist of as many as ten meetings). Each course may be offered at multiple times and locations. Each time/location a course is offered is called a "class." For each class, your computer system must store its location, maximum number of students allowed, instructor, and date/time of first meeting. All CJAE classes with multiple meetings are held once per week, at the same day of the week and time of day as the first meeting. For each location, you want to store a name, address information, and phone number. For each instructor, you want to store a first name, last name, address information, phone number, mobile phone number, and e-mail address. Each class has only one instructor, but instructors can teach more than one class. Students can enroll in more than one class, including classes that are offerings of the same course. For example, somebody might take "pottery studio" several times over the span of a year. However, it makes no sense for a student to enroll more than once in the same class. For each student, your system should store a first name, last name, address information, phone number, mobile phone number, and e-mail address. Students do not receive grades or college credits for CJAE's courses. Assume that you do have access to a zip code table.

Design a database to store this information. Draw an ER diagram, and write a database design outline. You may add "ID" fields wherever necessary.

7.6 **Doctors' office:** You are setting up an information system for a large doctors' office. For each of the many doctors working at the office, you want to store a first name, middle initial/name, last name, e-mail address, phone number, date they received their degree, and the name of the medical school granting their degree. For each patient, you want to store a first name, middle initial/name, gender, date of birth, address information, phone number, and e-mail address. You also want to store information about appointments: each appointment involves one patient being seen by one doctor; for every such appointment, your system needs to record the date and time, who the patient was, who the doctor was, and doctor notes (250 characters of text). For each appointment, the system should remember one or more diagnostic codes assigned by the physician (for example, diagnostic code "692.71" means "sunburn," while diagnostic code "463" means "tonsillitis"). For each code, the system should store the name of the corresponding disease (i.e., "tonsillitis") and a description. Each appointment may involve one or more procedures (for example, a throat culture or a smallpox vaccination); the system should remember which procedures were done at each appointment. For each procedure, it should store an identifying code, a procedure name, a description, and a price. Finally, a small minority of appointments (less than 1%) are observed by a second, "observer" doctor (usually more senior than the principal doctor for the appointment). For such appointments, the system should be able to identify the observing doctor and store observer comments (again, 250 characters of text).

Design a database to store this information. Draw an ER diagram, and write a database design outline. You may add "ID" fields wherever necessary. For the vast majority of appointments having no observing doctor, avoid having to store blank fields for the observing doctor comments.

7.7 Medical clinical trials: You work for a pharmaceutical research consortium that operates clinical trials for a variety of new medications. Each trial has a name, a date started, and a completion date. Each trial has a large number of patients, for each of whom you would like to store the following information: first name, middle name/initial, last name, phone number, address information, birth date, gender, and date of admission to the trial, along with the patient's height, weight, blood pressure, and cholesterol level at the date of admission. Each patient is allowed to serve in only one trial. For each trial, you wish to store a name, a date started, a completion date, and the identities of all physicians administering the trial. More than one physician can work on a trial, and a physician can work on more than one trial. For each physician, you want to store first name, middle name/initial, last name, employing institution, the institution from which they obtained their degree, phone number, e-mail, and address information. Draw an ER diagram, and write a database design outline for a database appropriate for this information.

7.8 Catering menu and orders: You operate a commercial catering business serving conferences and other similar events. For each dish on your menu, you want to store a name, description, and number of calories per serving. You do not charge customers by the individual dish, but by menu package (in the market niche you serve, your customers prefer the simplicity of ordering well-coordinated standard packages, rather than customizing their menus). Each menu package consists of multiple dishes, and each dish can be in a number of different menu packages. Each menu package has a name, description, and price per guest. For each customer, you want to store a name, address, city, state, zip, phone number, and contact person name. Each customer places one or more orders, each of which is for a single menu package. Each order also has a date placed, number of guests, time and date of event, delivery address information (not necessarily the same as the customer's address), and comments. Design a database to hold all this information. Draw an ER diagram, and write a database design outline.

7.9 Pollution monitoring: You have just taken a job working for the state department of environmental protection. The department has just taken delivery of 10 new mass-spectrometer air pollution measuring instruments, and is expecting to receive more during the next few fiscal years. The state legislature has just authorized the department to use the instruments in a new pollution monitoring program to scan for a "watch list" of several hundred dangerous air pollutants, and you expect this list to expand in the future. Each pollutant on the watch list has a name, a description, and a maximum "safe" reading in parts per billion (ppb). The measuring instruments can be programmed to detect new substances as they are added to the watch list. The department would like you to design a database to store the data collected in the course of the monitoring program.

Each instrument will be identified by a 4-digit "unit number." For each instrument, you also want to store its serial number and the date it was delivered to your department. The instruments come in several different models; each model is identified by its model number. For each model of instrument, you want to store its manufacturer's name and its recommended maintenance interval (in days). You may assume that two different manufacturers cannot make instruments with the same model number. Every time you perform maintenance on an instrument, you want to record which instrument was involved, the date, and the maintenance technician's comments. The measuring instruments will be rotated between about 400 monitoring sites the department has identified around the state; you hope to add more sites as the department acquires more instruments. Each monitoring site will be identified by a five-letter code; for each site, you also want to store a description, the name of the municipality it is located in, its elevation, its latitude, and its longitude.

A "reading" consists of placing one of the instruments at one of the monitoring sites for two hours. For each reading, you want to know which instrument and monitoring site were used, along with the time the reading started, and the average wind speed and direction. During any particular reading, the instrument may detect some of the pollutants on the watch list, but most of the pollutants on the watch list probably will not be present at detectable levels. For each pollutant the instrument does detect during a reading, you want to store the corresponding detected amount in parts per billion (ppb).

Design a database capable of storing all the information described above. Draw an ER diagram, and write a database outline description. You are allowed to create your own "ID" or key fields.

7.10 **Labor mediation records:** You work for an agency that mediates labor grievances between firms and employees, and you are trying to move some of the agency's basic recordkeeping from paper to electronic form, using Microsoft Access.

Your main unit of work is a "case," which is a dispute between a single employee and a single firm. A firm can be involved in more than one case. An employee can also be involved in more than one case and not always with the same firm (since employees can change jobs). There can sometimes be more than one case involving a given firm and employee. Each case is identified by a unique "docket number."

For each firm, you want to store a company name, address information, phone and fax numbers, and the name of a primary contact person. For each employee, you want to store first and last names, home address information, home phone number, and date of birth. For cases, you want to store the date opened, the date closed (if applicable), and a description of the case (as an Access "memo" or text field). At present, you do not have access a zip code table.

You employ a staff of mediators for whom you want to store names, office numbers, and telephone extensions. For each case, you hold a series of mediation sessions at which you attempt to resolve the case's dispute. For each session, you want to store the time started, the time ended, and a brief narrative of what was discussed (also as an Access "Memo" or "Long Text" field). You also want to keep records on which of your mediators attended which sessions. Sometimes more than one of your mediators will attend a session. A case can have only one session in progress at any given time.

Design a database to store all this information. Draw an ER diagram, and write a database design outline.

7.11 **Bakery recipes:** You have been hired to help operate a commercial baking plant. Currently, recipe information is kept in a collection of word processing files, one file per recipe. A typical file might look like this:

Recipe #801
Product Name: Whole grain rolls (product code WGR1)
Recipe Makes: 800
Work Time: 2 hours
Total Time: 10 hours

Equipment: Standard sifter (SIF001)
      Heavy-duty mixing machine (MIX002)
      Kneading/rising machine (KRM010)
      High-temperature bread oven (OVN003)

Ingredients: 40 pounds whole grain flour
      30 cakes #6 yeast
      1 pound sugar
      3 gallons whole milk
      5 pounds #3 vegetable shortening
      0.5 pound salt

Directions   Run flour through sifter. Transfer to mixer, crumble in
      yeast, stir in the sugar and ...

To help plan plant operations and materials purchasing, you would like to transfer this kind of information to a relational database. Each recipe makes one product, but there may be several different recipes for the same product, making different quantities, using different procedures, or requiring slightly different ingredients. Each ingredient is always measured in the same units; for example, sugar is always measured in pounds. You need to keep track of how much of each ingredient is in each recipe, and what pieces of equipment each recipe uses.

Draw an ER diagram, and write a database design outline for a database to store the recipe-related information. Assume that "directions" can be stored in a single "Long Text" or "Memo" field.

7.12 **Sales with multiple suppliers:** You operate a wholesale business. Your inventory consists of many items, each identified by an SKU code. For each SKU code, you want to store a description, a price, and the amount in inventory. Your customers place orders that can contain more than one item. In addition to the quantity of each item it contains, you want to keep track of the date each order was placed and the date it was delivered.

You obtain your inventory from multiple suppliers. Each supplier can sell you more than one item (but not every possible item), and many items can be obtained from more than one supplier. For each item, each supplier may have a different price and "lead time" (that is, the number of days it takes for them to deliver stock after you have ordered it).

You want to keep contact information on each supplier and each customer. Contact information for both suppliers and customers consists of a company name, the name of a contact person, a postal address, a telephone number, a fax number, and an e-mail. Assume all postal addresses are in the United States. You have access to a full zip code table and plan to include it in your database. Draw an ER diagram, and write a database design outline.

8

Multiple Relationships between the Same Pair of Tables

This chapter describes how to design databases when the business situation requires more than one relationship between the same two entities. Such multiple relationships are not common but are appropriate in specific situations. We begin with a review exercise.

Commuter Airline Example

Consider the following problem:

> Your firm operates a commuter airline covering portions of western Canada and the northwest United States. Presently, you store your schedule in a database with the following tables:
>
> FLIGHT(FlightNumber, OriginAirport, DepartureTime, DestinationAirport, ArrivalTime, PlaneCode)
>   PlaneCode foreign key to KINDOFPLANE
>
> FLIESONDAY(FlightNumber, Day)
>   FlightNumber foreign key to FLIGHT
>
> KINDOFPLANE(PlaneCode, FullPlaneName, SeatingCapacity)
>
> *OriginAirport* and *DestinationAirport* are standard three-letter airport codes (like "LAX" for Los Angeles or "EWR" for Newark). The permitted values of *Day* in the FLIESONDAY table are "Weekdays", "Saturday", or "Sunday". For instance, the records shown below indicate that Flight 123 operates between Calgary, Alberta (airport code YYC), and Helena, Montana (airport code HLN), departing 10:00 AM and arriving 12:30 PM on weekdays and Saturdays, but not operating on Sundays; the flight uses a De Havilland Dash 7 turboprop aircraft (plane code DH7) that

Introductory Relational Database Design for Business, with Microsoft Access, First Edition.
Jonathan Eckstein and Bonnie R. Schultz.
© 2018 John Wiley & Sons Ltd. Published 2018 by John Wiley & Sons Ltd.

seats 50 people. The records pertaining to other flights and kinds of aircraft are not shown.

FLIGHT: (123, YYC, 10:00, HLN, 12:30, DH7)

KINDOFPLANE: (DH7, "De Havilland Dash 7 Turboprop", 50)

FLIESONDAY: (123, Weekdays)
               (123, Saturday)

a) Draw an entity-relationship (ER) diagram for this database.

This is a simple review question. Examining the pattern of foreign keys, we obtain Figure 8.1.

Figure 8.1 ER diagram for initial design of commuter airline database.

Note that larger airlines may use the same flight number for several distinct flight "legs," for example, a flight from Newark that flies to Cleveland and then continues to Los Angeles (nowadays this kind of "continuation" is often illusory, because a different aircraft is actually used on the continuing flight leg). This practice introduces a minor additional level of complexity, but we need not deal with it in the case of this small airline: we will simply assume that each flight number corresponds to a unique trip from one departure airport to one arrival airport.

Next, we consider the following:

The operations department decides that Saturday demand for flight 123 is too small to justify a DH7 aircraft, and they want to substitute a smaller Saab 340 aircraft on Saturdays. They will continue to use the DH7 aircraft on weekdays.

b) With this change of aircraft, briefly explain why the database forces you to assign a different flight number to the Saturday flight, even though its scheduled arrival and departure information are identical to the weekday flight.

The problem here is that the *PlaneCode* foreign key field is in the table FLIGHT, meaning that it has to be fully determined by the primary key of FLIGHT, that is, *FlightNumber*. So, if we want a different kind of plane on the 10:00 am Alberta–Helena route on certain days, we have to assign a different flight number.

c) Redesign the database so the same flight number can be used on every day a flight operates, even if different aircraft are used. Draw a new ER diagram, and write a new database design outline.

To be able to use a different kind of aircraft for the same flight but on different days, we need to make *PlaneCode* a function of both *FlightNumber* and *Day*. That is, it should be in a table whose primary key consists of both *FlightNumber* and *Day*, namely, FLIESONDAY. Thus, we obtain the following outline:

FLIGHT(<u>FlightNumber</u>, OriginAirport, DepartureTime, DestinationAirport, ArrivalTime)

FLIESONDAY(<u>FlightNumber</u>, <u>Day</u>, PlaneCode)
    FlightNumber foreign key to FLIGHT
    PlaneCode foreign key to KINDOFPLANE

KINDOFPLANE(<u>PlaneCode</u>, FullPlaneName, SeatingCapacity)

The resulting ER diagram is shown in Figure 8.2.

Figure 8.2 Corrected ER diagram for commuter airline database.

We could also view FLIESONDAY as creating a many-to-many relationship between KINDOFPLANE and FLIGHT, although drawing the ER diagram in that manner could be misleading since its primary key is not (*FlightNumber*, *PlaneCode*).

We now proceed to the non-review portion of the exercise:

d) Suppose you want to be able to print reports in which you list not only the three-letter codes for airports but their full names. For example, a line of the report might read:

Flight 123 Departs Calgary, Alberta 10:00 am Arrives Helena, Montana 12:30 pm .

You plan to add a table to the database storing the name, state/province, altitude, latitude, and longitude of each airport (latitude and longitude are useful for calculating flight distance). Draw a new ER diagram and design outline for the database.

Clearly we need another table to store information about airports, such as:

AIRPORT(<u>AirportCode</u>, TownName, StateOrProvince, Altitude, Latitude, Longitude)

But what is the relationship between FLIGHT and AIRPORT? Corresponding to each airport, there may be an indefinitely large number of flights, but for each flight, there are exactly *two* airports, one for arrival and one for departure. Thus, we have a somewhat peculiar kind of situation, a "two-to-many" relationship.

Starting from the database as we have already designed it, the simplest way to implement this relationship is as follows: just include the AIRPORT table as defined above and require that the *OriginAirport* and *DestinationAirport* three-letter airport code fields in FLIGHT match a known airport. Thus, we have the following:

FLIGHT(<u>FlightNumber</u>, OriginAirport, DepartureTime, DestinationAirport,
     ArrivalTime)
  OriginAirport foreign key to AIRPORT
  DestinationAirport foreign key to AIRPORT

FLIESONDAY(<u>FlightNumber</u>, <u>Day</u>, PlaneCode)
  FlightNumber foreign key to FLIGHT
  PlaneCode foreign key to KINDOFPLANE

KINDOFPLANE(<u>PlaneCode</u>, FullPlaneName, SeatingCapacity)

AIRPORT(<u>AirportCode</u>, TownName, StateOrProvince, Altitude, Latitude,
     Longitude)

Do not be alarmed that the names of the foreign key fields *OriginAirport* and *DestinationAirport* in FLIGHT have different names from the primary key of AIRPORT they are supposed to match. Until now, we have usually used the same name for a foreign key and the primary key it is intended to match, but that is not possible here, because a table cannot contain two fields with the same name. As discussed earlier, having identical names is not in fact necessary to match a foreign and primary key; only the fields' datatypes actually need to match. The precise meaning of the annotation "*x* foreign key to *Y*" is as follows:

> The value of attribute *x* of each record in this table should equal the value of the primary key of some record in table *Y*.

Understood in this way, it is clear that "*x* foreign key to *Y*" does not require the name of attribute *x* be the same as the name of the primary key of *Y*. Since table *Y* has only one primary key, there is no ambiguity as to which attribute in *Y* the attribute *x* is supposed to match; thus, there is no need to make the names identical so that the attributes can "find" one another. In Access, the datatypes of the fields should be the same, but the names do not have to be: the "Edit Relationships" dialog box allows you to "pair up" fields with different names.

If we draw an ER diagram for the database we now have, we obtain Figure 8.3.

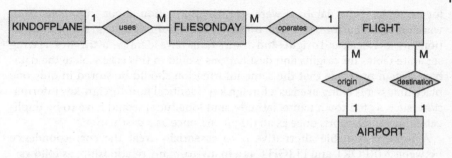

Figure 8.3 ER diagram for the commuter airline database with an AIRPORT table.

That is, we have *two* one-to-many relationships between AIRPORT and FLIGHT. Each flight has one origin airport and also one destination airport. Each airport may have many departing (origin) flights and many arriving (destination) flights. The two foreign keys in FLIGHT are not considered to be a repeating group because they are semantically distinct, that is, they have different meanings: each flight has an origin airport and a departure airport, with each having a fixed and distinct meaning.

To obtain a more familiar-looking diagram in situations like this, it may be tempting to instead draw an ER diagram as in Figure 8.4.

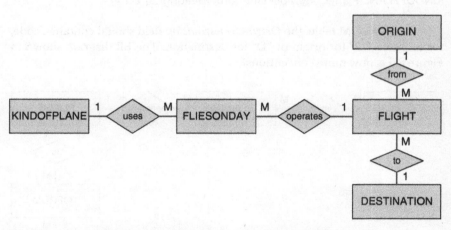

Figure 8.4 Incorrect approach to adding airport information to the commuter airline database.

This kind of approach would make sense only if there were no overlap between the set of possible origins and the set of possible destinations, or if origins and destinations had completely different attributes. Such a situation could happen, for example, if the database were storing information about shipments from warehouses to customers. Here, however, the set of origins and set of destinations are identical, and origins and destinations have identical attributes. Having separate tables for origins and destinations would in this case violate the database design principle that the same information should be stored in only one place unless it is being used as a foreign key: identical non-foreign-key information (such as the town name, latitude, and longitude) would have to be duplicated for each airport, once as an origin and once as a destination.

A more reasonable alternative is to essentially treat the correspondence between AIRPORT and FLIGHT as a many-to-many relationship, as follows:

FLIGHT(<u>FlightNumber</u>, DepartureTime, ArrivalTime)

TOFROM(<u>FlightNumber</u>, AirportCode, <u>OriginOrDestination</u>)
    FlightNumber foreign key to FLIGHT
    AirportCode foreign key to AIRPORT

AIRPORT(<u>AirportCode</u>, TownName, StateOrProvince, Altitude, Latitude,
        Longitude)

FLIESONDAY(<u>FlightNumber</u>, <u>Day</u>, PlaneCode)
    FlightNumber foreign key to FLIGHT
    PlaneCode foreign key to KINDOFPLANE

KINDOFPLANE(<u>PlaneCode</u>, FullPlaneName, SeatingCapacity)

In the TOFROM table, the *OriginOrDestination* field should contain a code, for example, "O" for origin or "D" for destination. The ER diagram shown in Figure 8.5 is now more conventional.

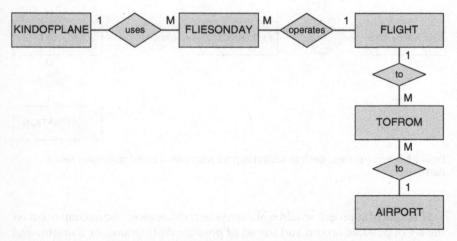

Figure 8.5 Alternative design of the commuter airline database with airports, using an intermediary table.

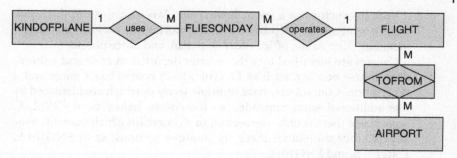

Figure 8.6 Intermediary table approach to the commuter airline database, depicted as a many-to-many relationship.

This diagram might also be rendered as in Figure 8.6. In this case, the first depiction is preferable, because the primary key of TOFROM is not (*FlightNumber, AirportCode*). This database design has both advantages and disadvantages as compared to using two parallel one-to-many relationships. Certain queries are easier to perform than in our original design, but some common-sense constraints present in our first design are not automatically enforced by the structure of the database. For example, one could create a flight with an origin but no destination. This kind of error would be impossible in the original design if we enforce referential integrity and prohibit blank values for the *OriginAirport* and *DestinationAirport* fields.

The College

We now consider a much more complicated example with some of the same features:

> We want to keep basic information about courses, instructors, departments, and student enrollments at a small college. We need to keep information about students' schedules for the current semester and their grades from prior courses (we may also store their schedules from prior semesters if we wish). We also want to store instructors' schedules for both the current semester and past ones.
>
> The college consists of *departments*, identified both by their full names and by unique three-letter codes such as ENG, MTH, CIS, MAN, and so forth. One particular instructor is designated as the *chairperson* of a department. We want our system to be able to store the current chairperson for each department (we do not need information about past chairpersons).

Each instructor has a *home department*. We wish to store the home department, and to keep basic contact information on each instructor, including their name, office address, e-mail, and office phone.

Courses are identified by a three-letter department code and a three-digit course number, such as ENG101. Each course has a name and a description. Courses may have multiple *sections*, which are identified by one additional letter appended to the course name, as in CIS223A. Sometimes there is only one section of a course (in which case it is usually "A"), but sometimes there are multiple sections, as in ENG101A, ENG101B, and ENG101C.

Each semester, a single instructor is responsible for each section. This instructor is usually in the same department as the course, but there may be exceptions. Each section also has a room number and a *time slot*, such as MWF10AM, for Monday/Wednesday/Friday at 10 a.m You want to store a table of time slot codes and their descriptions. Sometimes a course can have more than one section in the same time slot.

Each semester, a student can take multiple courses. You want to use the database to store student schedules, that is, the sections being taken by each student each semester. Once the semester is over, you want to store the student's grade for each class.

Finally, you want to store contact information for each student (name, campus address, phone number, and e-mail address). After their first few semesters, the students declare themselves as having a single *major* in a department. They may also declare a single *minor* in a different department. You want the system to store major and minor information for all students. Neither multiple majors nor multiple minors are allowed.

Draw an ER diagram, and write a database outline.

The ER diagram for this situation is shown in Figure 8.7.

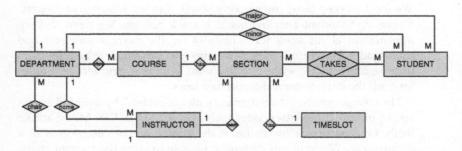

Figure 8.7 ER diagram for the college database.

Here is a corresponding database outline that makes extensive use of composite primary keys:

DEPARTMENT(<u>DeptCode</u>, DepartmentName, ChairID)
  ChairID foreign key to INSTRUCTOR

COURSE(<u>DeptCode</u>, <u>CourseNum</u>, Name, Description)
  DeptCode foreign key to DEPARTMENT

SECTION(<u>DeptCode</u>, <u>CourseNum</u>, <u>SectionLetter</u>, <u>Semester</u>, TimeCode,
      InstructorID RoomNumber)
  (DeptCode, CourseNum) foreign key to COURSE
  TimeCode foreign key to TIMESLOT
  InstructorID foreign key to INSTRUCTOR

TIMESLOT(<u>TimeCode</u>, TimeSlotDescription)

STUDENT(<u>StudentID</u>, FirstName, LastName, CampusAddress, Phone,
      Email, Major, Minor)
  Major foreign key to DEPARTMENT
  Minor foreign key to DEPARTMENT

TAKES(<u>StudentID</u>, <u>DeptCode</u>, <u>CourseNum</u>, <u>SectionLetter</u>, <u>Semester</u>, Grade)
  StudentID foreign key to STUDENT
  (DeptCode, CourseNum, SectionLetter, Semester) foreign key to SECTION

INSTRUCTOR(<u>InstructorID</u>, FirstName, LastName, HomeDepartment,
      OfficeAddress, OfficePhone, Email)
  HomeDepartment foreign key to DEPARTMENT

Some observations:

- As usual, the SECTION-TAKES-STUDENT arrangement could be viewed as two one-to-many relationships, instead of one many-to-many.
- When a table has a composite primary key and other tables have foreign keys "pointing" to it, those foreign keys must also be composite. For example, in SECTION, the combination (*DeptCode, CourseNumber*) is a foreign key to COURSE. In our outline notation, we denote this situation by writing "(DeptCode, CourseNumber) foreign key to COURSE." The drawback of heavy use of composite keys is that they can propagate and accumulate excessively — for instance, this database ends up with a five-part primary key in TAKES, of which four fields constitute a foreign key to SECTION.
- Note that there are two one-to-many relationships between DEPARTMENT and INSTRUCTOR, but they are oriented in opposite directions: the

"many" of one relationship is the "one" of the other. Each instructor has one home department, and each department will usually have many instructors. But to indicate who the chair of a department is, it makes the most sense to have a foreign key in the DEPARTMENT table. It is therefore possible (but unlikely in practice) that somebody could be the chair of more than one department. Having two one-to-many relationships in different directions between the same pair of tables is permissible but can lead to complications in creating records while maintaining referential integrity. It may be necessary to relax referential integrity or allow blank values for foreign keys in order to start entering records without encountering a "chicken and egg" situation.

- There is also a double relationship between STUDENT and DEPARTMENT, but more similar to the previous example since both relationships lead in the same direction; we place the appropriate three-letter code in *Major* or *Minor* to indicate a student's major or minor. If a student has no minor, or has not picked a major yet, we can leave the corresponding field blank, or have a special "unassigned" department code. Unfortunately, the structure of the database cannot inherently enforce the constraint that a student's major and minor should be in different departments; a special code module (in Access, a VBA procedure) would be needed to enforce this constraint.

Here is an alternate solution that instead uses synthetic keys wherever possible, except in the TAKES table:

DEPARTMENT(DeptCode, DepartmentName, ChairID)
   ChairID foreign key to INSTRUCTOR

COURSE(CourseID, DeptCode, CourseNum, Name, Description)
   DeptCode foreign key to DEPARTMENT

SECTION(SectionID, CourseID, SectionLetter, Semester, TimeCode,
         InstructorID, RoomNumber)
   CourseID foreign key to COURSE
   TimeCode foreign key to TIMESLOT
   InstructorID foreign key to INSTRUCTOR

TIMESLOT(TimeCode, TimeSlotDescription)

STUDENT(StudentID, FirstName, LastName, CampusAddress, Phone, Email,
         Major, Minor)
   Major foreign key to DEPARTMENT
   Minor foreign key to DEPARTMENT

TAKES(<u>StudentID</u>, <u>SectionID</u>, Grade)
    StudentID foreign key to STUDENT
    SectionID foreign key to SECTION

INSTRUCTOR(<u>InstructorID</u>, FirstName, LastName, HomeDepartment,
            OfficeAddress, OfficePhone, Email)
    HomeDepartment foreign key to DEPARTMENT

One could also use a synthetic key for TAKES, but that could have undesirable consequences, such as making it possible for a student to have two grades in the same section.

Clearly, the synthetic-key version has the advantage of being simpler and, depending on the datatypes involved, could use less storage. But there are also some less obvious disadvantages, again typical of many other situations. Suppose we would like to run a query returning all grades below C in mathematics (MTH) courses given last semester, along with the name of the student. With the synthetic-key approach, we must join the table TAKES to SECTION to determine the semester and join the result to COURSE to determine the department. Finally, we join the result to the STUDENT table to retrieve the student name. At a minimum, even a very smart "query engine" with a good query optimizer module would have to find all sections from last semester, all math courses, and all grades below C, and then perform a four-way join of these results with the STUDENT table.

With the composite-key design, the department and semester are already available in TAKES, so the query engine could simply scan TAKES for the correct semester, grade, and department, and join the result to STUDENT. Furthermore, if we wanted to include the course name in the output of the query, we could join TAKES directly to COURSE without having to do an extra join involving SECTION, because the course identifier (*DeptCode, CourseNumber*) is already available within TAKES. Such a process may be called a "shortcut join" because it directly joins tables that are only indirectly connected in the ER diagram.

Sports League Example

You have volunteered to automate the record keeping of a small recreational sports league. You are only concerned with this season's data and do not have a zip code table.

The league consists of teams, each of which has an ID number, a nickname, and a color scheme.

Each team has multiple players. For each player, you want to store the first name, last name, address, city, state, zip code, phone number, birth date, and skill rating. Each player is on only one team.

Each team also has multiple coaches. For each coach, you want to store the first name, last name, address, city, state, zip code, phone number, and "status" (which is 1 for less experienced coaches, 2 for more experienced coaches). Each coach is associated with at most one team per season.

You also want to keep track of games and their outcomes. Each game has a date, a home team, and a visiting team. For games that have been played already, you also want to store the points scored by each team.

Draw an ER diagram, and write a database design outline.

Here, we again have an example of a "two-to-many" relationship, in that each game involves exactly two teams, a home team and a visiting team, which are semantically distinct. Therefore, a reasonable ER diagram and database outline are as shown in Figure 8.8.

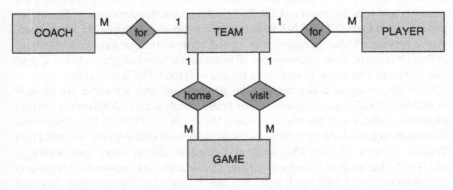

Figure 8.8 ER diagram for sports league database.

TEAM(<u>TeamID</u>, NickName, ColorScheme)

PLAYER(<u>PlayerID</u>, Fname, LName, Address, City, State, Zip, Phone, BirthDate,
     Rating, TeamID)
  TeamID foreign key to TEAM

COACH(<u>CoachID</u>, Fname, LName, Address, City, State, Zip, Phone, Status,
     TeamID)
  TeamID foreign key to TEAM

GAME(<u>GameID</u>, Date, HomeTeamID, HomeScore, VisitTeamID, VisitScore)
  HomeTeamID foreign key to TEAM
  VisitTeamID foreign key to TEAM

Instead of a synthetic key like *GameID*, various composite primary keys are also possible for GAME, depending on the details of the situation — for example, if each team can play at most one game per day, or we were to include not just the date but the exact start time of each game in the *Date* field, then (*Date, HomeTeamID*) would be a possible primary key.

Multiple Relationships in Access

The method of setting up these multiple relationships in Access is similar to setting up queries with multiple paths between tables. Download, save, and open the file `sports-with-games-clean.mdb` from the website. If the security banner appears, press its "enable" or "enable content" button. This file has all the tables described earlier, along with some sample data, but has no relationships defined.

Using the "Database Tools" tab, we open the Relationships window and start drawing the necessary relationships, including the home-team relationship between GAME and TEAM. We enforce referential integrity for each of these relationships (Figure 8.9).

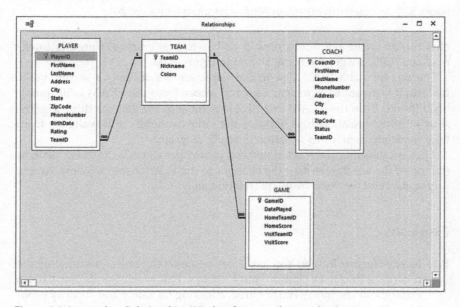

Figure 8.9 Incomplete Relationships Window for sports league database.

Establishing the second relationship between GAME and TEAM is a little tricky in Access. If we drag the *VisitTeamID* attribute over the *TeamID* attribute in TEAM, we get a warning that a relationship already exists. The dialog box asks if we want to edit the existing relationship, or create a new one. If we

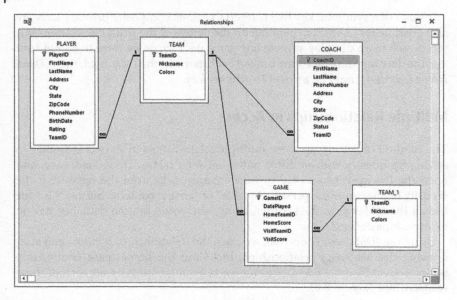

Figure 8.10 Completed Relationships Window for sports league database.

click "no" to create a new relationship, and then click "enforce referential integrity," and "OK," we get the result shown in Figure 8.10.

The second "table" TEAM_1 in this depiction is not really a second table. Instead, it is meant to represent a second record from the TEAM table, possibly different from the TEAM record. Thus, the way the Relationships window shows multiple relationships between the same two tables differs slightly from how we would depict this situation in an ER diagram.

After establishing these relationships, remember to click the "Save" icon at the top of the window to save the changes to the Relationship window. Access is now aware of the "two-to-many" relationship.

Exercises

8.1 Jersey Harbor Patrol: You have been assigned the task of automating the records of the Jersey Harbor Patrol Agency. This agency sends patrol boats throughout the Jersey Harbor area, checking for safety and security problems. The agency owns a fleet of boats; for each boat, you want to store its (unique) marine registration number, name, date built, and date acquired. The boats are operated by employees, for each of whom you want to store an employee number, first name, last name, date of birth, date hired, cell phone number, home phone number, and address information.

The employees use the boats to visit various sites around the harbor. Each site has a "site number," name, and description. Each instance of a boat leaving the agency's home dock is called a "patrol." Each patrol involves two employees, a "captain" and an "assistant." The captain is responsible for all decisions on the patrol, and the assistant must follow his orders. However, an employee who is the captain of one patrol might be the assistant on a different patrol. For each patrol, you want to record which boat was involved, who the captain and assistant were, what date and time the patrol started, and what date and time it ended. Each patrol involves visits to one or more sites; in general, the agency tries to visit each site at least once every few days. You want to record the set of sites visited by each patrol, and the exact date and time of each visit.

Design a database to store this information. Draw an ER diagram, and write a database design outline. You may add "ID" fields where necessary.

8.2 **Phone call logs:** Ginormous State University (GSU) maintains an office phone network. This question describes the database needed to keep track of individual phones. The university also keeps record of utilization of the network for internal calls. An internal call is one placed from one GSU office phone to another GSU office phone.

Each phone is identified by a unique phone number and is designated as either a personal phone or a common-area phone (the database should remember which). For each phone, the system should also store the date of installation and the employee "responsible" for the phone. For personal phones, the person responsible is typically the person in whose office the phone is located. Some employees may be responsible for more than one phone – for example, because the person has more than one office, each with its own phone, or because one person may be deemed responsible for more than one common-area phone.

Employees are identified by a unique university ID number. This database should store each employee's first name, middle name/initial, last name, and primary e-mail address.

The database should also remember in which room each phone is installed. Each building in the university has a unique building number, a building name (such as "McPherson Hall"), and a street address. All buildings in the university are located in the same city, state, and zip code, so the database need only store the street address. Each room has a number which is unique within its building (that is, there is only one "130 McPherson Hall," but there may be a room numbered "130" in a different building). The university physical plant department is able to supply a database containing all the valid room number/building combinations, along with the square footage and type (office, classroom, waiting area, etc.) for each room.

Finally, the database should keep a record of all internal calls, including from which phone the call was placed, to which phone it was placed, whether the call was answered (a yes/no field), the date and time the call started, and the date and time it ended. You may assume that only one call at a time can be placed from any given phone.

Design a database to store this information. Draw an ER diagram, and write a database design outline. You may add "ID" fields where necessary.

8.3 **Container shipping:** You have been asked to design part of a database an international shipping firm uses to track the movements of its cargo containers. In addition to the following attributes, you may create your own "ID" fields where necessary.

Each cargo container your firm owns has a unique ID number. For each container, you want to store this ID number, the date the container was built, and the date your firm acquired it (you occasionally buy used containers). You also want to store the "type" of the container. All containers of the same type have the same manufacturer, model number, length, width, height, and maximum weight capacity; you also want to store all this information.

A "terminal" denotes any place a container might be stored – for example, a port, a railroad yard, or a factory loading dock. Each terminal is identified by an eight-character ID code. For each terminal, you also want to store its latitude, its longitude, and a description. Containers are moved by "trips," which have a "type" that may be "truck," "rail," or "ship." Some trips (typically truck trips) move only one container, but others can move several containers or even hundreds or thousands of containers simultaneously. Naturally, containers can go on more than one trip. For all trips – past, present, and scheduled for the future – you want the database to keep be able to track of the following:

- The trip type (truck, rail, or ship)
- Departure terminal
- Arrival terminal
- Scheduled departure date/time
- Scheduled arrival date/time
- Actual departure time (blank for trips that have not departed yet)
- Actual arrival time (blank for trips that have not arrived yet)
- All containers moved (or scheduled to be moved) by the trip
- The carrier used

"Carriers" are companies with whom you contract to move containers. For each carrier, we want to store contact information including the company name, address, city, state/province, postal code, country, telephone number, and contact e-mail address.

Design a database to store all this information. Draw an ER diagram, and write a database design outline. You may add "ID" fields where necessary. Assume you do *not* have access to a table of postal or zip codes.

8.4 Sales visits: Your firm sells products to other businesses, and your marketing department would like to set up a database to track customer activity and marketing representative site visits. For each customer, you want to store a customer ID number, firm name, a description/comment field, contact person name, phone number, address, city, state, and zip code; assume that you do not have a zip code table. You also have sales representatives, identified by employee ID. For each sales representative, you want to store the first name, last name, date hired, date of birth, gender, and rank (such as "senior sales representative" or "associate sales representative"). Each customer is assigned a primary sales representative and a backup representative, for times when the primary representative is unavailable.

You also want to track sales representative visits to the customers. For each visit, you want to store the date it occurred, the amount of time spent at the customer site, and a comment field. Every visit has a single sales representative as "lead presenter"; usually the lead presenter is the primary representative for that customer, but there are fairly frequent exceptions to this rule. Sometimes, the lead presenter is accompanied by a second sales representative, who acts in the "technical support" role. Somebody may be a lead presenter on one visit and work as technical support on another visit. For each visit, you want the database to be able to remember the customer visited, lead presenter, and technical support person (if any).

You want to be able to tie your information on sales force activity with customer orders. Each order is placed by a single customer and has a unique order ID; you also want the database to remember the date the order was placed. An order consists of a number of products, each with a quantity. For each product, identified by a unique SKU (stock keeping unit) number, you want to store a name, description, and unit price.

Draw an ER diagram, and write a database design outline for this database.

8.5 Web security conference: You are setting up the database for a web security conference. A "participant" is defined to be a person who is involved in the conference in any way. You have decided to identify each participant by his or her e-mail address. For each participant, you also want to store the following contact information: last/family name, first/given name, additional/middle name, work affiliation, address information, and phone number.

Each presentation at the conference has a single speaker, who must be a participant. A participant is sometimes permitted to be the speaker for more than one presentation. Each presentation may also have an indefinite number of co-authors, who should also be participants. It is possible to be a co-author for more than one presentation, and the speaker for one presentation might be a co-author for another presentation. Each presentation may be given only once and has a title and an abstract.

Presentations are grouped into sessions; a session typically contains three presentations, but the number may vary. Each session has a title and also a chairperson, who must be a participant. Most sessions also have an organizer, who is also a participant. Typically, the organizer and the chairperson are the same person, but that is not always the case. A person may organize or chair more than one session. Other data pertinent to a session are its time slot and room. Time slots are identified by a two-letter code: for example, "MB" indicates the second session on Monday. For each time slot, you want to store a description; the description for "MB" might be "Monday 10:30 AM-12:00 PM". Rooms have a unique room code like "B203", a room name, a description, and a seating capacity. Several sessions may happen at the same time (in different rooms).

Design a normalized database that will store all this information. Draw an ER diagram, and write a database design outline. You may add "ID" fields where necessary.

9

Normalization

This chapter delves further into database design theory, specifically in regard to the process of *normalization*.

The first and most important database design principle for transaction databases is to avoid redundancy. Unless a field is a foreign key, it should be assigned to just one table.

A second principle is that your database should have no "bad" dependencies. In the dependency diagram of any table in the database, the determinant should be the whole primary key or a candidate key. Violations of this rule include partial dependencies and transitive dependencies.

Normalizing a database is the process of eliminating bad dependencies by splitting up tables and linking them through foreign keys. "Normal forms" are conceptual categories devised by database theorists to indicate how completely a database has been normalized.

There are six standard recognized normal forms (Figure 9.1). However, we will only cover first through third normal forms.

First Normal Form

A database is in *first normal form* (1NF) if all its table attributes are atomic. Attributes that are not considered atomic are nested relations, nested tables or sub-tables, repeating groups or sections, or list-valued attributes.

Table 9.1 shows an example of a table that has non-atomic attributes and therefore is not in first normal form. Its outline notation for may be written as follows:

CUSTOMER(CustomerID, CustomerName, BrokerID, BrokerName,
         HOLDING(SecID, SecName, SecType, NumShares))

Introductory Relational Database Design for Business, with Microsoft Access, First Edition.
Jonathan Eckstein and Bonnie R. Schultz.
© 2018 John Wiley & Sons Ltd. Published 2018 by John Wiley & Sons Ltd.

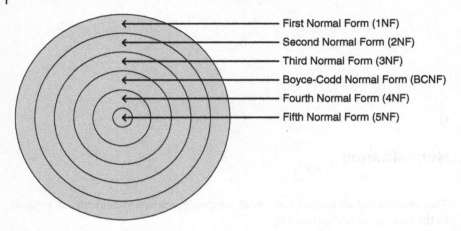

First Normal Form (1NF)
Second Normal Form (2NF)
Third Normal Form (3NF)
Boyce-Codd Normal Form (BCNF)
Fourth Normal Form (4NF)
Fifth Normal Form (5NF)

Figure 9.1 Hierarchy of normal forms.

As you can see, there is a subtable, which we call HOLDING, embedded inside the CUSTOMER table. That is, each record in CUSTOMER contains a subsidiary table indicating the securities held by the corresponding customer. This kind of nested or hierarchical form of design is a natural way for many people to view information. According to relational database theory, however, it is not the preferred format in which to store the underlying data. Historically, many information systems have stored data in hierarchical formats like this one, but they were not relational databases.

To normalize such a database, separate the "nested relation" to create a new table, and then link the two tables using a foreign key. In this case, the revised outline notation is as follows:

CUSTOMER(<u>CustomerID</u>, CustomerName, BrokerID, BrokerName)

HOLDING(<u>CustomerID</u>, <u>SecID</u>, SecName, SecType, NumShares)
    CustomerID foreign key to CUSTOMER

The HOLDING table in the new design consists of all records in the HOLDING sub-tables of the old design, "stacked" on top of one another. We include *CustomerID* in the new HOLDING table to indicate the owner of each block of securities. In the old, hierarchical design, this information was implicit in the location of each subtable. But once all the sub-tables are combined into a single table, this information would be lost unless we include *CustomerID* in the HOLDING table. This *CustomerID* field is a foreign key to the CUSTOMER table, because it must contain the ID of a valid customer.

Table 9.1 Investment holdings database that is not in first normal form.

Customer ID	Customer Name	Broker ID	BrokerName	SecID	SecName	SecType	NumShares
1006	Jane Golding	8791	Gerard Mills	875600	Allegiance	Fund	237
				431001	Apple	Stock	500
				438911	Citibank	Stock	788
2001	Carl Tate	9654	Alice Chan	43101	Apple	Stock	82
				430925	Oracle	Stock	530
3392	Shannon Lee	8923	Lisa Weitz	438390	IBM	Stock	120
				875600	Allegiance	Fund	387

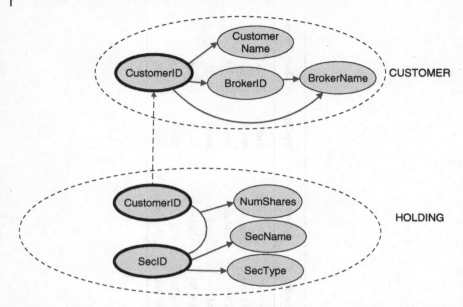

Figure 9.2 Dependency diagram of the investment holdings database after conversion to first normal form.

The dependency diagram for the revised database is shown in Figure 9.2. This financial services database is now in first normal form because it has no nested tables.

Second Normal Form

Remember that a *partial dependency* occurs when a table has a composite primary key and one of the table's attributes depends on a part of – but not all of – the primary key. A database is said to be in the *second normal form* (2NF) if it is in 1NF and does not contain any partial dependencies.

Our new investment holdings database is in first normal form, but it does have two partial dependencies, as indicated in Figure 9.3. In particular, *SecName* and *SecType* are both dependent on *SecID*, which is part of the primary composite key. The way to eliminate a partial dependency is to split up tables and introduce foreign keys so that the determinant of the partial dependency (in this case, *SecID*) becomes the primary key of a table and the attributes depending on it reside in the same table. In this example, if we create a new table called SECURITY, with *SecID* as its primary key, we can remove both of the partial dependencies by relocating *SecName* and *SecType* to the new table (Figure 9.4).

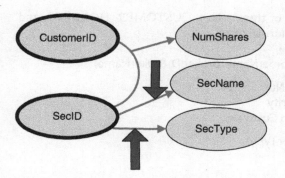

Figure 9.3 Partial dependencies in the HOLDING table.

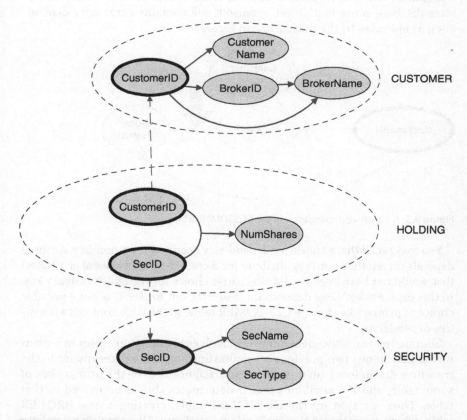

Figure 9.4 Dependency diagram of the investment holdings database after conversion to second normal form.

Our database now consists of three tables, CUSTOMER, HOLDING, and SECURITY, and is in second normal form:

CUSTOMER(<u>CustomerID</u>, CustomerName, BrokerID, BrokerName)

HOLDING(<u>SecID</u>, <u>CustomerID</u>, NumShares)
    SecID foreign key to Security
    CustomerID foreign key to Customer

SECURITY(<u>SECID</u>, SecName, SecType)

Third Normal Form

A database is said to be in the *third normal form* (3NF) if it is in 2NF and does not contain any transitive dependencies. While it is in 2NF, our financial services database is not in 3NF yet because it still contains a transitive dependency, as indicated by the thick arrow in Figure 9.5.

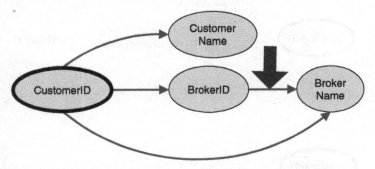

Figure 9.5 A transitive dependency in the CUSTOMER table.

You may recall that a transitive dependency occurs when a non-key attribute depends on another non-key attribute (or a composition of several attributes) that would not have been a valid alternative choice for the table's primary key. In this case, *BrokerName* depends on *BrokerID*, but *BrokerID* is not a possible choice of primary key for the CUSTOMER table, so the table contains a transitive dependency.

Eliminating transitive dependencies involves breaking up tables in a manner similar to our two previous normalization steps: the determinant in the transitive dependency (in this case, *BrokerID*) needs to be the primary key of some table, and the attributes that it determines should be moved to that table. Thus, we split up the CUSTOMER table, creating a new BROKER table, where we relocate the *BrokerName* attribute. Our resulting database now has the following four tables, and its entity-relationship (ER) diagram is shown in Figure 9.6.

CUSTOMER(<u>CustomerID</u>, CustomerName, BrokerID)
   BrokerID foreign key to BROKER

BROKER(<u>BrokerID</u>, BrokerName)

HOLDING(<u>SecID</u>, <u>CustomerID</u>, NumShares)
   SecID foreign key to Security
   CustomerID foreign key to Customer

SECURITY(<u>SECID,</u> SecName, SecType)

Figure 9.6 ER diagram for the investment holdings database converted to third normal form.

The dependency diagram is shown in Figure 9.7.

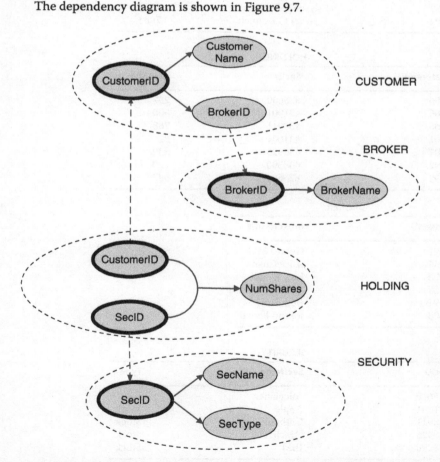

Figure 9.7 Dependency diagram of the investment holdings database in third normal form.

The financial services database is finally in third normal form, with the tables shown in Table 9.2 (here, we show a few more records than are necessary to reproduce the data shown earlier in the single nested table).

Table 9.2 Example data in the normalized investment holdings database.

CUSTOMER

CustomerID	CustomerName	BrokerID
1006	Jane Golding	8791
2001	Carl Tate	9654
3392	Shannon Lee	8923
7492	Isabelle Fuentes	9322
6103	James O'Donnell	7583

HOLDING

CustomerID	SecID	NumShares
1006	875600	237
1006	431001	500
1006	438911	788
2001	431001	82
2001	430925	530
3392	438390	120
3392	875600	387

BROKER

BrokerID	BrokerName
8791	Gerard Mills
9654	Alice Chan
8923	Lisa Weitz
7135	Achala Gupta
5294	Beth Levy
6503	Joseph Forelli

SECURITY

SecID	SecName	Type
875600	Allegiance	Fund
431001	Apple	Stock
438911	Citibank	Stock
430925	Oracle	Stock
438390	IBM	Stock

When you create the database's relationships in Access, the one-to-many relationships should display as shown in Figure 9.8.

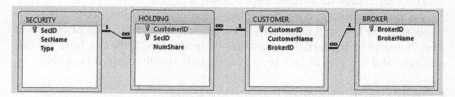

Figure 9.8 Relationships Window for the normalized investment holdings database.

This database consists of four entities, stored as separate tables:

- Security (SECURITY)
- Holding (HOLDING)
- Customer (CUSTOMER)
- Broker (BROKER)

There is no redundancy in the attributes in this database, since only foreign key attributes appear in more than one table. Furthermore, there are no repeating groups and there are no partial or transitive dependencies, so the database is in third normal form.

More Normal Forms

Database theorists define some additional normal forms: Boyce–Codd normal form (BCNF, a sort of 3.5th normal form), fourth normal form (4NF), and fifth normal form (5NF).

The distinctions between third normal form, Boyce–Codd normal form (BCNF), fourth normal form, and fifth normal form are subtle. They concern overlapping sets of attributes that could be used as primary keys (composite candidate keys) and are too technical to cover in this introductory textbook. Frequently, once a database has been converted to third normal form, it is already in the higher normal forms as well.

For the purposes of basic database design, you should know the following about 3NF:

- You need to be able to design a database in 3NF.
- You should be able to recognize when a database is in 3NF.
- You must be able to convert databases that are not in 3NF – also called "denormalized" – into 3NF. This process is called *normalization*.

It is also desirable to be able to recognize 1NF and 2NF, but it is not as important.

Key Factors to Recognize 3NF

When all attributes are atomic, the database is in 1NF.

If every determinant in every attribute relationship within each table is the whole primary key, or it could have been chosen as an alternative primary key, then there can be no partial or transitive dependencies. If the database has this property, and it is also in 1NF (every attribute is atomic), then it is in 3NF.

Example with Multiple Candidate Keys

Dependencies on a candidate key should not be considered transitive and should therefore not be considered violations of 3NF. For example, consider the following DRIVER table:

DRIVER(<u>License#</u>, SocialSecurity#, Gender, BirthDate)

Assuming that all the drivers described by the table are in the same state, then their license numbers must be unique and no two records can have the same value of *License#*. If all the drivers are currently alive, then their social security numbers should also be unique and no two records can have the same value of *SocialSecurity#*. In this situation, both *License#* and *SocialSecurity#* are possible choices of primary key, and the table has the following dependency diagram shown in Figure 9.9.

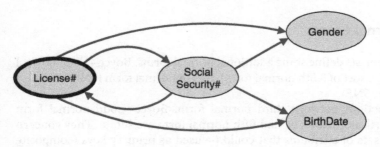

Figure 9.9 Dependency diagram for a table with multiple candidate keys.

The dependencies *SocialSecurity#* → *Gender* and *SocialSecurity#* → *BirthDate* are *not* considered transitive, because we could have chosen *SocialSecurity#* as the primary key for the table (although actually doing so would not generally be considered wise, because of the sensitivity of social security numbers).

Because the social security number value should be unique in every record, this kind of design is perfectly acceptable and will *not* give rise to anomalies.

Normalizing an Office Supplies Database

Here is a simplified example of an office supplies database. Suppose we have an ORDER table containing the data shown in Table 9.3.

Table 9.3 Office supply data before normalization.

Order Num	Cust Code	Order Date	Cust Name	ProdDescr	Prod Price	Quantity
10001	5217	11/20/15	Goldberg	Chair	$339.99	2
10001	5217	11/20/15	Goldberg	File Folders	$80.00	10
10002	5021	11/21/15	Sullivan	Stapler	$18.22	1
10002	5021	11/21/15	Sullivan	Desk Lamp	$27.49	1
10002	5021	11/21/15	Sullivan	Laser Paper	$45.29	1
10002	5021	11/21/15	Sullivan	Ink Cartridges	$287.85	3
10003	4118	11/21/15	Li	Chair	$339.99	1
10004	5217	11/22/15	Goldberg	Laser Paper	$45.29	7
10004	5217	11/22/15	Goldberg	Pens	$4.45	2
10005	6133	11/22/15	Chowdhury	Wireless Router	$34.95	1

In practice, we would also want to have product codes or SKUs as well as product descriptions, using the product codes as keys to identify products. Here, we identify products by their *ProdDescr* to limit the number of fields.

What is the best primary key for this table? The answer is a composite key consisting of (*OrderNumb, ProdDescr*). There is no reason for the table to have two records with the same combination of values for these two attributes: if it did, we could simply combine them by adding their *Quantity* fields. The outline description of the table is therefore as follows:

ORDER(OrderNum, CustCode, OrderDate, CustName, ProdDescr, ProdPrice,
      Quantity)

Note that since column order is unimportant in relational databases, it is of no concern that we did not list the two attributes making up the primary key next to one another in the table description.

This database is in 1NF because it contains no nested structures. The current dependency diagram is shown in Figure 9.10.

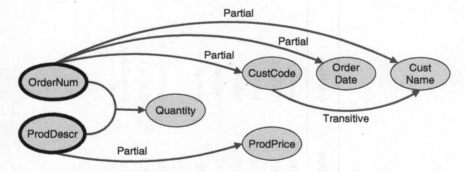

Figure 9.10 Dependency diagram for the office supply table, before normalization.

You can see from the diagram that the database contains multiple partial dependencies. To eliminate them, we create two new tables as follows:

QUANTITY(OrderNum, ProdDescr, Quantity)
      OrderNum foreign key to ORDERS
      ProdDescr foreign key to PRODUCTS

PRODUCT(ProdDescr, ProdPrice)

ORDERS(OrderNum, CustCode, OrderDate, CustName)

The dependency diagram now appears as shown in Figure 9.11. All the partial dependencies have been removed by breaking out the new tables ORDERS and PRODUCT, with the respective primary keys *OrderNum* and

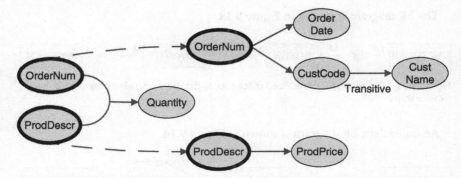

Figure 9.11 Office supply dependency diagram after removing partial dependencies.

ProdDescr. However, in the new ORDERS table, a transitive dependency exists between *CustCode* and *CustName*.

If we create a fourth table, CUSTOMER, we can remove this transitive dependency and convert our office supplies database to 3NF:

QUANTITY(<u>OrderNum</u>, <u>ProdDescr</u>, Quantity)
    OrderNum foreign key to ORDERS
    ProdDescr foreign key to PRODUCTS

PRODUCT(<u>ProdDescr</u>, ProdPrice)

ORDERS(<u>OrderNum</u>, CustCode, OrderDate)
    CustCode foreign key to CUSTOMERS

CUSTOMER(<u>CustCode</u>, CustName)

Our office supplies database dependency diagram is now in 3NF, and its dependency diagram is shown in Figure 9.12.

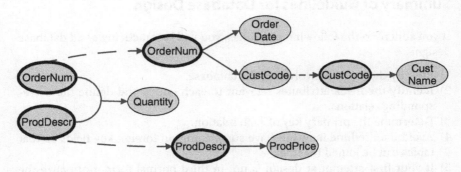

Figure 9.12 Office supply dependency diagram after conversion to third normal form.

The ER diagram is shown in Figure 9.13.

Figure 9.13 ER diagram for normalized office supply database, showing only one-to-many relationships.

An equivalent ER diagram is shown in Figure 9.14.

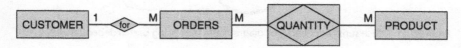

Figure 9.14 ER diagram for normalized office supply database, depicted with a many-to-many relationship.

In Access, we would set up this database's relationships as shown in Figure 9.15.

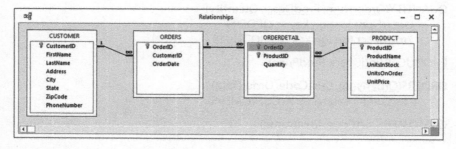

Figure 9.15 Relationships Window for normalized office supply database.

Summary of Guidelines for Database Design

If you adhere to the following principles, you will be practicing good database design:

1) Identify the entities involved in the database.
2) Identify the fields/attributes relevant to each entity, and define the corresponding relations.
3) Determine the primary key of each relation.
4) Avoid data redundancy, but have some common foreign key fields so that tables can be joined together.
5) If your first attempt at design is not in third normal form, normalize the database by splitting up relations.

Exercises

9.1 Temporary employment records: Table 9.4 keeps track of temporary worker assignments at a firm, one row per assignment. Note that the rate per hour is negotiated separately for each assignment. Design a third-normal-form database storing the same information. Draw an ER diagram, and write a database design outline.

9.2 Hospital blood tests: Consider Table 9.5, which gives information on blood tests ordered by doctors at a hospital. Only an illustrative subset of the rows are shown. A single test order may contain requests for multiple tests; for example, test order number R32501 includes both a lipid profile (code LIPP) and a sedimentation rate test (code ESR). Normalize this database so that it is in third normal form. Draw an ER diagram of the resulting database, and write a database design outline.

9.3 Express mail shipments: Download and examine the spreadsheet `express-mail.xslx` from the textbook website. This spreadsheet shows information about express mail packages being shipped between various post offices; only a small subset of the rows are included. Create a normalized database to hold the same information. Draw an ER diagram, and write a database design outline.

9.4 Car wash: Suppose that a car wash keeps records as shown in Table 9.6, using only one table, but with a repeating group.
The fields *AddOnCode*, *AddOnDescrip*, and *AddOnCharge* form a "repeating group," indicating which optional services were added to the basic wash operation. The interpretation of the data in this table is as follows:
- On March 5, Jane Wright washed her Honda Accord, with no optional services (so *AddOnCode*, *AddOnDescrip*, and *AddOnCharge* are blank).
- On March 8, Janet Wu washed her Toyota Camry, with two optional services: hot wax and undercoat.
- On March 12, Feliz Ortiz washed his Nissan Altima, with no optional services.
- On March 15, Janet Wu returned in a different car, this time a Honda Civic. She washed it with one optional service: hot wax.
- On March 15, Felix Ortiz returned with a different car, this time a Pontiac GTO. This time, he got three optional services: foam polish, hand wax, and tire seal.
- On March 16, Bill Shor washed his Dodge Magnum, with no optional services.
- On March 31, Jane Wright returned in the same Honda Accord. This time she washed it with one optional service: tire seal.

Table 9.4 Data for temporary employment record normalization exercise.

Assignment ID	Temp Code	Temp Name	Dept Code	Dept Name	Job Code	Job Description	Date	Hours Spent	Rate /hour
11772	1013	Bill Wong	ENG	Engineering	TC	Technical Consulting	2/27/2011	3	$100
11765	1015	Melanie East	MKT	Marketing	TC	Technical Consulting	1/25/2011	4	$120
11767	2051	Ed North	ACT	Accounting	CLR	Clerical	1/31/2011	2	$50
11768	2051	Ed North	MKT	Marketing	CLR	Clerical	2/10/2011	4	$55
11769	3356	John Edokway	SLS	Sales	SC	Strategic Consulting	2/15/2011	5	$90
11773	3356	John Edokway	MKT	Marketing	EDT	Editing	3/20/2011	6	$60
11771	4076	Marissa Estevez	ENG	Engineering	EDT	Editing	2/26/2011	7	$65
11766	4079	Hannah Goldberg	ENG	Engineering	TC	Technical Consulting	1/25/2011	4	$110
11770	4079	Hannah Goldberg	MKT	Marketing	EDT	Editing	2/25/2011	5	$70

Table 9.5 Data for hospital blood test normalization exercise.

Test Order Number	Date	Patient ID	Patient Name	Doctor ID	Doctor Name	Test Codes	Test Descriptions
R32493	4/22/2012	P0657	Martin Jones	D0076	Fernandez	BMP	Basic metabolic panel
R32497	4/22/2012	P0781	Isabel Fu	D0042	Scheimberg	ESR	Sedimentation rate
R32501	4/22/2012	P0897	Rajiv Patel	D0161	Wong	LIPP	Lipid profile
						ESR	Sedimentation rate
R32507	4/23/2012	P0684	Lyla Kahn	D0076	Fernandez	BMP	Basic metabolic panel
						HFP	Hepatic function panel
R32509	4/23/2012	P0657	Martin Jones	D0076	Fernandez	BMP	Basic metabolic panel
R32512	4/24/2012	P0657	Martin Jones	D0161	Wong	ESR	Sedimentation rate
						INR	Clotting time test
R32517	4/24/2012	P0844	Josh Strauss	D0042	Scheimberg	ADR	Adrenal function
						ALD	Aldosterone level
						ESR	Sedimentation rate
R32608	4/25/2012	P0897	Rajiv Patel	D0093	Galloway	LIPP	Lipid profile
						BMP	Basic metabolic panel
						CKT	Heart enzymes
						HFP	Hepatic function panel
R32069	4/25/2012	P0781	Isabel Fu	D0093	Galloway	ESR	Sedimentation rate

Table 9.6 Data for car wash normalization exercise.

Trans#	Date	License Plate	License State	Make	Model	Cust Code	Cust Name	AddOn Code	AddOn Descrip	AddOn Charge
T4561	3/5/2007	LDR47X	NJ	Honda	Accord	128	Jane Wright			
T4708	3/8/2007	378MXZ	NJ	Toyota	Camry	231	Janet Wu	HTWX	Hot Wax	$8.95
								UDCT	Undercoat	$6.95
T4915	3/12/2007	IYR32B	NY	Nissan	Altima	403	Felix Ortiz			
T4564	3/15/2007	PRQ19R	NJ	Honda	Civic	231	Janet Wu	HTWX	Hot Wax	$8.95
T4565	3/15/2007	ZZT342	NY	Pontiac	GTO	403	Felix Ortiz	FMPL	Foam Polish	$2.95
								HNWX	Hand Wax	$29.95
								TRSL	Tire Seal	$4.45
T4621	3/16/2007	AGX112	CT	Dodge	Magnum	334	Bill Shor			
T5102	3/31/2007	LDR47X	NJ	Honda	Accord	128	Jane Wright	TRSL	Tire Seal	$4.45

You may assume that the car wash always charges the same amount for each optional service, no matter the date of service, the kind of car, or the customer involved. Redesign this database so that it is in third normal form. Draw an ER diagram, and write a database design outline.

9.5 **Fire and rescue squad records:** Consider the spreadsheet-style information about fire and rescue squad dispatch events shown in Table 9.7. Sometimes several fire/rescue companies may be dispatched to the same event: this is the meaning of terms like "two-alarm fire" and "three-alarm fire." Here, event E3413 is a "two-alarm fire," and event E3415 is a "three-alarm fire." You may assume each fire company can only be in one place at any given time.

Write a database design outline that would allow this same information to be stored in third normal form, and draw a corresponding ER diagram.

9.6 **Temporary employment agency records:** A few years ago, you started a local temporary employment agency. You have been keeping records on the skills and work assignments of your employees in two spreadsheet tables that look like Table 9.8 (for brevity, many rows and some columns have been omitted).

For example, these tables say that Theresa Gillmore is skilled in general clerical jobs and is an expert in Microsoft Word. She worked 7 hours for Lawrence Engineering on February 12, applying her Word skills, and 8 hours for Western Legal February 14, applying her Word and general clerical skills. Note that the hourly rates are negotiated with clients and workers on an assignment-by-assignment basis. You may assume that each worker can have at most one work assignment per day.

You have decided that it is time to convert your record keeping to relational database form using Microsoft Access. Draw an ER diagram, and write a database design outline for a third-normal-form database to store the information shown in Table 9.8 (note: to store the information in third normal form, you should need more than two tables).

9.7 **Parking authorization:** Gotham City University grants parking privileges in various parking lots to faculty, staff, and students based on where they work or study, fees paid, and other factors. Access to each lot is controlled by an electronic gate at which drivers swipe their university ID cards. The parking department maintains its lot access privilege records in a "flat file" (single-table) database, some sample rows of which are shown in Table 9.9. Draw an ER diagram, and write a database design outline for a third-normal-form database to store this same information.

Table 9.7 Data for fire and rescue squad normalization exercise.

Event ID	Event Call-In Time	Event Address	Fire Company ID	Fire Company Name	Dispatch Time	Arrival Time
E3412	3/14/2012 10:20 am	234 River Road	C001	River Hook and Ladder	3/14/2012 10:21 am	3/14/2012 10:24 am
E3413	3/14/2012 5:17 pm	87 Stelton Road	C003	West Volunteer	3/14/2012 5:17 pm	3/14/2012 5:24 pm
E3413	3/14/2012 5:17 pm	87 Stelton Road	C001	River Hook and Ladder	3/14/2012 6:01 pm	3/14/2012 6:16 pm
E3414	3/15/2012 2:21 am	52 School Street	C002	Central Fire and Rescue	3/15/2012 2:23 am	3/15/2012 2:28 am
E3415	3/16/2012 8:22 pm	901 Plainfield Avenue	C002	Central Fire and Rescue	3/16/2012 8:23 pm	3/16/2012 8:27 pm
E3415	3/16/2012 8:22 pm	901 Plainfield Avenue	C001	River Hook and Ladder	3/16/2012 8:23 pm	3/16/2012 8:35 pm
E3415	3/16/2012 8:22 pm	901 Plainfield Avenue	C003	West Volunteer	3/16/2012 8:40 pm	3/16/2012 8:55 pm
E3416	3/17/2012 7:15 am	2304 Lincoln Highway	C004	East Volunteer	3/17/2012 7:17 am	3/17/2012 7:25 am
E3417	3/17/2012 3:02 pm	807 Plainfield Avenue	C003	West Volunteer	3/17/2012 3:03 pm	3/17/2012 3:12 pm
E3418	3/18/2012 10:43 am	6 Station Drive	C004	East Volunteer	3/18/2012 10:43 am	3/18/2012 10:50 am
E3418	3/18/2012 10:43 am	6 Station Drive	C002	Central Fire and Rescue	3/18/2012 11:00 am	3/18/2012 11:08 am

Table 9.8 Data for temporary employment agency normalization exercise.

Worker ID	First Name	Last Name	Joined Agency	Skill ID	Skill Name
W001	Theresa	Gillmore	6/1/2004	CLR	General Clerical
W001	Theresa	Gillmore	6/1/2004	WORD	MS Word Expert
W002	William	Duelker	11/6/1998	EMAC	Excel Macros
W002	William	Duelker	11/6/1998	EXL	MS Excel Expert
W002	William	Duelker	11/6/1998	WMAC	MS Word Macros
W002	William	Duelker	11/6/1998	WORD	MS Word Expert
W003	Ying-Fu	Lee	4/16/2009	EMAC	Excel Macros
W003	Ying-Fu	Lee	4/16/2009	EXL	MS Excel Expert
W004	Debratar	Srinivasan	7/15/2008	EDIT	Editing
W004	Debratar	Srinivasan	7/15/2008	WORD	MS Word Expert

Worker ID	First Name	Last Name	Client ID	Client Name	Date	Hours Worked	Hourly Rate	Skills Applied
W004	Debratar	Srinivasan	C003	MicroPharma	2/3/2010	8	$ 40.00	EDIT
W004	Debratar	Srinivasan	C003	MicroPharma	2/4/2010	7	$ 40.00	EDIT, WORD
W001	Theresa	Gillmore	C001	Lawrence Engineering	2/12/2010	7	$ 35.00	WORD
W001	Theresa	Gillmore	C002	Western Legal	2/14/2010	8	$ 35.00	WORD, CLR
W004	Debratar	Srinivasan	C001	Lawrence Engineering	3/15/2010	6	$ 50.00	WORD
W003	Ying-Fu	Lee	C001	Lawrence Engineering	3/15/2010	7	$ 40.00	EDIT
W002	William	Duelker	C003	MicroPharma	4/1/2010	8	$ 50.00	EMAC
W002	William	Duelker	C003	MicroPharma	4/5/2010	7	$ 50.00	EXL, EMAC
W002	William	Duelker	C001	Lawrence Engineering	4/7/2010	6	$ 55.00	EXL, EMAC, WMAC
W004	Debratar	Srinivasan	C003	MicroPharma	5/16/2010	5	$ 45.00	EDIT, WORD

Table 9.9 Data for parking authorization normalization exercise.

IDNumber	FamName	GivenName	LotCode	LotDescrip
105556002	Chen	Yu-Ping	202	East Campus
105556002	Chen	Yu-Ping	204	Engineering Center
105556002	Chen	Yu-Ping	500	Overflow
134738338	Studente	Joseph	301	Commuter North
174897434	Fleming	Jeanine	107	West Campus
174897434	Fleming	Jeanine	500	Overflow
249302923	Barski	Robert	001	Executive
249302923	Barski	Robert	107	West Campus
249302923	Barski	Robert	202	East Campus
457894873	Boghosian	Nadia	301	Commuter North
457894873	Boghosian	Nadia	310	Commuter South
576758823	Richards	Edward	001	Executive
576758823	Richards	Edward	107	West Campus
678843801	Patel	Jasmine	301	Commuter North
708091136	Secundo	Ellen	202	East Campus
708091136	Secundo	Ellen	500	Overflow

9.8 Marketing visits: Your firm markets specialty fabrics for demanding technical applications in the specialty clothing and outdoor equipment industries, as well as for other uses such as tents and sails. The group manager, a former fabric engineer, keeps records of customer visits by marketing representatives, and the resulting fabric orders, in a large spreadsheet (Table 9.10).

The proper interpretation of the first five rows is as follows:

- On October 23, 2004, Jill Strathdee visited Mountaineering, Inc., resulting in an order for 500 yards of Super Rip-Stop and 400 yards of Insulex.
- On November 1, 2004, Cecilia Lim visited West Lake Designs, resulting in an order for 1000 yards of Super Rip-Stop.
- On November 1, 2004, Jill Strathdee visited SailCo, resulting in an order for 800 yards of 20 Mil Ultra Rip-Stop and 400 yards of Canvasulon.

Also note that while Jill Strathdee visited SailCo on November 11, William Duffee visited the same company on January 22.

One defect of this spreadsheet-based system is that if a sales team visits a customer, but the customer does not order any fabric, either the

Table 9.10 Data for marketing visit normalization exercise.

Customer ID	Customer Name	Customer Contact	Date Visited	Market Rep ID	Market Rep First Name	Market Rep Last Name	Product ID	Product Name	Yards Ordered
C001	Mountaineering, Inc.	Barbara Mesirov	10/23/2004	E001	Jill	Strathdee	P002	Super Rip-Stop	500
C001	Mountaineering, Inc.	Barbara Mesirov	10/23/2004	E001	Jill	Strathdee	P005	Insulex	400
C002	West Lake Designs	Yusef Lateef	11/1/2004	E002	Cecilia	Lim	P002	Super Rip-Stop	1000
C003	SailCo	Archie Wright	11/1/2004	E004	Jill	Strathdee	P003	20 Mil Ultra Rip-Stop	800
C003	SailCo	Archie Wright	11/1/2004	E004	Jill	Strathdee	P010	Canvasulon	400
C001	Mountaineering, Inc.	Barbara Mesirov	11/28/2004	E001	Jill	Strathdee	P002	Super Rip-Stop	600
C004	BlowBack Corp.	Joe Young	12/3/2004	E004	William	Duffee	P006	GoreSnaz	250
C005	Lumberjack Outfitters	William McNeely	1/7/2005	E004	William	Duffee	P002	Super Rip-Stop	280
C005	Lumberjack Outfitters	William McNeely	1/7/2005	E004	William	Duffee	P003	20 Mil Ultra Rip-Stop	180
C003	SailCo	Archie Wright	1/22/2005	E004	William	Duffee	P010	Canvasulon	450
C003	SailCo	Archie Wright	1/22/2005	E004	William	Duffee	P006	GoreSnaz	100

information about the visit is lost, or you must enter a row in the spreadsheet with an order for a "dummy" product, or for zero yards of some existing product.

Design a third-normal-form relational database to hold the information shown in the table, making sure that it has a more natural way to keep track of visits that do not result in orders. Draw an ER diagram, and write a database outline description. You may create additional "ID" or key fields where necessary.

9.9 Pizza delivery: The tables shown in Table 9.11 (with only some of the rows shown) are part of the information system Checkers Pizza uses to track its home delivery business.

Table 9.11 Data for pizza delivery normalization exercise.

CustID	Name	Address	City	State	Zip	Phone
C1001	Lucinda Philip	123 Elm Road	Elmhurst	NJ	07802	(908) 678-0987
C1037	William Hurd	78 Wright Drive	Appleton	NJ	07930	(908) 776-8823
C1104	Yu-Ran Chen	90 Wright Drive	Appleton	NJ	07930	(908) 223-0904
C1161	Mohan Singh	211 Jones Court	Eastville	NJ	08023	(732) 778-7023

OrderNum	Date	CustID	PieNum	Size	ToppingCode	ToppingDescrip
7348	11/10/10	C1001	1	Large	PRI	Pepperoni
7348	11/10/10	C1001	2	Small	GAR	Garlic
7349	11/10/10	C1104	1	Large		
7350	11/10/10	C1161	1	Large	MUSH	Mushroom
7350	11/10/10	C1161	1	Large	PEP	Peppers
7350	11/10/10	C1161	2	Large	ART	Artichoke hearts
8001	11/11/10	C1037	1	Small	SAU	Sausage
8001	11/11/10	C1037	1	Small	MUSH	Mushroom
8001	11/11/10	C1037	1	Small	GAR	Garlic
8001	11/11/10	C1037	2	Large		
8052	11/12/10	C1001	1	Large	SAU	Sausage
8052	11/12/10	C1001	2	Large	EXC	Extra cheese
8052	11/12/10	C1001	3	Small	GAR	Garlic

The interpretation of the data shown is as follows:

- On November 10, Lucinda Philip placed an order for a large pepperoni pizza (*PieNum* = 1) and a small garlic pizza (*PieNum* = 2).
- On November 10, Yu-Ran Chen ordered a large plain pizza (with no toppings). Note that the *PieNum* field is only unique within a given order; thus, the first (and only) pizza in this order also has *PieNum* = 1.

Table 9.12 Data for ad placement normalization exercise.

Ad ID	Ad Description	Magazine ID	Magazine Name	Issue Date	Publisher Code	Publisher Name
101	Bears eating pizza	F&S	Field and Stream	6/2/1005	ZD	Ziff-Davis
101	Bears eating pizza	OW	Outdoor World	7/1/2015	NP	National Publishing Group
101	Bears eating pizza	BW	Business Week	7/15/2015	MH	McGraw-Hill
101	Bears eating pizza	F&S	Field and Stream	8/1/2015	ZD	Ziff-Davis
102	Spaceship	BW	Business Week	7/15/2015	MH	McGraw-Hill
102	Spaceship	PCW	PC World	8/1/2015	ZD	Ziff-Davis
102	Spaceship	AWST	Aviation Week	8/9/2015	MH	McGraw-Hill
103	Clown	NW	Newsweek	8/1/2015	NWI	Newsweek, Inc.
103	Clown	TIM	Time	8/7/2015	TW	Time-Warner
104	Chipmunks watching TV	F&S	Field and Stream	9/1/2015	ZD	Ziff-Davis
104	Chipmunks watching TV	TIM	Time	8/14/2015	TW	Time-Warner

- On November 10, Mohan Singh ordered a large mushroom and peppers pizza (two toppings on the same pizza, with *PieNum* = 1), along with a large artichoke hearts pizza (*PieNum* = 2). For this order, note that the lines with MUSH and PEP both have attribute *PieNum* equal to 1, meaning they are both for the first pizza in the order.
- On November 11, William Hurd ordered a small sausage, mushroom, and garlic pizza (three toppings on the same pizza – again, note there are multiple lines with the same value for *PieNum*), and a large plain pizza.
- On November 12, Lucinda Philip placed another order, this time for three pizzas: a large sausage, a large extra cheese, and a small garlic.

Design a third-normal-form database storing the same information as these two tables. Draw an ER diagram, and write a database design outline. You may add "ID" fields wherever necessary. This is a relatively challenging problem, so please read the above interpretation of the data carefully and be sure you understand it before proceeding with your normalization.

9.10 **Ad placements:** The one-table database shown in Table 9.12 keeps track of your firm's advertisement placements in various magazines.

For example, ad 101, a comical piece showing bears eating pizza, ran in the June *Field and Stream*, the July *Outdoor World*, the July 15 *Business Week*, and again in the August *Field and Stream* issues. You also ran another ad, a futuristic piece showing a spaceship, in the July 15 *Business Week* issue. You may run the same ad in several different issues of a magazine, or different ads in a single issue, but you never run the same ad more than once in a single issue of a magazine. Redesign this database so that it is in third normal form. Draw an ER diagram, and write a database design outline.

10

Basic Structured Query Language (SQL)

Structured Query Language (SQL) allows you to retrieve, manipulate, and display information from a database. MS Access lets you perform many of the same tasks using Query Design View, but other database software either lacks this capability or may implement it differently. If you understand the SQL language underlying Access queries, you will be able to formulate queries for essentially any relational database, including ones too large to store in Access. For most of this chapter, we will draw examples from the plumbing store database in Chapter 7, whose design is shown in Figure 10.1.

Using SQL in Access

You can easily display the SQL form of any query in Access. After pressing the "Query Design" button, you simply select "SQL View" from the "View" button at the left of the "Home" ribbon at the top of the window. When viewing the results of a query, you can also display its SQL form by selecting "SQL View" from the "Home" ribbon. When viewing the SQL form of any query, you may run it by selecting "Datasheet View" on the same "View" button, or by pressing the "!" (Run) button next to it.

The SELECT ... FROM Statement

The SELECT ... FROM statement is the core of SQL. It specifies which information you want to display. Although SQL has other statements, this book focuses on the SELECT statement.

The most basic form for the SELECT statement is:

```
SELECT expressions FROM data_source ;
```

Introductory Relational Database Design for Business, with Microsoft Access, First Edition.
Jonathan Eckstein and Bonnie R. Schultz.
© 2018 John Wiley & Sons Ltd. Published 2018 by John Wiley & Sons Ltd.

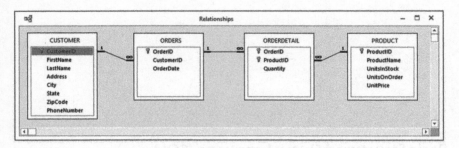

Figure 10.1 Relationships Window for plumbing supply store database.

In the simplest case, *expressions* is a single field name and *data_source* is a single table. For example, for the plumbing store database, the statement

```
SELECT OrderDate FROM ORDERS;
```

shows the *OrderDate* field for each row of the ORDERS table. The *expressions* specifier may also be a list of attribute names separated by commas. An example of such a query from the same database is:

```
SELECT City, State FROM CUSTOMER;
```

This query shows the *City* and *State* fields for each row of the CUSTOMER table. By default, SELECT does not eliminate duplicate rows in its output: for example, if there are three customers in the same city, then that city would appear three times in the output. However, SELECT has an optional DISTINCT modifier that removes any duplicate rows from the output table. Suppose we modify the above query to:

```
SELECT DISTINCT City, State FROM CUSTOMER;
```

The output of this query will consist of one row for each city in which customers are located, even if there is more than one customer in the same city.

A special possible value of *expressions* is "*", which displays every attribute in *data_source*. For example:

```
SELECT * FROM CUSTOMER;
```

displays the entire CUSTOMER table. The items in the *expressions* specifier need not be simple attribute names but may also be computed expressions. For example, the query

```
SELECT ProductName, UnitsInStock*UnitPrice FROM PRODUCT;
```

displays the name of each product in the PRODUCT table, along with the total value of inventory of the product on hand, computed as the product of the number of units in stock and the unit price. The syntax of the expressions allowed in the SELECT clause is similar to that of Microsoft Excel formulas, with "*" standing for multiplication. In the Access output for this query, the first column has the understandable heading "Product Name," but the second one has the cryptic heading "Expr1001." To provide a more understandable heading, we can add an AS modifier to the *expressions* specifier, as follows:

```
SELECT  ProductName,
        UnitsInStock*UnitPrice AS InventoryValue
FROM    PRODUCT;
```

This modification causes the second column to have the more understandable heading "InventoryValue." Note that there are no quotes or other special formatting around `InventoryValue` in this statement: the AS modifier effectively defines a new field name, which is formatted like any other field name. Here, we have broken the query into multiple lines to fit it on the page. You can insert line breaks and spaces anywhere in an SQL statement without changing its meaning, except in the middle of a word, table/field identifier, or number.

WHERE Conditions

Often you do not want to display data from every row of a table but only from rows that meet certain criteria. That is the purpose of SQL's WHERE clause. The most basic form of a SELECT query with a WHERE clause is:

```
SELECT expressions FROM data_source
  WHERE logical_expression ;
```

This statement functions much like the simplest SELECT statement, except that only information from the rows of *data_source* for which *logical_expression* evaluates to "true" appear in the output. A simple example of such a statement is:

```
SELECT ProductName FROM PRODUCT
  WHERE UnitsInStock >= 100;
```

This query displays the name of each product of which we have at least 100 units in stock. The `logical_expression` following WHERE may be arbitrarily complicated. For example:

```
SELECT  ProductName
FROM    PRODUCT
WHERE   UnitsOnOrder*UnitPrice > 5000;
```

shows the name of each product for which the total value of inventory on order is over $5,000. In addition to simple comparisons using = (equal), > (greater than), < (less than), <= (less than or equal to), and > = (greater than or equal to), SQL allows compound logical expressions constructed through AND and OR operations. For example:

```
SELECT  ProductName, UnitsOnOrder, UnitPrice
FROM    PRODUCT
WHERE   UnitsOnOrder >= 100 OR UnitPrice < 50;
```

displays the name, number of units on order, and unit price of each product that has at least 100 units on order or has a price less than $50. Note that OR in SQL is "inclusive," as in most computer languages, so that a record meeting both sub-conditions is considered to satisfy the OR condition. In the query above, for example, a product with at least 100 units on order and also costing less than $50 would be displayed in the query output. Here is another example of a compound condition:

```
SELECT  FirstName, LastName
FROM    CUSTOMER
WHERE   City="Hamilton" AND State="NJ";
```

This query will display the names of all customers from Hamilton, NJ; the database also contains a customer from Hamilton, NY, but this customer is not included in the query result because the *State* field value does not match the condition. When comparing text fields to literal character strings such as "CA", you should enclose the literal character strings in double quotes. Otherwise, SQL will try to interpret the character string as an attribute name.

Inner Joins

So far, this chapter has considered only queries drawn from a single table. We now discuss how SQL can express queries based on data from multiple tables. The most common technique for basing queries on multiple tables is called an *inner join.* An inner join consists of all combinations of rows selected from two tables that meet some matching condition, formally called a *join predicate.* One standard syntax for an inner join, of which we have already seen examples earlier in this book, is:

```
First_Table INNER JOIN Second_Table ON Condition
```

Formally, this syntax specifies that the query should form a table consisting of all combinations of a record from `First_Table` with a record from `Second_Table` for which `Condition` evaluates to "true." Most frequently, `Condition` specifies that a foreign key in one table should match a primary key in the other.

Here is an example of an inner join based on the plumbing store database:

```
SELECT FirstName, LastName, OrderDate
FROM    CUSTOMER INNER JOIN ORDERS
        ON CUSTOMER.CustomerID = ORDERS.CustomerID;
```

The INNER JOIN expression is now the `data_source` following the FROM keyword, where before we used a single table. This construction means that the data to be displayed is taken from the temporary table resulting from the inner join operation. The particular inner join expression, namely,

```
CUSTOMER INNER JOIN ORDERS
        ON CUSTOMER.CustomerID = ORDERS.CustomerID
```

specifies that the query should be based on all combinations of records from the CUSTOMER and ORDERS tables that have matching *CustomerID* fields. This kind of primary key to foreign key matching condition is by far the most common kind of inner join. `CUSTOMER.CustomerID` refers to the *CustomerID* field from the CUSTOMER table, while `ORDERS.CustomerID` refers to the *CustomerID* field from the ORDERS table. The use of " . " here is called *qualification.* It is required to eliminate ambiguity whenever several underlying tables have fields of the same name, as is the case for the *CustomerID* in this example: if we were to just write `CustomerID`, SQL would not be able to tell whether we were referring to the *CustomerID* field in the CUSTOMER table or the *CustomerID* field in the ORDERS table. To resolve this ambiguity, we preface an attribute name with a table name and " . ": for example, `CUSTOMER.CustomerID` means the *CustomerID* attribute of the CUSTOMER table.

Qualification is not required for field names that occur in only one of the underlying tables. While it can still be used in such cases – for example, one could say `CUSTOMER.FirstName` instead of `FirstName` in this query – it is not necessary, because there can be no ambiguity about which *FirstName* field is meant since this name occurs in only one underlying table.

The effect of this query is to display the date of each order, preceded by the first and last names of the corresponding customer (Table 10.1).

Just as for queries derived from just one table, we can use a WHERE clause to narrow the results of join-based queries. For instance, if we want to see the same information, but only for orders placed on or after April 28, 2013, we could write:

Table 10.1 Output from first SQL inner join example query.

First Name	Last Name	Order Date
Benjamin	Masterson	4/20/2013
Benjamin	Masterson	4/21/2013
Benjamin	Masterson	4/22/2013
Benjamin	Masterson	4/24/2013
Mary	Milgrom	4/21/2013
Mary	Milgrom	4/22/2013
Mary	Milgrom	4/22/2013
Leonard	Goodman	4/18/2013
Margerita	Colon	4/15/2013
Margerita	Colon	4/24/2013
Geoffrey	Hammer	4/18/2013
Geoffrey	Hammer	4/25/2013
Geoffrey	Hammer	4/26/2013
Geoffrey	Hammer	5/1/2013
Geoffrey	Hammer	5/1/2013
Ashley	Flannery	4/18/2013
Ashley	Flannery	4/24/2013
Joseph	Brower	4/30/2013
Xiaoming	Wang	4/25/2013
Derek	Escher	4/29/2013
Derek	Escher	4/29/2013
Laura	Ng	4/26/2013
Laura	Ng	4/26/2013
Robert	Sloan	4/27/2013
Robert	Sloan	4/28/2013

```
SELECT FirstName, LastName, OrderDate
FROM    CUSTOMER INNER JOIN ORDERS
        ON CUSTOMER.CustomerID = ORDERS.CustomerID
WHERE   OrderDate >= #4/28/2013#;
```

This query demonstrates the special syntax that SQL uses for dates, which is also used in the Access query grid: we enclose any date between "#" characters. Without this special syntax, SQL would mistake "4/28/2013" for the number 4 divided by 28, and then divided again by 2013.

When queries are based on more than one table, the "*" syntax can still be used to indicate "all fields." For example, we may write:

```
SELECT *
FROM    CUSTOMER INNER JOIN ORDERS
        ON CUSTOMER.CustomerID = ORDERS.CustomerID
WHERE   OrderDate >= #4/28/2013#;
```

In response, SQL displays all rows of the inner-joined table whose order date is on or after April 28, 2013. There is also a qualified form of "*". For instance, the query

```
SELECT FirstName, LastName, ORDERS.*
FROM    CUSTOMER INNER JOIN ORDERS
        ON CUSTOMER.CustomerID = ORDERS.CustomerID
WHERE   OrderDate >= #4/28/2013#;
```

shows the customer first name, customer last name, and all fields from the ORDERS table for orders placed on or after April 28, 2013. Here, ORDERS.* means "all fields from the ORDERS table."

Cartesian Joins and a Different Way to Express Inner Joins

In addition to INNER JOIN expressions, the FROM clause of a SELECT statement may contain a list of table names separated by commas. For example, it is possible to write:

```
SELECT FirstName, LastName, OrderDate
FROM    CUSTOMER, ORDERS;
```

However, this query does *not* behave the same way as the first query in the previous section. The construction "CUSTOMER,   ORDERS" in the FROM clause instructs SQL to form the table obtained by combining every possible row of the CUSTOMER table with every possible row of the ORDERS table, without checking whether the foreign key values linking the two tables match. Thus, if the CUSTOMER table contains 14 rows and the ORDERS table contains 25 rows, the resulting table contains $14 \times 25 = 350$ rows, most of which are essentially meaningless. This kind of join is called a *Cartesian join* or *cross join*.

The Cartesian join may seem like an unnatural way to interpret the above query, but the rationale is that an SQL statement's meaning should be the same no matter what relationships the database designer may have intended to exist between tables. More precisely, some early relational database systems maintained metadata describing the structure of each table but did not necessarily store metadata explicitly describing foreign keys. The interpretation of a query like the one above therefore needed to be independent of any intended foreign key relationships.

Cartesian joins are rarely useful in isolation but can be useful building blocks in various data manipulations. Typically one uses a WHERE clause to narrow down the result of a Cartesian join to something more useful. For example, we may change the above query to:

```
SELECT FirstName, LastName, OrderDate
FROM    CUSTOMER, ORDERS
WHERE   CUSTOMER.CustomerID = ORDERS.CustomerID;
```

This query specifies that SQL form the Cartesian join of the CUSTOMER and ORDER tables but then remove all rows violating the condition

```
CUSTOMER.CustomerID = ORDERS.CustomerID
```

The result is exactly the same temporary table as the INNER JOIN operation in the query in the previous section. The SELECT clause then specifies that SQL display first name, last name, and order date attributes from this temporary table, so the query generates exactly the same result as the first one in the previous section.

If interpreted literally, one might expect this query to run more slowly and require more memory than its equivalent INNER JOIN form, because of the potentially gigantic size of the Cartesian join table specified by the expression CUSTOMER, ORDERS. However, most SQL interpreters have a query optimizer module that analyzes queries and attempts to find efficient ways of producing the specified results. Most query optimizers would recognize that this query is equivalent to an inner join and execute it at approximately the same speed. In fact, when SQL was originally created, it had only WHERE; the explicit INNER JOIN syntax was introduced later.

To further illustrate the concept of a Cartesian join, temporarily consider the following very simple database:

PERSON(<u>PersonID</u>, FirstName, LastName)

EVENT(<u>EventID</u>, EventTime, PersonID)
   PersonID foreign key to PERSON

Suppose we execute the Cartesian join query:

```
SELECT * FROM PERSON, EVENT;
```

This query will create a temporary table from all possible combinations of a PERSON record and EVENT records, regardless of whether the foreign key *PersonID* has a matching value. The result of the query is illustrated in Figure 10.2 for the case that the PERSON table has two records and the EVENT table has three records.

PERSON		
PersonID	FirstName	LastName
P0001	Katya	Elmberg
P0002	Andrew	Kim

EVENT		
EventID	EventTime	PersonID
E0001	4/1/2016 4:32 PM	P0002
E0002	3/6/2016 9:17 AM	P0001
E0003	4/2/2016 3:22 PM	P0002

PERSON, EVENT					
PERSON.PersonID	FirstName	LastName	EventID	EventTime	EVENT.PersonID
P0001	Katya	Elmberg	E0001	4/1/2016 4:32 PM	P0002
P0002	Andrew	Kim	E0001	4/1/2016 4:32 PM	P0002
P0001	Katya	Elmberg	E0002	3/6/2016 9:17 AM	P0001
P0002	Andrew	Kim	E0002	3/6/2016 9:17 AM	P0001
P0001	Katya	Elmberg	E0003	4/2/2016 3:22 PM	P0002
P0002	Andrew	Kim	E0003	4/2/2016 3:22 PM	P0002

Figure 10.2 Example of a Cartesian join.

The query result has $6 = 2 \times 3$ rows, with half of them having non-matching *PersonID* fields. Suppose that we instead execute the query:

```
SELECT *
FROM    PERSON, EVENT
WHERE   PERSON.PersonID = EVENT.PersonID;
```

This query takes the result of the Cartesian join query above and removes the rows with non-matching *PersonID* fields. This process is depicted in Figure 10.3.

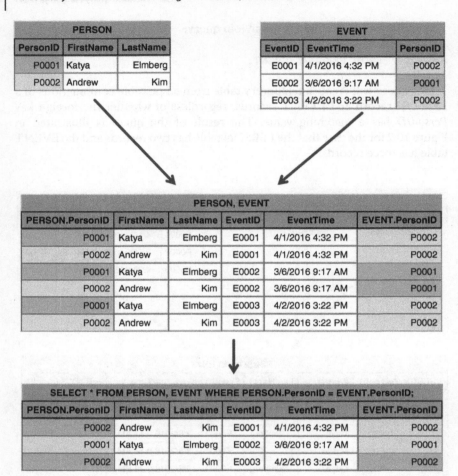

Figure 10.3 Example of a Cartesian join being reduced to an inner join through a WHERE condition.

The final result is the most common way to join the PERSON and EVENT tables, combining only pairs or rows that have common *PersonID* values. The result simply looks like the EVENT table, with the corresponding information from the PERSON table prepended to each row. It is identical to the output of the query:

```
SELECT *
FROM    PERSON INNER JOIN EVENT
            ON PERSON.PersonID = EVENT.PersonID;
```

The main advantage of expressing inner joins through a Cartesian join and WHERE clauses occurs when queries are based on more than two tables.

Suppose, returning to the plumbing store database example, that we want to display the *Quantity* field from each row of the ORDERDETAIL table, along with the name of the corresponding product and the date of the order. We may write this query as:

```
SELECT Quantity, ProductName, OrderDate
FROM   ORDERS, ORDERDETAIL, PRODUCT
WHERE  ORDERS.OrderID = ORDERDETAIL.OrderID AND
       ORDERDETAIL.ProductID = PRODUCT.ProductID;
```

Literally, the FROM clause in this query specifies that SQL form all possible combinations of rows from the three tables ORDERS, ORDERDETAIL, and PRODUCT, but the WHERE clause next indicates that it should only retain those combinations for which both foreign keys match. If interpreted literally, this query might be very slow and consume a huge amount of space. Properly analyzed by a query optimizer, however, it should run at about the same speed as the equivalent query constructed from inner joins, which looks like this:

```
SELECT Quantity, ProductName, OrderDate
FROM   (ORDERS INNER JOIN ORDERDETAIL
        ON ORDERS.OrderID = ORDERDETAIL.OrderID)
       INNER JOIN PRODUCT
        ON ORDERDETAIL.ProductID = PRODUCT.ProductID;
```

The first INNER JOIN clause in this query creates a temporary table that combines records from the ORDERS and ORDERDETAIL tables based on matching the *OrderID* foreign keys. The second INNER JOIN clause then combines rows of the resulting temporary table with rows of the PRODUCT table based on matching values of the *ProductID* field. The result is identical to the Cartesian join and WHERE combination in the previous example, but the SQL code may be harder for a human to read. Furthermore, if one omits the parentheses surrounding the first INNER JOIN clause, Access SQL will generate an error message instead of processing the query. If you inspect the SQL code automatically written by Access to implement queries constructed using the design grid, you will often see multiple inner join constructions like the one above, with multiple levels of nested parentheses if there are more than three tables. In this and the next chapter, we will concentrate on writing SQL directly, and will therefore prefer the more human-understandable form using WHERE. Some other dialects of SQL do not require parentheses when combining multiple INNER JOIN clauses, making the INNER JOIN option more attractive. Some IT departments therefore prefer using INNER JOINs because their efficiency is less reliant on query optimizer modules.

A compound WHERE clause can do "double duty" by both performing a join and filtering records. For example, suppose we want to perform the same query as above but wanted to see only cases in which at least 10 units of a product were in the same order. We could then write:

```
SELECT  Quantity, ProductName, OrderDate
FROM    ORDERS, ORDERDETAIL, PRODUCT
WHERE   ORDERS.OrderID = ORDERDETAIL.OrderID AND
        ORDERDETAIL.ProductID = PRODUCT.ProductID AND
        Quantity >= 10;
```

This query produces the results shown in Table 10.2.

Table 10.2 Results of query selecting products appearing at least 10 times in the same order.

Quantity	Product Name	Order Date
10	Replacement Valve Units Type A	4/21/2013
10	Frost-Free Outdoor Faucet Set	4/24/2013
10	Retro Nickel Bath/Shower Combo	4/24/2013
10	Flexible Spray Shower	4/24/2013
10	Budget Bath Sink Set	4/24/2013
25	Replacement Valve Units Type A	4/27/2013

Using WHERE to implement inner joins does have a potential pitfall, the unintentional Cartesian join. Suppose we want to use a more complicated, compound filtering condition in the above query: we want to see all order lines where the quantity is at least 10 or the order was placed on May 1, 2013. It may seem natural to write:

```
SELECT  Quantity, ProductName, OrderDate
FROM    ORDERS, ORDERDETAIL, PRODUCT
WHERE   ORDERS.OrderID = ORDERDETAIL.OrderID AND
        ORDERDETAIL.ProductID = PRODUCT.ProductID AND
        Quantity >= 10 OR OrderDate = #5/1/2013#;
```

There are only six records in the ORDERDETAIL table corresponding to the two orders placed on May 1, 2013, so one might expect this query to produce at most six more rows than the previous one. But instead it produces thousands of rows. The reason is that SQL, like most computer languages, processes AND before OR when interpreting compound logical expressions.[1]

Despite the way that we placed spaces and line breaks in the above query (which cannot alter its meaning), SQL interprets the above query as:

---

[1] The reason for this grouping is that AND and OR have analogous mathematical properties to multiplication and addition: essentially, AND is the multiplication of logic, while OR is the addition of logic.

```
SELECT Quantity, ProductName, OrderDate
FROM    ORDERS, ORDERDETAIL, PRODUCT
WHERE   (ORDERS.OrderID = ORDERDETAIL.OrderID AND
            ORDERDETAIL.ProductID = PRODUCT.ProductID AND
            Quantity >= 10)
        OR OrderDate = #5/1/2013#;
```

Thus, SQL forms the Cartesian join of the three tables ORDERS, ORDERDETAIL, and PRODUCT, which has thousands of rows, and then places two kinds of rows from this Cartesian join into the output:

- Rows where all the foreign keys match and the *Quantity* field is at least 10.
- Rows for which the order date is May 1, 2013, without any check that the foreign keys match.

The second variety of rows fills the query output with useless or misleading information. The solution to this misbehavior is simple: place parentheses within the WHERE condition to make sure it processes in the proper order. Therefore, we write:

```
SELECT Quantity, ProductName, OrderDate
FROM    ORDERS, ORDERDETAIL, PRODUCT
WHERE   ORDERS.OrderID = ORDERDETAIL.OrderID AND
        ORDERDETAIL.ProductID = PRODUCT.ProductID AND
        (Quantity >= 10 OR OrderDate = #5/1/2013#);
```

This small change restores sanity to the query output, producing the results in Table 10.3.

Table 10.3 Results of OR query after correcting inadvertent Cartesian join.

Quantity	Product Name	Order Date
10	Replacement Valve Units Type A	4/21/2013
10	Frost-Free Outdoor Faucet Set	4/24/2013
10	Retro Nickel Bath/Shower Combo	4/24/2013
10	Flexible Spray Shower	4/24/2013
10	Budget Bath Sink Set	4/24/2013
25	Replacement Valve Units Type A	4/27/2013
1	Omnidirectional Shower	5/1/2013
5.00	Massage Shower System	5/1/2013
3.00	Replacement Valve Units Type A	5/1/2013
1.00	Budget Bath Sink Set	5/1/2013
2.00	Spacesaver Toilet	5/1/2013
2.00	Retro Nickel Bath/Shower Combo	5/1/2013

Aggregation

In addition to the features we have discussed so far, SQL also allows queries to perform *aggregation*, which means computing summary information about all records or groups of records. Aggregation occurs when you use any aggregation function in your query. The most commonly used aggregation functions in SQL are shown in Table 10.4.

Table 10.4 Common SQL aggregation functions.

Function	Meaning
Sum ( )	Sum
Avg ( )	Average (sample mean)
Count ( )	Number of non-blank data items
Min ( )	Smallest or alphabetically first value
Max ( )	Largest or alphabetically last value
StDev ( )	Sample standard deviation
First ( )	First value encountered[2]
Last ( )	Last value encountered[2]

To give a simple example of using such functions, suppose we want to know the total number of items ordered over the entire history covered by the database. To display this information, we may write the query:

```
SELECT Sum(Quantity) FROM ORDERDETAIL;
```

This query adds up the *Quantity* field over all rows of the ORDERDETAIL table and produces (for the particular data in the example from Chapter 7) the single result "163." It is also possible to specify multiple aggregation operations in the same query. By way of illustration:

```
SELECT Sum(Quantity), Avg(Quantity), Max(OrderID)
FROM    ORDERDETAIL;
```

displays a single row of information showing the total number of items ordered, the average number of items per order detail line, and the alphabetically last *OrderID* value for which there are any order detail records (perhaps not a particularly useful piece of information).

---

2 The results of First () and Last () may be somewhat arbitrary, because the basic principles of relational databases do not allow full control over the order in which rows of a table are processed.

We may also apply aggregation functions to expressions rather than to just simple fields. For example, if we want to know the average difference (over all products) between the units in stock and the units on order, we can use the query:

```
SELECT Avg(UnitsinStock - UnitsonOrder) FROM PRODUCT;
```

Here, we are using the Avg aggregation function instead of the Sum aggregation function and a more complicated expression than a simple field as its argument. This query produces the single value 29.6451612903, meaning that the number of units in stock averages about 30 units higher than the number of units on order.[3]

Now suppose that we want to see the average order quantity per order line for products whose *ProductID* values are between 1 and 13. To accomplish this, we write:

```
SELECT  Avg(Quantity)
FROM    ORDERDETAIL
WHERE   ProductID >= 1 AND ProductID <= 13;
```

WHERE clauses always filter data source rows *before* any aggregation is performed, so that the average is now taken only for those products between P0001 and P0013 (inclusive), rather than all possible product IDs.[4] Incidentally, since applying a lower and upper limit to the same attribute is very common, SQL provides a special logical operator BETWEEN, which takes the form "x BETWEEN a AND b" and is equivalent to "$x >= a$ AND $x <= b$". You can use this kind of expression anywhere one might use a logical condition. Thus, we can also write the query as:

```
SELECT  Avg(Quantity)
FROM    ORDERDETAIL
WHERE   ProductID BETWEEN 1 AND 13;
```

This form of the query produces exactly the same result as the previous one (1.77272727273).

---

3 Since an average of a difference is identical to a difference of averages, we could also have expressed this query as SELECT Avg(UnitsinStock) - Avg(UnitsonOrder) FROM PRODUCT;

4 Since the *ProductID* field has the Long Integer datatype and the "P" symbols here are only part of the format specifier and not stored in the *ProductID* field, SQL manipulates *ProductID* values like numbers rather than character strings. Therefore, we do not use quotes and do not include a "P" when expressing SQL comparisons for *ProductID* values.

Another useful aggregation function is Count, which simply counts the number of non-blank data items in its argument. For example, the query

```
SELECT  Count(OrderID)
FROM    ORDERS
WHERE   OrderDate BETWEEN #4/22/2013# AND #4/28/2013#;
```

counts the number of orders received between April 22 and 28, 2013 (inclusive). The Count function should not be confused with the Sum function. Within a given set of records, Count will produce exactly the same result when applied to any argument that cannot be blank: in the above situation, it simply counts the number of records meeting the order date criterion. For example, the two queries

```
SELECT  Count(ProductID) FROM PRODUCT;
SELECT  Count(UnitsOnOrder) FROM PRODUCT;
```

will produce exactly the same result, namely the total number of rows in the PRODUCT table, as long as we do not allow the *UnitsOnOrder* field to contain blanks. A zero value is not considered to be blank, so even products with zero units on order will still contribute to the count. To add up the total number of units on order across all products, we would instead use the query:

```
SELECT Sum(UnitsOnOrder) FROM PRODUCT;
```

This query produces a totally different result from that using Count. In the next chapter, we will show some more advanced examples that take advantage of the fact that Count does not include blanks.

We may also apply aggregation across the rows of joined tables. Suppose we want to know the total revenue from orders placed between April 22 and April 29, 2013 (inclusive). We may calculate this information with the following query:

```
SELECT  Sum(UnitPrice*Quantity)
FROM    ORDERS, ORDERDETAIL, PRODUCT
WHERE   ORDERS.OrderID = ORDERDETAIL.OrderID AND
        ORDERDETAIL.ProductID = PRODUCT.ProductID AND
        OrderDate BETWEEN #4/22/2013# AND #4/29/2013#;
```

Here, the query applies aggregation to the result of a join operation. We start the query by (in principle) forming a Cartesian join with the ORDERS, ORDERDETAIL, and PRODUCT tables, and then use the same standard join conditions as in the previous section:

```
ORDERS.OrderID = ORDERDETAIL.OrderID AND
ORDERDETAIL.ProductID = PRODUCT.ProductID
```

These conditions ensure that we match up only triples of records that "make sense" together. The result consists basically of each row of the ORDERDETAIL table, augmented by the related information from the ORDER and PRODUCT tables. We then filter out the elements outside the date range that interests us with the additional condition:

```
AND OrderDate BETWEEN #4/22/2013# AND #4/29/2013#
```

This additional stipulation once again illustrates how both join-related conditions and other forms of criterion selection can be mixed in the same compound WHERE clause. It also once again shows how SQL uses "#" symbols around dates. The line

```
SELECT Sum(UnitPrice*Quantity)
```

indicates that SQL should take the sum of *UnitPrice* times *Quantity* over all the records of the joined and filtered table, resulting in a total of $36,583.65. This query is another example of applying aggregation to a computed expression rather than a simple field.

GROUP BY

More often than not, we do not want to aggregate information over the entire dataset but over multiple groups of records. Suppose that in the previous query, we do not want a single grand total but the total revenue for each day. To perform this kind of processing, we use another standard SQL feature, the GROUP BY clause. Suppose that we make the following additions to the previous query:

```
SELECT    OrderDate, Sum(UnitPrice*Quantity)
FROM      ORDERS, ORDERDETAIL, PRODUCT
WHERE     ORDERS.OrderID = ORDERDETAIL.OrderID AND
          ORDERDETAIL.ProductID = PRODUCT.ProductID AND
          OrderDate BETWEEN #4/22/2013# AND #4/29/2013#
GROUP BY OrderDate;
```

The most important addition here is the new clause "GROUP BY OrderDate." It works as follows: once the tables have been joined and the WHERE conditions have been applied, the query divides the rows of the joined and filtered table into groups. In this case, the GROUP BY clause specifies only the single expression OrderDate, so records are in the same group when they have the same order date. Each group is then condensed into a single row of query output, so we get as many rows of output as there are groups.

When GROUP BY is specified, aggregate functions like Sum no longer operate across the entire dataset but separately on each group. Thus, the query adds up *UnitPrice* times *Quantity* for all the records on a given date and reports a separate sum for each date, as shown in Table 10.5.

Table 10.5 Output of query computing revenue on each date.

Order Date	Expr1001
4/22/2013	$24,072.95
4/24/2013	$7,833.70
4/25/2013	$359.75
4/26/2013	$1,082.60
4/27/2013	$249.75
4/28/2013	$569.95
4/29/2013	$2,414.95

The "Expr1001" heading on the second columns is not very explanatory, a minor issue we can fix by adding an optional AS clause:

```
SELECT    OrderDate, Sum(UnitPrice*Quantity) AS Revenue
FROM      ORDERS, ORDERDETAIL, PRODUCT
WHERE     ORDERS.OrderID = ORDERDETAIL.OrderID AND
          ORDERDETAIL.ProductID = PRODUCT.ProductID AND
          OrderDate BETWEEN #4/22/2013# AND #4/29/2013#
GROUP BY OrderDate;
```

This query produces the more aesthetic output shown in Table 10.6.

Table 10.6 Query computing revenue on each date, using AS to obtain a more understandable column name.

Order Date	Revenue
4/22/2013	$24,072.95
4/24/2013	$7,833.70
4/25/2013	$359.75
4/26/2013	$1,082.60
4/27/2013	$249.75
4/28/2013	$569.95
4/29/2013	$2,414.95

We include the *OrderDate* field in the SELECT clause so that each row of output includes the date to which it applies. Otherwise, we would just see a column of revenue totals without any dates attached.

Conceptually, this query works by first forming a huge Cartesian join on the ORDERS, ORDERDETAIL, and PRODUCT tables, discarding all the resulting rows that have non-matching foreign keys or do not meet the date window condition, then forming groups, and finally summing up *UnitPrice* times *Quantity* over each group. In practice, and depending on the exact database software that you use, a query optimizer module in the SQL language processing system might rearrange the query's operations to make it more efficient. For example, it might filter the ORDERS table based on order date *before* performing the join.

Next, suppose we want to display the total revenue for each day recorded in the database, but organized by customer rather than by date, and showing the customer's first and last name. We may attempt to implement this query as follows:

```
SELECT    FirstName, LastName,
          Sum(UnitPrice*Quantity) AS Revenue
FROM      CUSTOMER, ORDERS, ORDERDETAIL, PRODUCT
WHERE     CUSTOMER.CustomerID = ORDERS.CustomerID AND
          ORDERS.OrderID = ORDERDETAIL.OrderID AND
          ORDERDETAIL.ProductID = PRODUCT.ProductID
GROUP BY FirstName, LastName;
```

We now join records from all four tables in the database, based on all the respective foreign keys matching – we need to include the CUSTOMER table in this query, because we need to output the name of the customer, which resides only in that table. More importantly, this query illustrates the use of GROUP BY with more than one attribute. When multiple attributes are specified in a GROUP BY clause, groups are formed based on *all* the specified attributes being identical. In this case, two records of the joined table are placed into the same group if both their *FirstName* and *LastName* fields have identical contents. If any of their grouped-by fields are not the same, the query places the records into different groups. For example, the above query would place data for two people with the same last name but different first names into different groups.

For a larger store than the one in our database, the above query has a high chance of producing misleading results because two customers might well have the same name. For example, if our database contained two customers named "William Jones," their purchases would form a single group, and they would appear to be a single customer in the query output. To prevent this behavior, we modify the query as follows:

```
SELECT    FirstName, LastName,
          Sum(UnitPrice*Quantity) AS Revenue
FROM      CUSTOMER, ORDERS, ORDERDETAIL, PRODUCT
WHERE     CUSTOMER.CustomerID = ORDERS.CustomerID AND
          ORDERS.OrderID = ORDERDETAIL.OrderID AND
          ORDERDETAIL.ProductID = PRODUCT.ProductID
GROUP BY  CUSTOMER.CustomerID, FirstName, LastName;
```

This query specifies that two records be placed in the same group only if they have the same *CustomerID*, the same first name, and the same last name. Since no two customers can have the same *CustomerID*, two different customers can no longer be placed in the same group. If there were two customers with the same name, they would appear on different lines of the output. We obtain the output shown in Table 10.7.

Table 10.7 Output of query showing revenue aggregated by customer.

First Name	Last Name	Revenue
Benjamin	Masterson	$7,293.60
Mary	Milgrom	$23,783.75
Leonard	Goodman	$3,982.95
Margerita	Colon	$5,141.26
Geoffrey	Hammer	$8,670.27
Ashley	Flannery	$8,246.50
Joseph	Brower	$225.85
Xiaoming	Wang	$249.90
Derek	Escher	$2,414.95
Laura	Ng	$822.70
Robert	Sloan	$819.70

Since the query contains the WHERE constraint CUSTOMER.CustomerID = ORDERS.CustomerID, it does not matter if we group by CUSTOMER.CustomerID or ORDERS.CustomerID because, after applying the WHERE criteria, these attributes will have the same value in every retained row of the joined table. However, we must still apply some qualification to this identifier, because there are two tables mentioned in the query that have a field called *CustomerID*: if we just tried to group on CustomerID with no qualification, we would receive an error message (at least in the Access dialect of SQL).

It may seem redundant that we are grouping by the combination of *CustomerID*, *FirstName*, and *LastName*, because *CustomerID* determines

FirstName and *LastName*. That is, if two records have the same *CustomerID* value, then they must have the same *FirstName* and *LastName* values. Thus, while the query says "GROUP BY CUSTOMER.CustomerID, FirstName, LastName", it is effectively grouping only by *CustomerID*. In Access, however, if we try to simplify the query to

```
SELECT    FirstName, LastName,
          Sum(UnitPrice*Quantity) AS Revenue
FROM      CUSTOMER, ORDERS, ORDERDETAIL, PRODUCT
WHERE     CUSTOMER.CustomerID = ORDERS.CustomerID AND
          ORDERS.OrderID = ORDERDETAIL.OrderID AND
          ORDERDETAIL.ProductID = PRODUCT.ProductID
GROUP BY CUSTOMER.CustomerID;
```

we get a rather cryptic error message relating to the attribute *FirstName*. The problem is that standard SQL must be able to verify a query's correctness without knowing the primary and foreign key structure of the underlying database. Therefore, Access' SQL language "parser" does not take into account that *CustomerID* determines *FirstName* and *LastName*, and thus cannot verify whether the query above has an unambiguous meaning. As a result, it produces an error message instead of processing the query. In general, there is a rule that whenever any form of aggregation is present, every attribute appearing in the SELECT part of the query must be either within an aggregation function (like Sum), or be grouped by.

While this restriction is part of standard SQL, some database systems do not enforce it. For example, the above query would run and produce the expected results in the popular open-source MySQL system that is built into many websites. When it encounters a non-aggregated and non-grouped-by attribute in the SELECT clause, MySQL will just select an arbitrary representative of the group to display. In cases like the one above, where every member of any given group must have exactly the same value of *FirstName* and *LastName*, the only value that could possibly be displayed is the one that we would expect.

However, if we display just the *CustomerID* rather than the first and last name, then there would be no problem in any version of SQL. That is, the query

```
SELECT    CUSTOMER.CustomerID,
          Sum(UnitPrice*Quantity) AS Revenue
FROM      CUSTOMER, ORDERS, ORDERDETAIL, PRODUCT
WHERE     CUSTOMER.CustomerID = ORDERS.CustomerID AND
          ORDERS.OrderID = ORDERDETAIL.OrderID AND
          ORDERDETAIL.ProductID = PRODUCT.ProductID
GROUP BY CUSTOMER.CustomerID;
```

runs with no problem in Access, although the output is not as human-friendly as before, showing only customer IDs but no name information (see Table 10.8).

Table 10.8 Output of simpler query computing revenue per customer, but identifying customers only by *CustomerID*.

CustomerID	Revenue
C0001	$7,293.60
C0002	$23,783.75
C0003	$3,982.95
C0004	$5,141.26
C0006	$8,670.27
C0007	$8,246.50
C0008	$225.85
C0009	$249.90
C0010	$2,414.95
C0011	$822.70
C0012	$819.70

As an aside, this version of the query is unnecessarily complicated, because it does not really need the CUSTOMER table, since the *CustomerID* attribute is already present in ORDERS. Dispensing with the CUSTOMER table, we obtain exactly the same output through the simpler query:

```
SELECT    CustomerID, Sum(UnitPrice*Quantity) AS Revenue
FROM      ORDERS, ORDERDETAIL, PRODUCT
WHERE     ORDERS.OrderID = ORDERDETAIL.OrderID AND
          ORDERDETAIL.ProductID = PRODUCT.ProductID
GROUP BY CustomerID;
```

But if we wish to display customer name information, we must use the CUSTOMER table. Returning to the version of the query that displays customer names, an alternative to using a seemingly redundant GROUP BY clause is to apply some unnecessary aggregation operation in the SELECT clause. For example, we could write:

```
SELECT    Min(FirstName), Min(LastName),
          Sum(UnitPrice*Quantity) AS Revenue
FROM      CUSTOMER, ORDERS, ORDERDETAIL, PRODUCT
WHERE     CUSTOMER.CustomerID = ORDERS.CustomerID AND
          ORDERS.OrderID = ORDERDETAIL.OrderID AND
          ORDERDETAIL.ProductID = PRODUCT.ProductID
GROUP BY CUSTOMER.CustomerID;
```

The Min operation, when applied to text data, selects the alphabetically first value within each group. But since *FirstName* and *LastName* take the same value throughout each group, the output for each group contains the only possible applicable first name and last name. This query is probably more confusing to a human than the original one, however. If we were to take this approach, we would also need to use more AS modifiers to make the column names in the output more readable.

We do not give an example here, but it is possible to GROUP BY not only by the values of simple attributes, but the values of general expressions (computed fields).

When you use GROUP BY, one should have at least one aggregation function such as Sum or Avg somewhere in your query, typically in the SELECT clause. Without any aggregation functions, GROUP BY will either cause an error message, have no effect, or operate in the same way as SELECT DISTINCT, which is simpler to use.

HAVING

Suppose we are interested in performing the same query, but we want to see only customers who have spent a total of at least $7,000. This restriction cannot be imposed by a WHERE clause, because WHERE restrictions are always applied *before* grouping and aggregation occur. Here, we need to instead apply a criterion to the *result* of the Sum aggregation function, which can only be known after the grouping and aggregation steps. To apply criteria after grouping and aggregation, SQL provides an additional clause called HAVING. To implement this query, we add the clause

```
HAVING Sum(UnitPrice*Quantity) >= 7000
```

to the query, resulting in:

```
SELECT    FirstName, LastName,
          Sum(UnitPrice*Quantity) AS Revenue
FROM      CUSTOMER, ORDERS, ORDERDETAIL, PRODUCT
WHERE     CUSTOMER.CustomerID = Orders.CustomerID AND
          Orders.OrderID = ORDERDETAIL.OrderID AND
          ORDERDETAIL.ProductID = PRODUCT.ProductID
GROUP BY  CUSTOMER.CustomerID, FirstName, LastName
HAVING    Sum(UnitPrice*Quantity) >= 7000;
```

This clause specifies that, after grouping and aggregation, we retain only output rows for which the sum of the unit price multiplied by quantity is at least 7,000. Now, only "big spenders" appear in the output, as shown in Table 10.9.

Table 10.9 Output of query identifying high-spending customers.

First Name	Last Name	Revenue
Benjamin	Masterson	$7,293.60
Mary	Milgrom	$23,783.75
Geoffrey	Hammer	$8,670.27
Ashley	Flannery	$8,246.50

HAVING and WHERE perform similar functions, but WHERE filters records *before* aggregation and HAVING filters records *after* aggregation. Both can be used in the same aggregation query (as is the case above). In queries without aggregation, there is no difference between HAVING and WHERE, but it is customary to use only WHERE. The logical expression appearing after HAVING should customarily include an aggregation function, since otherwise we could accomplish the same result with WHERE.

Since the computed field *Revenue* is already defined by an AS clause, one might expect to be able to substitute "HAVING Revenue >= 7000" for the HAVING clause in the above query. Unfortunately, this technique does not work properly in Access, although it may work in other SQL dialects. In Access, AS modifiers within the SELECT clause do not influence expressions in other clauses, so we instead get a request to enter the value of the undefined parameter "Revenue."

ORDER BY

SQL's ORDER BY clause sorts the output of a query and can be used in queries with or without aggregation. Despite its superficial resemblance to GROUP BY, it performs a completely different function: GROUP BY establishes groups over which aggregation functions operate, whereas ORDER BY places the final query results in a specified sequence. ORDER BY sorting happens after aggregation when aggregation is present, so it occurs after the grouping specified by GROUP BY. The existence of the ORDER BY clause is the reason our plumbing store database violates our usual naming conventions by calling order table ORDERS rather than ORDER. Because ORDER, being part of ORDER BY, is a "reserved word"[5] in SQL, calling a table ORDER can badly confuse the SQL parser.

For example, if we want to see "big spenders" in the previous query in order of spending, with biggest spenders first, we would write:

---

5 In a computer language, a *reserved word* is one that has a predefined, special meaning and cannot be redefined by the programmer. For example, SELECT, AS, FROM, and WHERE are all reserved words in SQL. Using such words as the name of a table or attribute can badly confuse SQL and will result in syntax errors.

```
SELECT    FirstName, LastName,
          Sum(UnitPrice*Quantity) AS Revenue
FROM      CUSTOMER, Orders, ORDERDETAIL, PRODUCT
WHERE     CUSTOMER.CustomerID = Orders.CustomerID AND
          Orders.OrderID = ORDERDETAIL.OrderID AND
          ORDERDETAIL.ProductID = PRODUCT.ProductID
GROUP BY  CUSTOMER.CustomerID, FirstName, LastName
HAVING    Sum(UnitPrice*Quantity) >= 7000
ORDER BY  Sum(UnitPrice*Quantity) DESC;
```

This query's results are shown in Table 10.10.

Table 10.10 Output of query showing high-spending customers sorted by expenditure.

First Name	Last Name	Revenue
Mary	Milgrom	$23,783.75
Geoffrey	Hammer	$8,670.27
Ashley	Flannery	$8,246.50
Benjamin	Masterson	$7,293.60

The DESC modifier here specifies a sort in descending order, meaning that the largest or alphabetically last values should appear first. Note that we can ORDER BY any combination of aggregated and non-aggregated expressions that could appear in the SELECT clause. For example, if we wanted to order the same query alphabetically primarily by last name, and then secondarily by first name,[6] we would change the query to:

```
SELECT    FirstName, LastName,
          Sum(UnitPrice*Quantity) AS Revenue
FROM      CUSTOMER, Orders, ORDERDETAIL, PRODUCT
WHERE     CUSTOMER.CustomerID = Orders.CustomerID AND
          Orders.OrderID = ORDERDETAIL.OrderID AND
          ORDERDETAIL.ProductID = PRODUCT.ProductID
GROUP BY  CUSTOMER.CustomerID, FirstName, LastName
HAVING    Sum(UnitPrice*Quantity) >= 7000
ORDER BY  LastName, FirstName;
```

This version of the query results in the different ordering shown in Table 10.11.

---

6 That is, among people with the same last name, we order by first name.

Table 10.11 High-spending customers sorted by their names.

First Name	Last Name	Revenue
Ashley	Flannery	$8,246.50
Geoffrey	Hammer	$8,670.27
Benjamin	Masterson	$7,293.60
Mary	Milgrom	$23,783.75

The sorting priority is always from left to right in the ORDER BY clause, but you can specify the expressions in the ORDER BY clause in a different sequence than in the SELECT clause. By default, numerical values are sorted from smallest to largest, dates are sorted from earlier to later, and text is sorted from alphabetically first to alphabetically last. The modifier DESC may be appended to any individual sort expression to reverse the default order. You may use the modifier ASC to specify the normal, ascending order, but only to clarify the intent of the query to human readers, since ascending order is the default.

You can use ORDER BY in queries either with or without aggregation. As an example of an ORDER BY query without aggregation, consider:

```
SELECT    FirstName, LastName, OrderDate
FROM      CUSTOMER, ORDERS
WHERE     CUSTOMER.CustomerID = ORDERS.CustomerID
ORDER BY OrderDate DESC, LastName, FirstName;
```

This query displays the customer first name, customer last name, and date of each order, sorted from the most recent orders to the oldest. Orders placed on the same date are presented alphabetically by customer last name; orders placed on the same date by customers with the same last name are presented alphabetically by customer first name (although this consideration does not affect this particular small database). This query produces the output shown in Table 10.12.

The Overall Conceptual Structure of Queries

In summary, SQL queries have the following general form:

```
SELECT {DISTINCT} expressions1   "{}" means DISTINCT is
                                 optional

FROM     data_source
WHERE    conditions1             Optional
GROUP BY expressions2            Optional
HAVING   conditions2             Optional
ORDER BY expressions3            Optional
;
```

Table 10.12 Orders sorted by customer name and date.

First Name	Last Name	Order Date
Geoffrey	Hammer	5/1/2013
Geoffrey	Hammer	5/1/2013
Joseph	Brower	4/30/2013
Derek	Escher	4/29/2013
Derek	Escher	4/29/2013
Robert	Sloan	4/28/2013
Robert	Sloan	4/27/2013
Geoffrey	Hammer	4/26/2013
Laura	Ng	4/26/2013
Laura	Ng	4/26/2013
Geoffrey	Hammer	4/25/2013
Xiaoming	Wang	4/25/2013
Margerita	Colon	4/24/2013
Ashley	Flannery	4/24/2013
Benjamin	Masterson	4/24/2013
Benjamin	Masterson	4/22/2013
Mary	Milgrom	4/22/2013
Mary	Milgrom	4/22/2013
Benjamin	Masterson	4/21/2013
Mary	Milgrom	4/21/2013
Benjamin	Masterson	4/20/2013
Ashley	Flannery	4/18/2013
Leonard	Goodman	4/18/2013
Geoffrey	Hammer	4/18/2013
Margerita	Colon	4/15/2013

Conceptually, the sequence of operations is as follows:

1) We form the Cartesian join of the tables appearing in the FROM clause. This table consists of all possible combinations of records from the constituent tables of the query. If we use the INNER JOIN syntax instead of separating tables with commas, those specific inner joins are made.[7]

---

7 In the next chapter, we will revisit the concept of an outer join, which SQL expresses using the LEFT JOIN or RIGHT JOIN syntax. Such joins also happen in the first step of the conceptual query sequence.

2) We drop any rows that do not meet the WHERE conditions. If the FROM clause is made up of Cartesian joins, the WHERE conditions typically include checks to make sure that foreign keys match, as well as any other desired conditions.

3) We perform any specified grouping and aggregation. We form groups based on the concatenated values of all the expressions in the GROUP BY clause, and then condense each group to a single row. Any expressions involving aggregation functions specified in the SELECT or HAVING clauses are computed at this time.

4) We apply the post-aggregation criteria specified by the HAVING clause, dropping (aggregated) rows that do not met the specified criteria.

5) We sort the resulting rows as specified in the ORDER BY clause.

6) We delete all columns/attributes not appearing in the SELECT clause. Although we associate this step with the SELECT clause, database theorists call it a "project" or "projection" operation (as in projection of a three-dimensional image to a two-dimensional image).

7) Finally, if the query includes DISTINCT, we delete any rows that are exact duplicates of some preceding row after the dropping of columns in the previous step.

Figure 10.4 shows a graphical depiction of this sequence of operations.

Figure 10.4 Conceptual order of query processing steps.

While the above steps are the conceptual sequence of operations, the query optimizer module of the database system is free to find a more efficient way to compute the same result. The effectiveness of query optimization may vary depending on the complexity of your query and which database software you are using.

One immediate consequence of this conceptual sequence is that it is not possible to use an aggregation function such as Sum within a WHERE condition or in the ON condition of a join, because joins and WHERE occur before aggregation. If you need to perform such operations, then your query requires query nesting or chaining, both of which are described in the next chapter.

Another consequence of the conceptual ordering of queries is that expressions appearing in ORDER BY are subject to the same rules as those appearing in SELECT, because queries evaluate both kinds of expressions after aggregation. Specifically, if a query uses GROUP BY, then every attribute appearing in SELECT or ORDER BY must either be grouped by or should be within an aggregation function. For example, consider the hypothetical query:

```
SELECT    FirstName, LastName,
          Sum(UnitPrice*Quantity) AS Revenue
FROM      CUSTOMER, Orders, ORDERDETAIL, PRODUCT
WHERE     CUSTOMER.CustomerID = Orders.CustomerID AND
          Orders.OrderID = ORDERDETAIL.OrderID AND
          ORDERDETAIL.ProductID = PRODUCT.ProductID
GROUP BY  CUSTOMER.CustomerID, FirstName, LastName
ORDER BY  ProductName;                               (Incorrect)
```

This query will generate an error message because we are not grouping by *ProductName*. Fundamentally, this query makes no sense, because we cannot sort the grouped output by the value of an attribute that can take many different values within each group: each order may contain more than one product, so there is often no single appropriate product name to associate with a particular order. Therefore, we cannot use *ProductName* in the SELECT or ORDER BY clauses unless it appears within an aggregation function.

Exercises

10.1 (Queries of a single table without filtering conditions) Based on the plumbing supply store database from Chapter 7, write SQL SELECT queries that display the following information:

  A The name of each product.

  B All days on which orders have been placed, with no duplicate entries in the case of more than one order placed on the same day.

  C The entire PRODUCT table.

  D For each product, the product ID, product name, and the ratio of the number of units on order to the number of units in stock.

10.2 (Queries of a single table without filtering conditions) Based on the conference database `conference.mdb` on the book website, write SQL SELECT queries to display the following information:

  A The first and last name of each speaker.

  B A list of all areas of expertise claimed by speakers, with no repetition in the case of multiple speakers with the same expertise area.

  C The entirety of the rooms table.

10.3 (Queries of a single table with filtering conditions) Based on the plumbing supply store database from Chapter 7, write SQL queries that perform the following tasks:

  A Show the name and unit price of all products priced below $50 (note: SQL treats currency amounts like any other number, so you should *not* use a $ sign or quotes in your query.)

B Show the product name, units on order, and units in stock for all products for which the number of units on order is at least 40% of the number of units in stock.

C Show the same information as in part (b), but with the additional restriction that the number of units on order is no more than 10.

D Show the first name, last name, city, and state of all customers outside New Jersey (state code "NJ").

E Show the first name, last name, city, and state of all customers who are outside New Jersey or have the first name "Robert" (or both).

10.4 (Queries of a single table with filtering conditions) Based on the conference database on the website, write SQL SELECT queries to display the following information:

A The titles, dates, and start times of all sessions in room "101"; note that the *RoomID* field in this database is text, not a number.

B The room IDs, capacities, and notes for all rooms with a capacity below 100.

C The same information as in part (b), but only for rooms capable of serving refreshments; note that in SQL the possible values of a yes/no field are `True` and `False` (without quotes).

10.5 (Simple inner joins) Based on the plumbing supply store database from Chapter 7, write SQL queries that use an INNER JOIN clause to perform the following tasks:

A Show the entirety of each combination of a record from the ORDERDETAIL table and a record from the PRODUCT table for which the *ProductID* fields match.

B For the same combinations of ORDERDETAIL and PRODUCT records as in part (a), show the entirety of the ORDERDETAIL record, but only the product name and unit price fields from the PRODUCT record.

C Show the same information as in part (b), but only for items costing at least $1,000 (again, note that you do not use $ signs in front of currency amounts in SQL).

D Produce the same output as in part (c), but with an additional column showing the unit price of the product multiplied by the quantity ordered.

E For all combinations of a record from the ORDERDETAIL table and a record from the PRODUCT table that have matching *ProductID* fields and also have a quantity ordered that is at least half the number of units now in stock, show the quantity ordered, the product name, and the number of units in stock.

10.6 (A Cartesian join) Based on the plumbing supply store database from Chapter 7, write a query that shows the first name, last name, and product name for all possible combinations of a record from the CUSTOMER table and record from the PRODUCT table, without regard to whether the customer has ever ordered the product.

10.7 (Inner joins using WHERE) Repeat all the queries from Problem 5, but use a WHERE clause instead of an INNER JOIN clause.

10.8 (Compound joins using WHERE) Based on the plumbing supply store database from Chapter 7, write SQL queries to perform the following tasks:

  A Write a query that shows, for each row of the ORDERDETAIL table, the first and last name of the corresponding customer, the date of the order, the quantity ordered, and the name of the product. Use only WHERE conditions to join the tables.

  B Create a query producing the same output as part (a) using MS Access Query Design View. Switch to SQL view and compare the contents of the FROM clause to what you wrote in part (a).

  C Perform the same query as part (a), using WHERE to join tables, but only include rows for which the quantity ordered is at least 5.

  D Repeat the query from part (a), but showing all rows for which the quantity ordered is at least 5 or the unit price is over $1,500.

10.9 (More compounds joins) Based on the conference database on the website, and using WHERE to express joins between tables, write SQL queries for the following tasks. A "presentation" consists of a single speaker appearing in a single session.

  A Show the title, starting time, room ID, and room capacity for each session.

  B For each presentation at the conference, show the speaker first name, speaker last name, speaker area of expertise, session title, room ID, and session start time.

  C Show the same information as part (b), but only for speakers from Florida (state code "FL").

  D Show the same information as part (b), but only for speakers who are from Florida or whose area of expertise is "Wellness."

  E For each presentation being given in a room with a capacity of at least 100, show the speaker ID, speaker first name, speaker last name, room ID, and room capacity.

  F Show the speaker ID, first name, and last name for all speakers giving any presentations in a room with a seating capacity of at least 100.

10.10 (Simple aggregation without grouping) Based on the plumbing supply store database from Chapter 7, write SQL queries to perform the following tasks:

    A Show the total number of units of held in stock (summed across all products).

    B Show the total value of inventory held, with each unit of inventory valued at its unit price.

    C Show the total value of inventory held in products whose price is below $50.

    D Show the total value of inventory held in products whose price is between $100 and $750 (inclusive).

    E Show the number of products whose unit price is under $200.

10.11 (More simple aggregation without grouping) Based on the conference database on the website, and using WHERE to express joins between tables, write SQL queries to display the following information. A "presentation" consists of a single speaker appearing in a single session.

    A The total combined seating capacity of all rooms.

    B The smallest room seating capacity, the average room seating capacity, and the largest room seating capacity.

    C The number of speakers attending the conference.

    D The number of presentations being given at the conference.

    E The number of presentations being given in rooms whose capacity is below 100.

    F The number of sessions taking in place in rooms that can serve refreshments.

10.12 (Aggregation with grouping) Based on the plumbing supply store database from Chapter 7, write SQL queries to perform the following tasks:

    A For each customer, show the Customer ID, first name, last name, and the total number of orders placed.

    B Show the same information about customers as in part (a), but count only orders placed since April 28, 2013; if a customer has placed no orders since that time, they need not appear in the output.

    C Show the same information as in part (b), but also include the date of each customer's most recent order.

    D For each product, show its name and average quantity ordered when it appears in orders placed by customers from New Jersey (state code "NJ").

10.13 (More aggregation with grouping) Based on the conference database on the website, and using WHERE to express joins between tables, write SQL queries for the following tasks:

A For each room in which any session is being held, show the room ID and the number of sessions being held there (with the column heading *NumSessions*).

B Show the same information as part (a), but also show the capacity of each room.

C For each room, show its ID, capacity, and the number of *presentations* being given there (the heading for this column should be *NumPresentations*).

D For each speaker, show their first name, last name, the number of presentations they are giving (with the column heading *NumPresentations*). Make sure that if the conference were large enough to have two speakers with the same name, each would appear on a different line of the output.

10.14 (More aggregation with grouping) Download, save, and open the database `bookstore-2000.mdb` from the website. This database is a somewhat more complicated retail database than our plumbing database. The price actually charged the customer is the *cost_of_ each* attribute in the ORDERLINES table, and can be lower than the *retail_price* attribute in the BOOKS table, reflecting occasional discounts. The database contains a small amount of redundancy, in that *cost_line* in the ORDERLINES table is always equal to *quantity*cost_each*. Using WHERE to express joins between tables, write SQL queries to for the following tasks:

A Show the name of each author, the number of books written by the author (labeled *numb_books*), the most recent year of publication for such books (labeled *most_recent*), and their average retail price (labeled *avg_price*).

B For each combination of publisher and year after 1985 for which any books were published, show the publisher name, the year, and the number of books published by that publisher in that year (labeled *numb_books*).

C For each customer, show their customer number, first name, last name, and the total dollar value of discounts they have received; note that the total discounts received is equal to the sum of *quantity*(retail_price − cost_each)*, or equivalently the sum of *quantity*retail_price − cost_line*. Note that the total discounts received are zero for most customers. The discounts column should have the heading *discounts*.

D For each publisher, show its name and the total value of inventory on hand from that publisher, which is the total of *retail_price* number_on_hand* for each book by that publisher. This column should have the label *inventory_value*.

10.15 (Criteria after aggregation) Based on the plumbing supply store database from Chapter 7, write SQL queries to perform the following tasks:

   A Show the name and total revenue for each product from which you have at least $2,000 in revenue.

   B Show the name and total revenue between April 22 and 27, 2013 (inclusive) for each product for which you have at least $1,500 in revenue between those dates.

   C Show the first name, last name, and number of orders for all customers who have placed at least 3 orders.

   D Show the first name, last name, and number of orders placed on or after April 25, 2013, for all customers who have at least 2 such orders.

10.16 (Criteria after aggregation) Based on the conference database on the website, write SQL queries to for the following tasks:

   A Show the first and last name of all speakers who are appearing in least three sessions. Also show the number of sessions each such speaker is appearing in, labeled *NumSessions*.

   B Show the first and last name of all speakers who are appearing at least two sessions being held in rooms with a large screen. Also show the number of such sessions, labeled *NumLargeScreen*.

   C Show the ID and capacity for each room in which at least three sessions are being held. Also show the number of sessions being held in each of these rooms, labeled *NumSessions*.

10.17 (Simple sorting) Based on the plumbing supply store database from Chapter 7, write SQL queries to perform the following tasks:

   A Show the name, unit price, units in stock, and units on order for each product, sorted alphabetically by product name.

   B Show the same information as in part (a), but sorted from the largest number of units in stock to the smallest. For products with the same number of units in stock, sort the rows of output from the largest number of units on order to the smallest.

   C Show the same information as in parts (a) and (b), and also the *inventory position*, which is the sum of the units in stock and the units on order. Sort the output from largest to smallest inventory position.

   D Show the same information as in part (c), and in the same order, but only for products with a unit price of at least $1,000.

10.18 (Sorting information extracted from multiple tables) Based on the plumbing supply store database from Chapter 7, write SQL queries to perform the following tasks:

A Show the name of each product and the total amount of revenue it has generated (labeled *Revenue*). The output should be sorted by revenue, with the highest-revenue products first; products that have never been ordered need not appear in the output.

B Show the same information as in part (a), but only for items that have generated at least $1,000 of revenue.

C Show the same information as part (a), but including only revenue from orders placed April 27, 2013, or later; products not ordered since that date need not appear in the output.

D Show the same information as part (a), but only for items for which at least four total units have been ordered, and also showing the total number of units ordered for each product (labeled *UnitsOrdered*). Sort the output from the largest to the smallest total number of units ordered; within products with the same total number of units ordered, sort from the largest to smallest total revenue.

10.19 (Mixed queries on the bookstore database) Download the `bookstore-2000.mdb` sample database from the textbook website. Write SQL queries to show the following:

A Show the first name, last name, and e-mail of each customer in New Jersey.

B For each order, list the customer first and last name, customer phone, and order date.

C Repeat the query from part (b), but only show orders placed on or after July 1, 2000.

D Show all book titles ordered on or after March 1, 2000. Do not list any title more than once.

E Show the title, author name, publisher name, publication year, and number on hand for all books of which there are at least 8 copies on hand, and which were published by Knopf or published after 1980 (or both). Sort the output by the number of copies on hand, with the largest number of books on hand coming first. Books with the same number of copies on hand should appear in alphabetical order by title.

F For each author with any books with a publication year before 1950, give the author's name and the number of such books. Sort the results in order of the number of books, with the largest number of books appearing first. The number of books column should have the heading *number_of_books*.

G Show the number of titles and total number of copies on hand of books that have a retail price less than $20. These results should respectively be labeled *number_of_titles* and *number_of_copies*.

H Compute the total value of current inventory (based on retail prices), labeled as *total_inventory_value*.

I Show the title, author, and number of copies of each book ordered (labeled *number_sold*) in the period January–June 2000. Books not ordered during this period need not appear. Sort the result alphabetically by author name, with books having the same author sorted alphabetically by title.

J Show the first name, last name, and number of physical books ordered (labeled *num_ordered*) for all customers who have ordered at least 10 physical books. Sort the results alphabetically by last name, with customers having the same last name sorted alphabetically by first name.

K Show the first name and last name of each customer who has spent at least $45 on books published in 1980 or later. Also show the total amount of such spending. Sort the results from the most spent to the least. Among customers whose spending is identical, display them alphabetically by last name.

10.20 (Mixed queries on the conference database) From the textbook website, download the conference database. Write SQL queries for the following:

A Show a "master schedule" for the conference. For each presentation at the conference, this query should list the date, session start time, session title, room, speaker first name, and speaker last name. It should be sorted by date, then by session start time, then by session title, then by speaker last name.

B Show the ID, name, date, and start time of each session, along with the number of speakers scheduled for the session. Sort the results from the largest number of speakers to the smallest.

C Show the ID, name, date, and start time of each session, along with the number of speakers scheduled, for each session with at least two speakers. Sort the results from the largest number of speakers to the smallest.

D Show a schedule for room 101. For each presentation at the conference in room 101, show the session start date, session start time, session title, speaker first name, and speaker last name. Sort the results by order of occurrence (earliest first) and then by speaker last name.

E Show all rooms with capacity of at least 75 people in which at least 6 presentations are being given. Show the room ID, the room capacity, whether or not the room has a large screen, and the number of presentations. Sort the results by the number of presentations, with the largest number of presentations first. The number-of-presentations column should have the heading *NumberOfPresentations*.

F Show the average capacity of rooms that either have a large screen or have the ability to serve refreshments (or both). The result of this query should be a single cell.

G For each session, show the title of the session and a single count of the number of speakers in the session whose expertise is either "Student Life" or "Residence Halls." If there are no such speakers in a given session, then that session need not appear in the query output.

H For each room, show the room ID and the number of talks being given in the room by speakers from Pennsylvania ("PA") or Georgia ("GA"). Display only one count per room, not separate counts for the two states. Rooms with no such talks need not appear in the output. Sort the results by the number of talks, with the largest number first. The column heading for the number-of-talks column should be *PAGATalks*.

11

Advanced Query Techniques

SQL is a powerful language. We have seen some of its basic capabilities in prior chapters, but there are many more that we have not yet examined. This chapter explores some additional features of SQL, such as more advanced techniques for joining tables and combining multiple queries to perform a computation too elaborate for a single query.

Outer Joins

Consider the sports league and games database from Chapter 8. The COACH and TEAM tables are shown in Tables 11.1 and 11.2.

Suppose we wish to show the first name, last name, and team nicknames for all coaches, sorted by coach last name. For coaches not presently assigned to a team, we want to display a blank team nickname. In Chapter 5, we saw how to display such a table using the Access graphical interface, but it is also possible directly from SQL. In SQL, we write:

```
SELECT FirstName, LastName, NickName
FROM   COACH LEFT JOIN TEAM ON COACH.TEAMID = TEAM.TEAMID;
```

The LEFT JOIN syntax specifies that the join result always contain at least one representative of each record in the left table (in this case, COACH), even if there is no matching record in the right-hand table to satisfy the ON condition. When there is no matching query in the right-hand table, SQL supplies blank values for its attributes. Running this query results in the output shown in Table 11.3.

Introductory Relational Database Design for Business, with Microsoft Access, First Edition.
Jonathan Eckstein and Bonnie R. Schultz.
© 2018 John Wiley & Sons Ltd. Published 2018 by John Wiley & Sons Ltd.

Table 11.1 The COACH table.

CoachID	First Name	Last Name	Phone Number	Address	City	State	Zip Code	Status	Team ID
C01	Steve	Zion	(954) 753-9999	6754 Lakeview Dr.	Coral Springs	FL	33071	1	T01
C02	Michael	Moldof	(954) 753-8888	100 Oak Lane	Coral Springs	FL	33071	2	
C03	Neil	Goodman	(954) 752-7777	3800 Westview Dr.	Coral Springs	FL	33071	2	T01
C04	David	Stone	(954) 753-6666	550 Sample Road	Coral Springs	FL	33067	1	
C05	Frank	Barber	(954) 752-5555	4545 Westview Dr.	Coral Springs	FL	33071	2	
C06	Curtis	Kimble	(954) 344-4444	1101 Ramblewood Rd.	Coral Springs	FL	33071	1	T07
C07	Caren	Zarinsky	(954) 753-3333	4532 Maplewood Dr.	Coral Springs	FL	33065	2	
C08	Derek	Anderson	(954) 344-2222	1345 University Dr.	Coral Springs	FL	33071	2	T03
C09	Karen	Kinzer	(954) 752-1111	922 Sample Road	Coral Springs	FL	33067	1	T06
C10	Alex	Fraser	(954) 344-0000	4566 Parkside Dr.	Coral Springs	FL	33071	1	T04
C11	Lorenzo	Pearson	(954) 752-1234	2450 Maplewood Dr.	Coral Springs	FL	33065	1	T03
C12	Shira	Citron	(954) 753-5678	500 Oak Lane	Coral Springs	FL	33071	2	T06

Table 11.2 The TEAM table.

TeamID	Nickname	Colors
T01	Rockets	Red/White
T02	Comets	Blue/White
T03	Bulldogs	Red/Black
T04	Hurricanes	Orange/Green
T05	Tornadoes	Blue/Gold
T06	Gators	Orange/Blue
T07	Seminoles	Maroon/Gold

Table 11.3 Result of a LEFT JOIN of the COACH and TEAM tables.

First Name	Last Name	NickName
Michael	Moldof	
David	Stone	
Frank	Barber	
Caren	Zarinsky	
Steve	Zion	Rockets
Neil	Goodman	Rockets
Derek	Anderson	Bulldogs
Lorenzo	Pearson	Bulldogs
Alex	Fraser	Hurricanes
Karen	Kinzer	Gators
Shira	Citron	Gators
Curtis	Kimble	Seminoles

There is also a RIGHT JOIN version that is similar but reverses the roles of the "left" and "right" tables. Generically, such operations are called "outer joins," and in some dialects of SQL these operations instead use the syntax LEFT OUTER JOIN and RIGHT OUTER JOIN. Note that outer joins require an explicit join verb – unlike for an inner join, there is no equivalent way of applying WHERE conditions to the result a Cartesian join to obtain a result equivalent to an outer join.

Outer Joins and Aggregation

Outer joins are particularly useful when combined with aggregation. On the same database, suppose we want a query showing the ID and name of each team, together with the number of coaches assigned to it. We start with the query:

```
SELECT    TEAM.TeamID, Nickname, Count(CoachID) AS NumCoaches
FROM      TEAM, COACH
WHERE     TEAM.TeamID = COACH.TeamID
GROUP BY  TEAM.TeamID, Nickname;
```

This query produces the result shown in Table 11.4.

Table 11.4 Teams with no coaches do not appear in the query output when using a conventional join.

TeamID	Nickname	NumCoaches
T01	Rockets	2
T03	Bulldogs	2
T04	Hurricanes	1
T06	Gators	2
T07	Seminoles	1

Although there are seven teams, only five appear in the output of the query. The reason is that two teams, the Comets (T02) and Tornadoes (T05) do not currently have any coaches assigned to them. There is therefore no combination of a team and coach meeting the join condition TEAM.TeamID = COACH.TeamID for which the team is T02 or T05. Conceptually, the query works by first forming a Cartesian join table whose rows consist of all possible combinations of a team record and a coach record, then deleting all rows of this table violating the condition TEAM.TeamID = COACH.TeamID, then grouping the remaining rows by *TeamID*, and finally condensing each of these groups into one output row. After applying the WHERE condition, no rows remain to form a group for which *TeamId* is T02, and the same holds for T05. Consequently, these teams "disappear" from the query output.

Rather than have teams with no coaches simply vanish, it might be more intuitive to have them appear in the output, but with a zero as their coach count. Outer joins provide a way of obtaining this kind of result. Let us modify the query to

```
SELECT    TEAM.TeamID, Nickname, Count(CoachID) AS NumCoaches
FROM      TEAM LEFT JOIN COACH
                ON TEAM.TeamID = COACH.TeamID
GROUP BY TEAM.TeamID, Nickname;
```

The result of this query is just what we want (see Table 11.5).

Table 11.5 Using an outer join causes teams with no coaches to appear in the query output.

TeamID	Nickname	NumCoaches
T01	Rockets	2
T02	Comets	0
T03	Bulldogs	2
T04	Hurricanes	1
T05	Tornadoes	0
T06	Gators	2
T07	Seminoles	1

How did this change make the query produce the results we wanted? First, the entire result of the outer join operation TEAM LEFT JOIN COACH ON TEAM.TeamID = COACH. TeamID is as shown in Table 11.6.

Most of the rows of this table consist of information about a team and one of the team's coaches, but for the two teams without a coach, we get a record consisting of team information coupled with blank coach information. When we next form groups using the attributes *TeamID* and *Nickname*, each of the two coach-less teams is placed in a group consisting of one of these records. When the Count ( ) function counts the *CoachID* field from this group, it obtains a count of zero, rather than one, because it does not count blanks. However, if we had counted *TeamID* rather than *CoachID*, we would have obtained a count of one.

You can use outer joins with aggregation functions other than Count ( ). Returning to the plumbing store database of Chapter 7, suppose we attempt to issue a query to identify low-revenue products, as follows:

```
SELECT    PRODUCT.ProductID, PRODUCT.ProductName,
          Sum(Quantity*UnitPrice) AS Revenue
FROM      PRODUCT, ORDERDETAIL
WHERE     PRODUCT.ProductID = ORDERDETAIL.ProductID
GROUP BY PRODUCT.ProductID, PRODUCT.ProductName
ORDER BY Sum(Quantity*UnitPrice);
```

Table 11.6 Immediate result of the outer join operation between TEAM and COACH.

TeamID	Nickname	Colors	CoachID	First Name	Last Name	Phone Number	Address	City	State	Zip Code	Status	Team ID
T01	Rockets	Red/White	C01	Steve	Zion	(954) 753-9999	6754 Lakeview Dr.	Coral Springs	FL	33071	1	T01
T01	Rockets	Red/White	C03	Neil	Goodman	(954) 752-7777	3800 Westview Dr.	Coral Springs	FL	33071	2	T01
T02	Comets	Blue/White										
T03	Bulldogs	Red/Black	C08	Derek	Anderson	(954) 344-2222	1345 University Dr.	Coral Springs	FL	33071	2	T03
T03	Bulldogs	Red/Black	C11	Lorenzo	Pearson	(954) 752-1234	2450 Maplewood Dr.	Coral Springs	FL	33065	1	T03
T04	Hurricanes	Orange/Green	C10	Alex	Fraser	(954) 344-0000	4566 Parkside Dr.	Coral Springs	FL	33071	1	T04
T05	Tornadoes	Blue/Gold										
T06	Gators	Orange/Blue	C09	Karen	Kinzer	(954) 752-1111	922 Sample Road	Coral Springs	FL	33067	1	T06
T06	Gators	Orange/Blue	C12	Shira	Citron	(954) 753-5678	500 Oak Lane	Coral Springs	FL	33071	2	T06
T07	Seminoles	Maroon/Gold	C06	Curtis	Kimble	(954) 344-4444	1101 Ramblewood Rd.	Coral Springs	FL	33071	1	T07

Table 11.7 First seven rows of output of the initial version of low-selling product query.

ProductID	Product Name	Revenue
P0018	Unclogger Tool Set	$59.95
P0028	Leak Fixer System	$89.85
P0026	Flow Regulator Valve	$151.90
P0019	Nickel Finish Shower Head	$159.80
P0025	Waterfall Bath Faucet Set	$191.90
P0027	Budget Filter System	$231.90
P0023	Victorian Kitchen Faucet with Spray	$249.95

The first few rows of the result of this query are as shown in Table 11.7. This output only includes products that a customer has ordered at least once. Therefore, its top rows of output consist of the products that have generated the least revenue over the time period covered by the database, among those that have been ordered at least once. However, there are in fact three products that have no orders in the time period covered by the database. By a similar mechanism to the previous query, these products simply disappear from the output, because they are not represented by any rows in the ORDERDETAIL table and hence no longer remain after the WHERE condition is applied. To include these products in the output, we modify the query to:

```
SELECT    PRODUCT.ProductID, PRODUCT.ProductName,
          Sum(Quantity*UnitPrice) AS Revenue
FROM      PRODUCT LEFT JOIN ORDERDETAIL
            ON PRODUCT.ProductID = ORDERDETAIL.ProductID
GROUP BY PRODUCT.ProductID, PRODUCT.ProductName
ORDER BY Sum(Quantity*UnitPrice);
```

Now, the top output rows are as shown in Table 11.8. The LEFT JOIN operation gives these products a representative in its output, but with the Quantity field blank. The blank value of *Quantity* results in a blank value for *Quantity*UnitPrice*, which curiously results in a blank value of the Sum( ) function. Fortunately, the ORDER BY clause treats these blank values the same way as zeroes, so we obtain essentially the result we want.[1]

---

1 SQL also has explicit ways of converting a blank to a zero if necessary, although they may vary with the SQL dialect.

Table 11.8 Output of low-selling product query using an outer join.

ProductID	Product Name	Revenue
P0017	Utility Sink set	
P0015	Replacement Valve Units Type B	
P0031	Circulator Pump Fitting	
P0018	Unclogger Tool Set	$59.95
P0028	Leak Fixer System	$89.85
P0026	Flow Regulator Valve	$151.90
P0019	Nickel Finish Shower Head	$159.80
P0025	Waterfall Bath Faucet Set	$191.90
P0027	Budget Filter System	$231.90
P0023	Victorian Kitchen Faucet with Spray	$249.95

Joining Multiple Records from the Same Table: AS in the FROM Clause

Returning to the sports team database, suppose that we want to write a query showing, for each game played, the home team nickname, home team score, visiting team nickname, and visiting team score. If we wanted only to show team IDs, instead of team nicknames, we could base our query on just the GAME table, which is shown in Table 11.9.

But if we want display the team nicknames, we also need information from the TEAM table. A feature of this query that we have not encountered before is that each row of the query output needs to contain information from two different rows of the TEAM table, one for the home team and one for the visiting team. We set up this query as follows:

```
SELECT  HOMETEAM.Nickname, HomeScore,
        VISITTEAM.Nickname, VisitScore
FROM    GAME, TEAM AS HOMETEAM, TEAM AS VISITTEAM
WHERE   GAME.HomeTeamID = HOMETEAM.TeamID AND
        GAME.VisitTeamID = VISITTEAM.TeamID;
```

Here, the FROM clause specifies that each row of output is based on a record from the GAME table, a record from TEAM table that is given the name HOMETEAM, and another record from the TEAM table that is given the name VISITTEAM. This is the first time we have seen AS used outside the SELECT clause: in the FROM clause, it gives a second, "alias" name to the table specifier that precedes it. The WHERE clause then enforces the following

Table 11.9 The GAME table.

Games					
GameID	**DatePlayed**	**HomeTeamID**	**HomeScore**	**VisitTeamID**	**VisitScore**
G001	9/5/2015	T01	4	T04	2
G002	9/5/2015	T02	2	T05	0
G003	9/5/2015	T03	4	T06	4
G004	9/12/2015	T07	1	T01	4
G005	9/12/2015	T02	2	T03	0
G006	9/12/2015	T04	2	T05	3
G007	9/19/2015	T05	1	T01	0
G008	9/19/2015	T06	4	T02	0
G009	9/19/2015	T07	3	T04	3
G010	9/26/2015	T01	5	T02	3
G011	9/26/2015	T03	2	T04	0
G012	9/26/2015	T05	3	T07	3
G013	10/2/2015	T06	2	T07	1

commonsense constraints: GAME.HomeTeamID = HOMETEAM.TeamID specifies that the TEAM record called HOMETEAM really does correspond to the home team of the GAME record, and by specifying GAME.VisitTeamID = VISITTEAM.TeamID, we require that the TEAM record called VISITTEAM really does correspond to the game record's visiting team. After application of the WHERE clause, the data source consists of records from the GAME table, each concatenated with the TEAM record for its home team, and also with the TEAM record for its visiting team. Running the query produces the output shown in Table 11.10.

Whenever a query's data source contains two records from the same table, we must use an AS modifier to assign an alias to at least one of them, or references to the table become ambiguous: if we had just written FROM GAME, TEAM, TEAM, SQL would have no way of telling which of the two TEAM records was being requested by an expression like TEAM.TeamID. In this particular query, we went further and applied AS modifiers to both TEAM records to make the query more understandable. Using an AS modifier in the FROM clause makes the alias it defines available in the rest of the query; this use of AS is unlike column labels defined by AS in the SELECT clause, which (in Access) are not usable elsewhere in the query.

Table 11.10 Output of query showing games with the nicknames of both participating teams.

HOMETEAM.Nickname	HomeScore	VISITTEAM.Nickname	VisitScore
Rockets	4	Hurricanes	2
Comets	2	Tornadoes	0
Bulldogs	4	Gators	4
Seminoles	1	Rockets	4
Comets	2	Bulldogs	0
Hurricanes	2	Tornadoes	3
Tornadoes	1	Rockets	0
Gators	4	Comets	0
Seminoles	3	Hurricanes	3
Rockets	5	Comets	3
Bulldogs	2	Hurricanes	0
Tornadoes	3	Seminoles	3
Gators	2	Seminoles	1

Another Use for AS in the FROM Clause

A different, less sophisticated use of AS is to condense a long or awkward table name. For example (for a different, hypothetical database), we could condense a query like

```
SELECT SuperLongTableName.Date, OtherTable.Quantity
FROM   SuperLongTableName, OtherTable
WHERE  SuperLongTablename.ProductID = OtherTable.ProductID;
```

to:

```
SELECT SLT.Date, OtherTable.Quantity
FROM   SuperLongTableName AS SLT, OtherTable
WHERE  SLT.ProductID = OtherTable.ProductID;
```

Here, the AS modifier simply makes the query more concise.

An Introduction to Query Chaining and Nesting

The standard sequence of operations in a SQL query is extremely powerful, and you can use it to implement highly sophisticated queries. But it cannot manage every possible task. In the plumbing store database from

Chapter 7, for example, suppose that we want to see a list of customers with each row showing the customer's first name, their last name, and the dollar amount of their largest order (as measured in dollars). Given the way the database has been structured, a single SQL SELECT statement cannot implement this query because it requires two different kinds of aggregation: first we need to add up *Quantity*UnitPrice* for the products in each order to obtain the total dollar amount of each order, and then we have to take the maximum (a different kind of aggregation operation) across the dollar amounts of the orders corresponding to each customer. A single SQL SELECT query has only one aggregation step and so cannot possibly perform this calculation.

Fortunately, relational database systems permit a technique we may call *query chaining*, in which the results of one query may be fed into another query as if they were a table. This technique allows you to piece together a more complicated query out of simpler subqueries.

In this particular case, for example, one can easily combine two queries to produce the result we want. To understand this process, we may start by realizing that if the total order price were included in the ORDERS table, say as an attribute called *OrderPrice*, we would be able to obtain the desired result by a simple aggregation of the CUSTOMER and ORDERS tables, applying the Max ( ) aggregation function to *OrderPrice*. Although we do not actually have such an attribute, we can use a query to compute one by writing:

```
SELECT    OrderID, Sum(Quantity*UnitPrice) AS OrderPrice
FROM      ORDERDETAIL, PRODUCT
WHERE     ORDERDETAIL.ProductID = PRODUCT.ProductID
GROUP BY OrderID;
```

This query produces a table consisting of the ID of each order in the database and its total price, which it calls *OrderPrice*. We save this query and call it ORDERPRICE. If we connect this query to the existing CUSTOMER and ORDERS tables, we can then easily derive what we want, as follows:

```
SELECT    FirstName, LastName,
          Max(OrderPrice) AS BiggestOrder
FROM      CUSTOMER, ORDERS, ORDERPRICE
WHERE     CUSTOMER.CustomerID = ORDERS.CustomerID AND
          ORDERS.OrderID = ORDERPRICE.OrderID
GROUP BY CUSTOMER.CustomerID, FirstName, LastName;
```

This query joins together the CUSTOMER and ORDERS tables in the same way we have seen many times before. However, we also include the query ORDERPRICE in the FROM clause, as if it were a table. In the WHERE clause, the condition ORDERS.OrderID = ORDERPRICE.OrderID links the result of this query to the ORDERS table by matching the *OrderID* fields. We can then use the *OrderPrice* field of the query as if it were an ordinary attribute, applying the Max ( ) function to it. We obtain the result shown in Table 11.11.

Table 11.11 Result of chained query showing each customer's largest order.

First Name	Last Name	BiggestOrder
Benjamin	Masterson	$5,055.90
Mary	Milgrom	$17,931.00
Robert	Goodman	$3,982.95
Margerita	Colon	$4,535.40
Geoffrey	Hammer	$4,183.95
Ashley	Flannery	$5,688.00
Joseph	Brower	$225.85
Xiaoming	Wang	$249.90
Derek	Escher	$2,299.00
Laura	Ng	$742.80
Robert	Sloan	$569.95

If we had decided to just compute and store *OrderPrice* in the ORDERS table whenever an order is finalized, we could have produced the same output with only a single non-chained query. However, we would then be storing redundant information, since *OrderPrice* can be recomputed from other information in the database. In practice, one might opt to allow this modest amount of redundancy in order to simplify a variety of queries. One could also argue that once a customer places an order, its price is a fact experienced by the customer, and should thus be preserved in the database in a way that cannot be inadvertently changed.

Finally, SQL makes it possible to write our chained query as a single "nested" statement. Essentially we can write one query inside another, with a general structure like this:

```
SELECT    FirstName, LastName, Max(OrderPrice) AS BiggestOrder
FROM      CUSTOMER, ORDERS, (Subquery) AS ORDERPRICE
WHERE     CUSTOMER.CustomerID = ORDERS.CustomerID AND
          ORDERS.OrderID = ORDERPRICE.OrderID
GROUP BY CUSTOMER.CustomerID, FirstName, LastName;
```

Here, *Subquery* is a SELECT statement equivalent to the order price query. Specifically, we may write:

```
SELECT     FirstName, LastName, Max(OrderPrice) AS BiggestOrder
FROM       CUSTOMER, ORDERS,
           (SELECT    OrderID,
                      Sum(Quantity*UnitPrice) AS OrderPrice
            FROM      ORDERDETAIL, PRODUCT
            WHERE     ORDERDETAIL.ProductID = PRODUCT.ProductID
            GROUP BY OrderID) AS ORDERPRICE
WHERE      CUSTOMER.CustomerID = ORDERS.CustomerID AND
           ORDERS.OrderID = ORDERPRICE.OrderID
GROUP BY CUSTOMER.CustomerID, FirstName, LastName;
```

This query produces exactly the same result with only one statement, albeit a rather complicated one.

A More Complicated Example of Query Chaining: The League Standings

Let us return now to the sports league database that we studied earlier. A very reasonable thing to want to do with our database is to generate a league standings report showing the games won, lost, and tied by each team. Again, this result is not something that you can easily achieve in a simple SELECT query, despite the numerous options available. However, we can produce the desired results in a fairly straightforward way if we use query chaining. In this section, we will explore one possible way of using query chaining to compute a league standings table.

While computing the entire league standings in one SELECT seems a daunting task, computing just the number of games won by each team is manageable. A reasonable first attempt is as follows:

```
SELECT     TeamID, NickName, Count(GameID) AS Won
FROM       TEAM, GAME
WHERE      (TeamID = HomeTeamID AND HomeScore > VisitScore) OR
           (TeamID = VisitTeamID AND VisitScore > HomeScore)
GROUP BY TeamID, Nickname;
```

Here, we arrange the FROM and WHERE clauses so that we combine each record in the TEAM table with each of the GAME records corresponding to the games that the team won. The FROM clause is a conventional Cartesian join of the TEAM and GAME tables, but the WHERE clause is more interesting. We combine a team record with a game record if the team's *TeamID* matches the game's *HomeTeamID* and the home team won the game, or the team's *TeamID* matches the game's *VisitTeamID* and the visiting team won the game. We end up with a table consisting of the GAME record for each non-tied game, joined with the TEAM record for the winning team. We group this table by *TeamID*, and then display the *TeamID*, the team *Nickname*, and a count of games that we label as Won. Since the AND processes before OR by default, the parentheses in the join condition are not strictly necessary, but we include them for clarity.

Note that we need to group by *Nickname* as well as by *TeamID*, because of the standard SQL convention that any displayed field must be either grouped by or aggregated. This query produces the output shown in Table 11.12.

Table 11.12 Query output showing games won by each team, but omitting winless teams.

TeamID	NickName	Won
T01	Rockets	3
T02	Comets	2
T03	Bulldogs	1
T05	Tornadoes	2
T06	Gators	2

There is one problem with this query, which is that winless teams do not appear at all. To be able to produce a proper standings table, we need every team to appear in the output, with zeroes for winless teams. We have already seen how this kind of issue can be addressed with an outer join: instead of the more comfortable FROM-WHERE pattern, we need to use an outer join to combine records from the TEAM and GAME table, in such a way that we force in at least one record for every team. Thus, we formulate the following query:

```
SELECT    TeamID, NickName, Count(GameID) AS Won
FROM      TEAM LEFT JOIN GAME ON
            (TeamID = HomeTeamID AND
              HomeScore > VisitScore) OR
            (TEAM.TeamID = GAME.VisitTeamID AND
              VisitScore > HomeScore)
GROUP BY TeamID, Nickname;
```

Instead of a Cartesian join, we use LEFT JOIN, with the same complicated condition that we formerly used in the WHERE clause. This join syntax tells the query to join records from the TEAM table for which the complicated condition holds, but for teams for which no game fulfills the complicated condition to include it anyway, with blank game data (this is a somewhat atypical use of LEFT JOIN). However, due to a quirk of Access's SQL interpreter, we get an error message about an "unsupported join condition" unless we fully qualify the references to the *TeamID* and *VisitTeamID* attributes in the second part of the condition. The result of this join is the same as the result of the join in the previous query, except that winless teams are represented by a single record with blank game data.

Next, as earlier in this chapter, we rely on the way Count ( ) works: it counts the number of data elements fed to it, but it does not count blanks. This means that the winless teams, which are represented by only one row of the join with the *GameID* left blank, yield a count of zero. Thus, the output is as shown in Table 11.13.

Table 11.13 Query output correctly showing wins for each team.

TeamID	NickName	Won
T01	Rockets	3
T02	Comets	2
T03	Bulldogs	1
T04	Hurricanes	0
T05	Tornadoes	2
T06	Gators	2
T07	Seminoles	0

Note that all seven teams are now represented, with zeroes for the winless teams. We save this query and call it WINS.

By essentially the same approach, we can make a query to compute the losses of each team. We simply take the Wins query, change the alias *Won* to *Lost*, and reverse the directions of the score comparisons:

```
SELECT    TeamID, NickName,
          Count(GameID) AS Lost
FROM      TEAM LEFT JOIN GAME ON
             (TeamID = HomeTeamID AND
              HomeScore < VisitScore) OR
             (TEAM.TeamID = GAME.VisitTeamID AND
              VisitScore < HomeScore)
GROUP BY TeamID, Nickname;
```

This query produces the output shown in Table 11.14. We save this query under the name LOSSES.

Our next task is to compute the number of tied games. We can accomplish this by changing both "<" operators to "=", but we can also simplify the condition a little:

```
SELECT    TeamID, NickName, Count(GameID) AS Tied
FROM      TEAM LEFT JOIN GAME ON
             (VisitScore = HomeScore AND
                (TeamID = HomeTeamID OR
                 TEAM.TeamID = GAME.VisitTeamID))
GROUP BY TeamID, Nickname;
```

Table 11.14 Query output showing losses for each team.

TeamID	NickName	Lost
T01	Rockets	1
T02	Comets	2
T03	Bulldogs	1
T04	Hurricanes	3
T05	Tornadoes	1
T06	Gators	0
T07	Seminoles	2

Table 11.15 Results of the completed league standings query chain.

Nickname	Won	Lost	Tied
Gators	2	0	1
Rockets	3	1	0
Tornadoes	2	1	1
Bulldogs	1	1	1
Comets	2	2	0
Seminoles	0	2	2
Hurricanes	0	3	1

Again, due to a quirk of the Access SQL interpreter, we need to fully qualify the *TeamID* and *VisitTeamID* references at the end of the join condition. The extra parentheses around the join condition are needed for a similar reason. We save this query under the name TIES.

We now have three queries that respectively compute the wins, losses, and ties for every team, including zeroes when appropriate. Armed with these three queries, it is a simple matter to combine them into the team standings table shown in Table 11.15, by using the following SQL query:

```
SELECT    Wins.Nickname, Won, Lost, Tied
FROM      WINS, LOSSES, TIES
WHERE     WINS.TeamID = LOSSES.TeamID AND
          WINS.TeamID = TIES.TeamID
ORDER BY (Won + 0.5*Tied)/(Won + Lost + Tied) DESC, Lost, Tied;
```

This query is another example of query chaining: in the FROM clause, we simply use the results of other queries as if they were tables. Our new query simply matches up the rows of the output of the wins, losses, and ties queries we have already created. Checking that WINS.TeamID=LOSSES.TeamID and WINS.TeamID=TIES.TeamID automatically implies that LOSSES.TeamID =TIES.TeamID, so we need to check for only two matching keys, not three (we can pick any two pairs that we like). When we display the *Nickname*, we need to qualify it, because all three data sources contain a *Nickname* field (it does not matter which one we choose, since they all have to be the same in each combination passing the WHERE test).

The somewhat complicated ORDER BY expression shows the results in the standard "winning percentage" order: the "winning percentage" is the fraction of its games a team has won, with ties counting as winning half a game. We present the teams in order of winning percentage, with the highest percentage first, hence the DESC modifier. For teams with an identical winning percentage, we follow the convention that teams that have lost fewer games (are "ahead in the loss column") should have higher standing. For teams with identical winning percentages and losses, we then follow the convention that the team that has tied fewer games should be ahead.

We may depict the flow of information in our league standings calculation as in Figure 11.1.

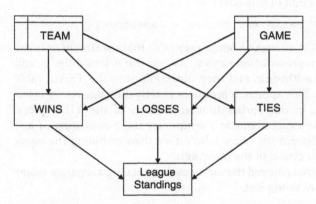

Figure 11.1 Flow of information between tables and queries when computing the league standings.

There are several other ways in which one can combine multiple queries to arrive at a league standings table; we have tried to show what seems to be the conceptually simplest one. In general, when one passes from issuing individual SELECT statements to chaining and combining multiple queries, the process of querying becomes more complicated and starts to acquire the flavor of classical computer programming involving procedural languages like C++, Java, or Python.

Like regular queries, chained queries in Access are "live" functions of the underlying table data. For example, if we had the result of the league standings query open, and we were to enter a new game into the GAME table, the result of the standings query would update essentially instantaneously.

Subqueries and Back to the Plumbing Store Database

As we have already seen, SQL provides a mechanism for writing one SELECT statement inside another. We may call this technique *nested queries* or *subqueries*. To give a further simple illustration of subqueries, here is an alternative way to implement the Ties query from the previous example:

```
SELECT TEAM.TeamID, NickName, Count(GameID) AS Tied
FROM TEAM LEFT JOIN
        (SELECT * FROM GAME
            WHERE VisitScore = HomeScore) AS TiedGames
        ON TEAM.TeamID = TiedGames.HomeTeamID OR
            TEAM.TeamID = TiedGames.VisitTeamID
GROUP BY TEAM.TeamID, Nickname;
```

Here, the subquery portion of this query is:

```
(SELECT * FROM GAME WHERE VisitScore = HomeScore)
```

This expression tells SQL to make a temporary table that consists of only the GAME table rows that represent tied games. We use the AS modifier to call this temporary table TiedGames, and then outer-join it to the TEAM table using the *TeamID* fields. This approach produces exactly the same result as the single complicated join in our earlier implementation of the TIES query. The difference is that we explicitly form a temporary table consisting of just tied games, and then perform the outer join, rather than including the equal score condition in the ON clause of the outer join.

Of course, we could have achieved the same result by having a separate query called TIEDGAMES, containing just

```
SELECT * FROM GAME WHERE VisitScore = HomeScore;
```

and then chaining it to the rest of the query by running:

```
SELECT    TEAM.TeamID, NickName, Count(GameID) AS Tied
FROM      TEAM LEFT JOIN TIEDGAMES ON
            TEAM.TeamID = TIEDGAMES.HomeTeamID OR
            TEAM.TeamID = TIEDGAMES.VisitTeamID
GROUP BY TEAM.TeamID, Nickname;
```

The subquery approach works exactly the same way, but it simply embeds commands generating the "upstream" query into the main, "downstream" query.

Subqueries can also work in a "parameterized" way, which we will illustrate shortly. At this point, we return to the plumbing supply store database from Chapter 7:

Our plumbing supply store needs to keep track of its customers, including their names, address, city, state, zip code, and phone number (assume we do not have a zip code table). We also need to keep track of the products we stock, including name, description, and list price. At any given time, a customer may place an *order* that may consist of more than one product – for example, an order could consist of a bathtub, a sink, and a faucet set.

The solution we have seen to this problem uses four tables, CUSTOMER, ORDERS, PRODUCT, and ORDERDETAIL (which according to several other standard conventions could also be called LINEITEM, ORDERPRODUCT, or QUANTITY), with prices stored in PRODUCT. Suppose that on April 25, we lower the price of a particular sink by changing its *UnitPrice* attribute in the PRODUCT table. If we then try to calculate the total price of an order placed April 18, it will reflect the new price, not the price in effect on April 18. That will be wrong unless we give the customer a retroactive refund.

Redesign the database so it stores the entire price history for each product – that is, for each product, we store all prices we have ever charged, each with the date/time the price became effective.

Our previous solution to this problem looked like the following, with the ER diagram in Figure 11.2:

CUSTOMER(CustomerID, FName, LName, Address, City, State, Zip)

ORDERS(OrderID, CustomerID, OrderDate)
  CustomerID foreign key to CUSTOMER

PRODUCT(ProductID, Namew, UnitsInStock, UnitPrice)

ORDERDETAIL(OrderID, ProductID, Quantity)
  OrderID foreign key to ORDERS
  ProductID foreign key to PRODUCT.

Figure 11.2 ER diagram for the original design of the plumbing store database.

In practice, this design has the defect that it is not consistent in its treatment of time. It records sales activity over time (in the ORDERS and ORDERDETAIL tables), but information about products is stored only "in the now." We know the current units in stock and current unit price, but we do not store the past histories of inventory levels and prices. Suppose we drop the price of a particular sink from \$300 to \$250 on a particular date, say, April 1. If, after April 1, we formulate a query to compute the value of an order from *before* April 1 that contained that particular sink, the query will use the new lower price, which will be incorrect unless we give retroactive refunds. The problem is that *ProductID* is not really sufficient to determine the *UnitPrice* attribute. In order to really know the price for an item, we need to know both what item it was (that is, the *ProductID*, often called the SKU) and the date.

We need a new PRICE entity, in a one-to-many relationship with PRODUCT – that is, for each product, there are many prices, depending on the date. So, we have the following, with the ER diagram in Figure 11.3:

CUSTOMER(<u>CustomerID</u>, FName, LName, Address, City, State, Zip)

ORDERS(<u>OrderID</u>, CustomerID, OrderDate)
   CustomerID foreign key to CUSTOMER

PRODUCT(<u>ProductID</u>, Name, UnitsInStock, UnitPrice)

PRICE(<u>ProductID</u>, <u>EffectiveDate</u>, UnitPrice)
   ProductID foreign key to PRODUCT

ORDERDETAIL(<u>OrderID</u>, <u>ProductID</u>, Quantity)
   OrderID foreign key to ORDERS
   ProductID foreign key to PRODUCT.

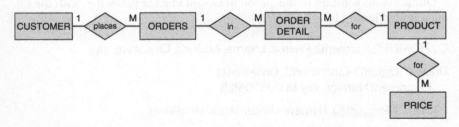

Figure 11.3 ER diagram for the plumbing store database with an additional table for prices.

This design raises the practical question of how often to make entries in the PRICE table. There are several possibilities, of which the conceptually simplest solution is to make a separate entry every day for every product offered for sale; this approach will make queries easy to perform but will lead to a gigantic and constantly growing PRICE table. A more realistic alternative would be to make a single entry each time the price of a product changes.

Suppose you have taken the latter approach of only storing prices when they change, and you want to create a query that gives the *OrderID*, *OrderDate*, customer first and last name, and total price for each order. Basically, we need to group records of the ORDERDETAIL table by order, and sum up *Quantity*UnitPrice* for each group. However, we have to be careful to use the most recent price in effect on or before the date of the order. To find that price, it is convenient to use a subquery:

```
SELECT    ORDERS.OrderID, OrderDate, FirstName, LastName,
          Sum(Quantity*UnitPrice) AS OrderPrice
FROM      CUSTOMER, ORDERS, ORDERDETAIL, PRICE
WHERE     CUSTOMER.CustomerID = ORDERS.CustomerID AND
          ORDERS.OrderID = ORDERDETAIL.OrderID AND
          ORDERDETAIL.ProductID = PRICE.ProductID AND
          EffectiveDate =
             (SELECT Max(EffectiveDate)
              FROM    PRICE
              WHERE   ORDERDETAIL.ProductID = PRICE.ProductID
                      AND EffectiveDate <= Orders.OrderDate)
GROUP BY ORDERS.OrderID, OrderDate, FirstName, LastName;
```

Let us examine the elements of this query one by one. In the FROM clause, we make a Cartesian join of the CUSTOMER, ORDERS, ORDERDETAIL, and PRICE tables. Note that we do not need any attributes in the PRODUCT table for this query, so we can just "shortcut-join" the ORDERDETAIL table to the PRICE table, even though they are not directly adjacent in the ER diagram. The first three WHERE conditions (shown below) simply ensure that the foreign keys match between the CUSTOMER, ORDERS, and ORDERDETAIL records, and that if we match a PRICE record to an ORDERDETAIL record, they pertain to the same product:

```
WHERE   CUSTOMER.CustomerID = ORDERS.CustomerID AND
        ORDERS.OrderID = ORDERDETAIL.OrderID AND
        ORDERDETAIL.ProductID = PRICE.ProductID
```

The last part of the WHERE clause contains the subquery. If we just left the WHERE clause as immediately above, each ORDERDETAIL record would be joined to every price that ever applied to the corresponding product. For example, if there were three different prices for a product (effective on different days), we would get three different combinations of a row from ORDERDETAIL and row from PRICE. Then, when computing Sum(Quantity*UnitPrice) and grouping by *OrderID*, each order line item corresponding to that product would contribute to the sum three times instead of once, and we would get a much larger sum than desired.

To avoid this problem, we want to only join a row of ORDERDETAIL to the price most recently in effect at the time of the order. This is precisely the purpose of the last condition in the WHERE:

```
AND EffectiveDate =
        (SELECT Max(EffectiveDate)
         FROM    PRICE
         WHERE   ORDERDETAIL.PRODUCTID = PRICE.PRODUCTID
                 AND EffectiveDate <= ORDERS.OrderDate)
```

This condition says to join a record from PRICE if its date is the one computed by the subquery enclosed in the parentheses. The `Max(EffectiveDate)` expression in the subquery finds the latest date from the PRICE table that is for the product currently being considered (since `ORDERDETAIL.ProductID = PRICE.ProductID`) and falls on or before the date of the order (because `EffectiveDate <= ORDERS.OrderDate`). Here, the values of the expressions `ORDERDETAIL.ProductID` and `ORDERS.OrderDate` come from the join being performed by the outer main query: thus, they form "parameters" for the subquery, and we can think of the subquery as being performed repeatedly for each record in the ORDERDETAIL table. Because it uses parameters from the surrounding query, this subquery is not interchangeable with a separately saved chained query, as our earlier subquery examples have been.

Practical Considerations and "Bending the Rules" Against Redundancy

The database we just designed above hews strictly to the "official" rule against redundancy, which says that you should not store computed fields that may be recomputed from the base data. In practice, however, one may "bend" this rule somewhat, depending on how easy it is to recompute the required information. If information is relatively difficult to recompute and storing it is not likely to lead to anomalies, we may consider "bending the rules" in the interest of efficiency and convenience. For example, we could imagine duplicating the *UnitPrice* field in the ORDERDETAIL table: whenever an order is finalized, we just copy current *UnitPrice* values from the PRODUCT table into each of the order's ORDERDETAIL records. The database would then remember the exact unit price actually charged to the customer on each order, no matter what subsequent changes were made to the PRICE table. Furthermore, the sales report we just created, and many similar queries, could now be computed without having to resort to query chaining or subqueries. In some sense, we could now be viewed as storing redundant information, but it is relatively difficult to imagine how this particular redundancy could lead to anomalies or other operational problems. Furthermore, we may view ourselves as storing the prices actually experienced by the customer, which are properties of a past event that cannot be altered.

We will not go into great depth, but similar issues are associated with the *UnitsInStock* attribute in the PRODUCT table. Suppose we were to augment the database to keep track of arriving shipments of inventory. Then, we would not, strictly speaking, need the *UnitsInStock* field in the PRODUCT table: to compute the current units in stock for a particular product, we would simply perform a query adding up the quantities of all its prior incoming shipments and subtract from the results the outcome of a query adding up the quantities of all the product's prior sales. For a large database stretching far back in time, however, this process could be quite lengthy and resource-consuming, and we would ideally like inventory-level queries to be easy and quick to perform. So, for practical efficiency, we might again "bend the rules" and keep a current stock level explicitly in the database, even though in principle it is redundant and could be computed from the other available data.

Exercises

11.1 (Bookstore) Download the sample database `bookstore-2000.mdb` from the book website. Write SQL to perform the following queries:

  A Consider all pairs of books with the following properties: they have the same author name, the second book's publication year is later than the first book's, and the second book's retail price is at least $5 more than the first book's retail price. For each such pair, display the author name, first book title, second book title, first book publication year, second book publication year, first book retail price, and second book retail price. Sort the results alphabetically by author name, then by the first book title, and then by the second book title.

  B Show the first name and last name of each customer, and the total number of orders they have placed (labeled *orders_placed*). Customers who have placed no orders should still appear in the output, with zero in the *orders_placed* column.

  C Write a query that retrieves all rows of the *Orders* table that correspond to orders placed in the year 2000. Save it under the name *Orders2000*. Then use it as subquery in a query that shows the first and last name of every customer, and the number of orders they placed in the year 2000. Customers who did not place an order in 2000 should still appear in the output, but with a count of zero.

  D If you just append a WHERE condition on the order dates to your answer for (b), do you obtain exactly the same output as in part (c)? *Briefly* explain why or why not.

11.2 (Conference database): From the textbook website, download the file `conference.mdb`, which describes the sessions and speakers at a conference. Write SQL queries for the following:

  A Show the first name, last name, e-mail address, and area of expertise for every speaker, along with the number of sessions they are speaking in, labeled *NumSessions*. If a speaker is not yet scheduled as appearing in any sessions, they should still appear, but the number of session should be zero. Sort the output from most session appearances to least session appearances; for speakers with the same number of session appearances, sort them alphabetically by last name.

B Show the ID, capacity and number of sessions (labeled *NumSessions*) being held in each room, sorted alphabetically by room ID. Rooms with no sessions should still appear in the output, but with a zero for their number of sessions.

C A "presentation" consists of a speaker appearing in a session. Create a query called *Presentations* which shows, for every presentation in the conference, all the associated fields from the Speakers table and the Sessions table. Using this query as a subquery, write a query that shows the ID of each room, its capacity, and the number of presentations taking place in it.

D Write a query called *SpeakersRooms* that shows every possible combination of *SpeakerID* and *RoomID* for which the speaker is appearing in a session being held in the room. If a speaker is appearing more than once in a room, the combination should only appear once (hint: use SELECT DISTINCT).

E Using the *SpeakersRooms* query from part (d) as a subquery, write a query that shows the first name and last name of each speaker and the number of different rooms in which they are giving presentations (if a speaker is giving multiple talks in the same room, the query should only count the room once). This last information should be labeled *NumDifferentRooms*. Speakers who are not yet scheduled as appearing in any sessions should still appear in the output, but with a *NumDifferentRooms* being zero. The output should be sorted from the largest to smallest number of different rooms. Within speakers speaking in the same number rooms, sort alphabetically by speaker last name.

11.3 (Sports league): Download the sports league database on the book website, and write SQL queries for the following:

A Show the first names, last names, and phone numbers of all players with skill level "A," followed by their team nicknames. Sort the results alphabetically first by team nickname and then by player last name.

B Show the nicknames and number of players for all teams with at least three players, sorted alphabetically by team nickname.

C Create a query producing a list of team IDs and nicknames, with a count of their players whose ranking is either "A" or "B." We want one count per team, including all players who have either ranking. The results should appear sorted by the number of such players, with largest number of players first. Teams with the same number of such players should be listed in alphabetical order by nickname. If a team has no "A"- or "B"-rated players, it need not appear.

D Create a query showing for each game the date played, the home team nickname, the home team score, the visiting team nickname, and the visiting team score. Sort the result from earliest to latest date played, and within the same date played, sort alphabetically by home team nickname.

E Create a query that shows the ID and name of each team, along with the number of home games it has won.

F Create a query that shows the ID and name of each team, along with the number of away games it has won.

G Write a chained query that combines the two previous queries and the TEAM table to produce a table showing the following for each team:

- The team name
- The team colors
- The number of home games the team won, labeled *HomeWins*
- The number of away games the team won, labeled *AwayWins*

Sort the results alphabetically by team nickname.

12

Unary Relationships

This chapter will cover the last topic in this book: situations in which a table is in a relationship "with itself." In relational database theory, this situation is called a *unary relationship*. We will discuss several examples and cover three different aspects of the topic: conceptual design, the mechanics of setting up databases with unary relationships in Access, and the details of formulating SQL queries of such databases.

We begin with a simple one-to-many example of a unary relationship.

Employee Database

Consider the following problem:

> You are creating a database for your company's Human Resources department. Each employee is identified by an ID number, and you want to store each employee's first name, last name, salary, gender, and performance rating.
>
> You also want to keep track of each employee's location and job title. Each employee is assigned to a single location and has a single job title. For each location, you want to store a name, address, state, zip code, and phone number. For each job title, you want to store a name, description, education requirement, minimum required salary, and maximum allowable salary. Assume that you do not want to include a separate zip code table in the database.
>
> Every employee except the CEO has one supervisor (the CEO does not have a supervisor). The database should be able to answer queries like "Who is the supervisor of employee X?", "What are the first and last names of employees who directly supervise at least four other employees?", or "Who are all the employees supervised by somebody whose supervisor is employee Z?"

Introductory Relational Database Design for Business, with Microsoft Access, First Edition.
Jonathan Eckstein and Bonnie R. Schultz.
© 2018 John Wiley & Sons Ltd. Published 2018 by John Wiley & Sons Ltd.

Other than the issue of keeping track of supervisory relationships, this problem consists of familiar material. Let us for the moment set aside the problem of supervisory relationships and model the rest of the database, obtaining the following database, whose ER diagram is shown in Figure 12.1:

Figure 12.1 Entity-relationship (ER) diagram for the employee database (incomplete).

LOCATION(<u>LocationID</u>, LocName, Address, City, State, Zip, Phone)

TITLE(<u>TitleID</u>, TitleName, Description, EdRequired, MinSalary, MaxSalary)

EMPLOYEE(<u>EmployeeID</u>, FirstName, LastName, Salary, Gender, PerfRating,
        LocationID, TitleID)
  LocationID foreign key to LOCATION
  TitleID foreign key to TITLE

The question remains of how to handle supervisor relationships. One's first impulse, taking into account that each employee has at most one supervisor, might be as in the ER diagram in Figure 12.2.

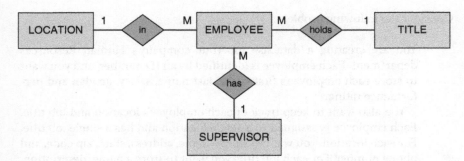

Figure 12.2 ER diagram for the employee database with separate tables for employees and supervisors (not recommended).

LOCATION(<u>LocationID</u>, LocName, Address, City, State, Zip, Phone)

TITLE(<u>TitleID</u>, TitleName, Description, EdRequired, MinSalary, MaxSalary)

EMPLOYEE(<u>EmployeeID</u>, FirstName, LastName, Salary, Gender, PerfRating,
        LocationID, TitleID, SupervisorID)
  LocationID foreign key to LOCATION
  TitleID foreign key to TITLE
  SupervisorID foreign key to SUPERVISOR

SUPERVISOR(<u>SupervisorID</u>, ?????)

As suggested by the "*?????*" above, it is problematic to decide which fields should be in the SUPERVISOR table. Since supervisors are also regular employees, should we repeat all the fields *FirstName, LastName, Salary, Gender, PerfRating, LocationID,* and *TitleID* in the SUPERVISOR table? For people who are both supervisors and have a supervisor of their own, we would then be breaking the basic database design rule of not storing the same information (for example, *Salary*) in more than one table. In a normalized database, storing the same attribute in multiple tables is only permitted for foreign keys, so we would no longer have a normalized database design. To get around this problem, we could instead have a foreign key pointing back to EMPLOYEE, as in:

SUPERVISOR(SupervisorID, EmployeeID)
    EmployeeID foreign key to EMPLOYEE

This setup essentially directs one back to EMPLOYEE table to find specific information about a supervisor and results in the rather peculiar ER diagram of Figure 12.3.

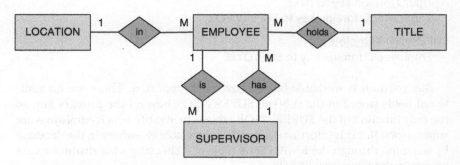

Figure 12.3 More complicated ER diagram for employee database with separate tables for employees and supervisors (also not recommended).

This diagram shows a second one-to-many relationship from EMPLOYEE to SUPERVISOR, reversed from the original one, because that is literally what having an *EmployeeID* foreign key in SUPERVISOR means. The result is rather strange, and conceivably we could have several entries in SUPERVISOR pointing to the same employee. That would mean that several different "supervisors" in the SUPERVISOR table were actually the same person.

To simplify this approach, we may realize that supervisors are just a subset of employees, and use a subtype. Specifically, this means that we do not have to assign supervisors two ID codes, one as employee and one as a supervisor, and then have to manage the relationships between these multiple codes. We can just use the same *EmployeeID* codes to identify supervisors that we use to identify employees, since they are already employees (see Figure 12.4).

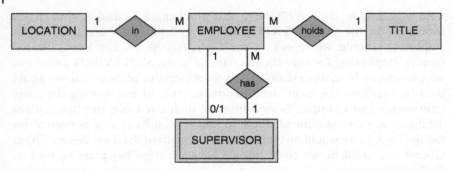

Figure 12.4 Representing supervisors through a subtype.

LOCATION(<u>LocationID</u>, LocName, Address, City, Stat, Zip, Phone)

TITLE(<u>TitleID</u>, TitleName, Description, EdRequired, MinSalary, MaxSalary)

EMPLOYEE(<u>EmployeeID</u>, FirstName, LastName, Salary, Gender, PerfRating,
           LocationID, TitleID, SupervisorID)
  LocationID foreign key to LOCATION
  TitleID foreign key to TITLE
  SupervisorID foreign key to SUPERVISOR

SUPERVISOR(<u>EmployeeID</u>)
  EmployeeID foreign key to EMPLOYEE

This solution is workable but still overly complicated. There are no additional fields stored in the subtype SUPERVISOR beyond the primary key, so the only function of the SUPERVISOR table is to identify which employees are supervisors. But this information is already available elsewhere in the database by scanning through the EMPLOYEE table and checking what distinct values appear in the *SupervisorID* field.

This situation suggests a simpler solution, which is to dispense with the SUPERVISOR table entirely, and just have *SupervisorID* in EMPLOYEE match the primary key of a presumably different record in EMPLOYEE. We describe the database as follows:

LOCATION(<u>LocationID</u>, LocName, Address, City, State, Zip, Phone)

TITLE(<u>TitleID</u>, TitleName, Description, EdRequired, MinSalary, MaxSalary)

EMPLOYEE(<u>EmployeeID</u>, FirstName, LastName, Salary, Gender, PerfRating,
           LocationID, TitleID, SupervisorID)
  LocationID foreign key to LOCATION
  TitleID foreign key to TITLE
  SupervisorID foreign key to EMPLOYEE

This arrangement might seem to "break the rules," but remember that the annotation "*x* foreign key to *Y*" means that "the value of attribute *x* of each record in this table should equal the value of the primary key of some record in table *Y*." There is no restriction that *Y* has to be a different table from the current one. So, "SupervisorID foreign key to EMPLOYEE" means that the value of *SupervisorID* in each record in EMPLOYEE must match the value of the primary key of some (presumably different) record in EMPLOYEE.

This kind of situation is called a *unary relationship* and may be depicted as in Figure 12.5.

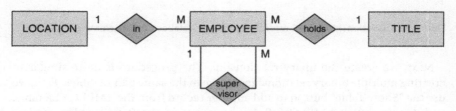

Figure 12.5 ER diagram for the employee database with a unary relationship.

The diagram indicates that the EMPLOYEE table is in a one-to-many relationship with itself. This is a simpler solution; the only advantage to the subtype approach would be if we wanted to pre-designate a subset of employees allowed to be supervisors; then we could use referential integrity to prevent somebody who is not a designated supervisor from being referenced in the *SupervisorID* field.

If an employee does not have a supervisor, then we leave the *SupervisorID* field blank – in this case, only the CEO is in this situation. In Access, fields have a property called "required" that you can set to "no" if you want it be possible to leave the field blank.

Setting Up and Querying a Unary Relationship in Access

We now open the `emp-self-clean.accdb` database from the book website. This database has all the tables defined and contains some sample data, but the relationships are missing. First, we create the standard, "binary" relationships in the usual manner:

1) Click the "Relationships" button on the "Database Tools" ribbon tab.
2) Show all three tables using the "Show Table" button.
3) Draw the usual relationships, and enforce referential integrity (Figure 12.6).

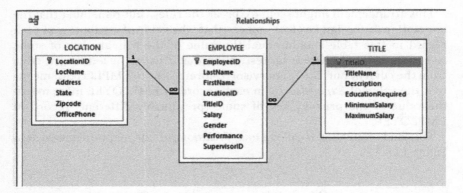

Figure 12.6 Relationships Window for the employee database, before creating the unary relationship.

Next, we create the unary relationship. The procedure is quite similar to creating multiple binary relationships between the same pair of tables. First, we use the "Show Table" button to add another record from the EMPLOYEE table, and Access calls it EMPLOYEE_1 (unfortunately, the Relationships window does not have an alias feature allowing one to choose a more understandable name). See Figure 12.7.

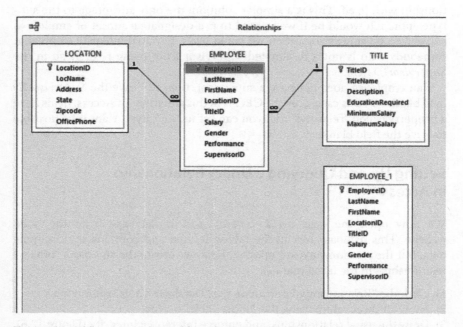

Figure 12.7 Adding a second record from the EMPLOYEE table to the Relationships Window.

Finally we link the *SupervisorID* field in the EMPLOYEE record with the *EmployeeID* field in the EMPLOYEE_1 record, and enforce referential integrity (Figure 12.8).

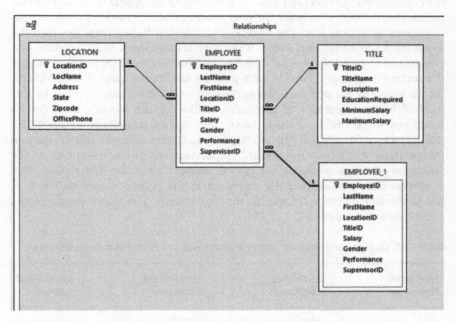

Figure 12.8 Completed employee database Relationships Window showing a unary relationship.

This step completes the process of creating a unary relationship. In the properties of the *SupervisorID* field of the EMPLOYEE table, note that the "required" property is set to "no," to allow some employees (like the CEO) not to have a supervisor; allowing a blank field does not interfere with referential integrity, which is enforced only if the foreign key field is non-blank. When entering additional data into the EMPLOYEE table, we need to be sure that the record for an employee's supervisor exists before filling in that employee's *SupervisorID* field. Otherwise, we would encounter problems with referential integrity. Now let us perform some queries. First, let us produce the following:

- The first name and last name of each person who has a supervisor, along with the first and last name of their supervisor.

To perform this query, we can use the following SQL:

```
SELECT  EMPLOYEE.FirstName, EMPLOYEE.LastName,
        SUPERVISOR.Firstname, SUPERVISOR.LastName
FROM    EMPLOYEE, EMPLOYEE AS SUPERVISOR
WHERE   EMPLOYEE.SupervisorID = SUPERVISOR.EmployeeID;
```

The logic of this query is as follows: each line of output needs to contain information from two different employee records, one for the employee and one for the corresponding supervisor. Formally, writing FROM EMPLOYEE, EMPLOYEE means that the data source for the query consists of a Cartesian join of all possible pairs of records from the EMPLOYEE table, including pairs in which the same exact record appears twice. If we have n employees, this Cartesian join consists of n^2 pairs of records. The AS modifier in the FROM clause assigns the second employee record in each pair the alternative name SUPERVISOR. As we noted in the previous chapter, we can use table aliases created by this method in the remainder of the query, unlike column labels created by AS modifiers in SELECT clauses. Next, the WHERE condition EMPLOYEE. SupervisorID = SUPERVISOR.EmployeeID eliminates all pairs in the join except those for which the second (supervisor) record corresponds to the employee who is supervising the person referred to in the first record. This condition thus ensures that the employee in the second record definitely is the supervisor of the employee in the first record. The query produces the output shown in Table 12.1.

Table 12.1 Query output showing names of employees and names of their supervisors.

EMPLOYEE. FirstName	EMPLOYEE. LastName	SUPERVISOR. FirstName	SUPERVISOR. LastName
Ann	Manin	Pamela	Milgrom
Patricia	Rubin	Pamela	Milgrom
Kenneth	Charles	Pamela	Milgrom
Kelly	Marder	Pamela	Milgrom
Pamela	Milgrom	Tracey	Coulter
James	Johnson	Tracey	Coulter
Susan	Wong	Tracey	Coulter
Marietta	Brown	Tracey	Coulter
David	Adamson	Tracey	Coulter
Billy	Marlin	Tracey	Coulter
Jennifer	Adams	Frank	Smith
Imani	Sumner	David	Adamson
Vernon	Frank	David	Adamson

In this sample dataset, the "big boss" is Tracey Coulter. Note that she does not appear in the left-hand columns, because there is no supervisor to match with her. If we want the "big boss" to appear with blank entries for her supervisor, we must use an outer join instead of a standard Cartesian join / WHERE condition combination (or equivalently an inner join). Using LEFT JOIN, we may write:

```
SELECT  EMPLOYEE.FirstName, EMPLOYEE.LastName,
        SUPERVISOR.Firstname, SUPERVISOR.LastName
FROM    EMPLOYEE LEFT JOIN EMPLOYEE AS SUPERVISOR
        ON EMPLOYEE.SupervisorID =
                SUPERVISOR.EmployeeID;
```

The LEFT JOIN forces every record in the left-hand table (here, the first use of the EMPLOYEE table) to have a representative in the output, even if there is no matching second record satisfying the ON condition; in such cases, all fields in the nonexistent matching right-hand record are treated as blanks. The output of the modified query is the same, except that the "big boss" now appears, joined to blank supervisor information (Table 12.2).

Table 12.2 Query output showing names of employees and supervisors, using an outer join to avoid excluding the highest-level supervisor.

EMPLOYEE. FirstName	EMPLOYEE. LastName	SUPERVISOR. FirstName	SUPERVISOR. LastName
Tracey	Coulter		
Ann	Manin	Pamela	Milgrom
Patricia	Rubin	Pamela	Milgrom
Kenneth	Charles	Pamela	Milgrom
Kelly	Marder	Pamela	Milgrom
Pamela	Milgrom	Tracey	Coulter
James	Johnson	Tracey	Coulter
Susan	Wong	Tracey	Coulter
Marietta	Brown	Tracey	Coulter
David	Adamson	Tracey	Coulter
Billy	Marlin	Tracey	Coulter
Jennifer	Adams	Frank	Smith
Imani	Sumner	David	Adamson
Vernon	Frank	David	Adamson

For our next query, consider the following:

- Show the first name, last name, and location name for all employees whose supervisor is in a different location, along with the first name, last name, and location name for the supervisor.

To set up this query, we need two records from EMPLOYEE and two records from LOCATION, appropriately aliased and related. One EMPLOYEE record is for the employee, and the other for the supervisor; one LOCATION record is for the employee's location, and the other is for the supervisor's location. The SQL is as follows:

```
SELECT  EMPLOYEE.FirstName, EMPLOYEE.LastName,
        LOCATION.LocName,
        SUPERVISOR.FirstName, SUPERVISOR.LastName,
        SUPERVISORLOCATION.LocName
FROM    EMPLOYEE, EMPLOYEE AS SUPERVISOR,
        LOCATION, LOCATION AS SUPERVISORLOCATION
WHERE   EMPLOYEE.SupervisorID = SUPERVISOR.EmployeeID AND
        EMPLOYEE.LocationID = LOCATION.LocationID AND
        SUPERVISOR.LocationID = SUPERVISORLOCATION.LocationID AND
        EMPLOYEE.LocationID <> SUPERVISOR.LocationID;
```

Here, EMPLOYEE, EMPLOYEE AS SUPERVISOR in the FROM clause, along with the first WHERE condition EMPLOYEE.SupervisorID = SUPERVISOR.EmployeeID, perform exactly the same role as in our first query: matching up employees with their supervisors. Since we need to include information from two different records of the LOCATION table, we also include LOCATION, LOCATION AS SUPERVISORLOCATION in the FROM clause. Here, the AS modifier gives an explanatory name to the second record from the LOCATION table. There are also two additional WHERE conditions:

```
EMPLOYEE.LocationID = LOCATION.LocationID AND
SUPERVISOR.LocationID = SUPERVISORLOCATION.LocationID
```

These conditions ensure that the first LOCATION record matches the EMPLOYEE record and that the second LOCATION record matches the SUPERVISOR record. The final WHERE condition EMPLOYEE.LocationID <> SUPERVISOR.LocationID enforces the query's requirement that the employee and supervisor be in different locations. Rather than comparing location names to ensure that the two locations are different, we compare the *LocationID* fields: although it would be unlikely and inadvisable to have two locations with the same name, comparing primary keys makes absolutely sure the locations are different. Note that there are various pairs of *LocationIDs* that we could compare − basically, we have to compare either the field EMPLOYEE.LocationID or the field LOCATION.LocationID (which must equal one another) with either the field SUPERVISOR.LocationID or the field SUPERVISORLOCATION.LocationID (which also must equal one another).

The results of this query are shown in Table 12.3.

Table 12.3 Output of query showing employees and supervisors in different locations.

EMPLOYEE. FirstName	EMPLOYEE. LastName	LOCATION. LocName	SUPERVISOR. FirstName	SUPERVISOR. LastName	SUPERVISOR LOCATION. LocName
Pamela	Milgrom	Boston	Tracey	Coulter	Atlanta
James	Johnson	Chicago	Tracey	Coulter	Atlanta
David	Adamson	Chicago	Tracey	Coulter	Atlanta
Billy	Marlin	Miami	Tracey	Coulter	Atlanta
Kelly	Marder	Chicago	Pamela	Milgrom	Boston
Vernon	Frank	Miami	David	Adamson	Chicago

Next, consider the following query:

- Show the first name, last name, job title, and number of people directly supervised for each person who directly supervises at least four people.

We need two records from EMPLOYEE, one aliased with the name SUPERVISOR, and one record from TITLE, in order to supply the job title. The query required is as follows:

```
SELECT     SUPERVISOR.FirstName, SUPERVISOR.LastName,
           TitleName,
           Count(EMPLOYEE.EmployeeID) AS NumberSupervised
FROM       EMPLOYEE, EMPLOYEE AS SUPERVISOR, TITLE
WHERE      EMPLOYEE.SuperVisorID = SUPERVISOR.EmployeeID AND
           SUPERVISOR.TitleID = TITLE.TitleID
GROUP BY   SUPERVISOR.EmployeeID,
           SUPERVISOR.FirstName, SUPERVISOR.LastName,
           TitleName
HAVING     Count(EMPLOYEE.EmployeeID) >= 4;
```

Here, the join of pairs of records from the EMPLOYEE table and the first WHERE condition `EMPLOYEE.SuperVisorID = SUPERVISOR.EmployeeID` work in exactly the same way as in the previous queries. However, we also join a single record from the TITLE table, making sure that it corresponds to the supervisor, rather than the employee, by specifying the WHERE condition `SUPERVISOR.TitleID = TITLE.TitleID`. In this query, however, we need to perform aggregation. We group by *EmployeeID* from SUPERVISOR and then count the number of employees in each group using the `Count()` function. Although `EMPLOYEE.EmployeeID` is an intuitive attribute to use within `Count()`, any field that is guaranteed to be non-blank would serve just as well. In the GROUP BY clause, we include `SUPERVISOR.EmployeeID` so that there is no possibility of two supervisors with the same name being consolidated into a single group (although that will not happen in this specific sample dataset). By the conventions of standard SQL, we must also group by the other attributes displayed outside an aggregation function, even though every one of them is determined by SUPERVISOR.EmployeeID.[1] Finally, we use a HAVING clause to filter out supervisors with fewer than four subordinates. This filtering cannot be performed by a WHERE condition, because the relevant information becomes known only after aggregation.

The output is shown in Table 12.4.

Table 12.4 Output of query showing employees who directly supervise at least four others.

FirstName	LastName	Title	Number Supervised
Pamela	Milgrom	Manager	4
Tracey	Coulter	Manager	6

Finally, consider the following:

- Show the first name and last name of everybody at least two levels down in the management hierarchy, along with the first and last name of their supervisor's supervisor.

This query requires *three* records from EMPLOYEE, appropriately related and aliased. The SQL implementation is as follows:

```
SELECT EMPLOYEE.FirstName, EMPLOYEE.LastName,
       BOSSOFBOSS.FirstName, BOSSOFBOSS.LastName
FROM   EMPLOYEE, EMPLOYEE AS BOSS, EMPLOYEE AS BOSSOFBOSS
WHERE  EMPLOYEE.SupervisorID = BOSS.EmployeeID AND
       BOSS.SupervisorID = BOSSOFBOSS.EmployeeID;
```

For brevity, we use the alias BOSS instead of SUPERVISOR and call the record for the supervisor's supervisor BOSSOFBOSS. We join the first two EMPLOYEE-table records much as in the earlier queries, except for this name change, and then we join the BOSSOFBOSS record to the BOSS record in much the same way: a record corresponds to a "boss of boss" if its *EmployeeID* matches the *SupervisorID* of the boss. The output of the query is shown in Table 12.5.

---

1 In some SQL implementations, as we have mentioned before, this extra grouping is not required.

Table 12.5 Output of query showing employees and their supervisors' supervisors.

EMPLOYEE. FirstName	EMPLOYEE. LastName	BOSSOFBOSS. FirstName	BOSSOFBOSS. LastName
Ann	Manin	Tracey	Coulter
Patricia	Rubin	Tracey	Coulter
Kenneth	Charles	Tracey	Coulter
Kelly	Marder	Tracey	Coulter
Jennifer	Adams	Tracey	Coulter
Imani	Sumner	Tracey	Coulter
Vernon	Frank	Tracey	Coulter

The Course Catalog Database

We consider the following problem:

> A university is transferring its course catalog to an automated online system. Courses are offered by departments, which are identified by codes of between two and four letters, such as ENG for English, MATH for mathematics, JOUR for journalism, or CS for computer science. For each department, we want to store a name, description, and the location and phone number of the department office.
>
> The college has a notion of a *degree-granting program*, which is not identical to a department. Each degree-granting program is administered by a single department, but a department can run more than one program. For example, the computer science department offers a regular bachelor's degree in computer science and a certificate in website administration. For each program, we want to store its name, description, and type of degree (such as certificate, bachelor's, master's, or doctoral).
>
> Each department offers multiple courses, identified by the department code and an additional three-digit number: for example ENG 412, CS 111, or MATH 201. For each course, we want to store a name and description.
>
> Each program has a set of required courses, which may be from various departments. It also has a required number of electives and a set of allowed elective courses.
>
> Some courses have prerequisites: for example, students must complete CS 111 before enrolling in CS 112, or ENG 101 before enrolling in JOUR 200. Some courses have more than one prerequisite, and some are prerequisites for more than one other course.

You wish to create a database storing the above information and describing the relationships between courses, departments, and programs, along with the prerequisite relationships between courses. Write a database outline, and draw an ER diagram.

The main entities in this problem are DEPARTMENT, PROGRAM, and COURSE. Each course is offered by a single department, and each program is administered by a single department, so we have two standard one-to-many relationships. The relationship between courses and programs is many-to-many, because a program clearly can have more than one course, and a course can be in more than one program. Setting aside for the moment the issue of course prerequisites, we have the design shown below (see Figure 12.9):

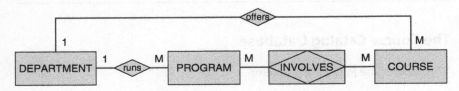

Figure 12.9 ER diagram of course catalog database without course prerequisite information.

DEPARTMENT(<u>DeptCode</u>, Name, Description, Location, Phone)

PROGRAM(<u>ProgramID</u>, Name, Description, Type, DeptCode, NumElectives)
  DeptCode foreign key to DEPARTMENT

COURSE(<u>DeptCode</u>, <u>CourseNum</u>, Name, Description)
  DeptCode foreign key to DEPARTMENT

INVOLVES(<u>ProgramID</u>, <u>DeptCode</u>, <u>CourseNum</u>, Required)
  ProgramID foreign key to PROGRAM
  (DeptCode, CourseNum) foreign key to COURSE

Here, we use the composite key (*DeptCode*, *CourseNum*) for courses, with a matching composite foreign key in INVOLVES, because this is a very natural way for people to refer to courses. We could also use a synthetic key for COURSE, which would simplify the INVOLVES table. In the INVOLVES table, *Required* is a yes/no field indicating whether a course is required for a program; if its value is "no," then the course is an elective for the program.

One could also model required and elective courses as two different, parallel, many-to-many relationships between PROGRAM and COURSE, but doing so would have a number of drawbacks: it is more complicated, we would not automatically implement the inherent constraint that a course cannot be both elective and required for the same program, and certain queries would become much more difficult to perform, possibly requiring query chaining. Note that *NumElectives* is a property of a program and is thus stored in the PROGRAM table. Strictly speaking, it is not necessary to store the number of required courses for a program, since we can determine this number by simply counting matching required courses in INVOLVES.

Now consider the matter of courses being prerequisites for other courses. A course could conceivably have multiple prerequisites and could in turn be a prerequisite for several other courses. So, we must have some kind of many-to-many relationship. We should not introduce a new entity for prerequisites, because prerequisites are just courses, and all their attributes are already stored in the COURSE table. The most straightforward thing to do is to introduce an additional table:

PREREQ(<u>DeptCode</u>, <u>CourseNum</u>, <u>PrereqDept</u>, <u>PrereqNum</u>)
   (DeptCode, CourseNum) foreign key to COURSE
   (PrereqDept, PrereqNum) foreign key to COURSE

The presence of a record in this table indicates that course (*PrereqDept*, *PrereqNum*) is a prerequisite for course (*DeptCode*, *CourseNum*). For example, if PREREQ contains the record (JOUR, 200, ENG, 101), that indicates that ENG 101 is a prerequisite for JOUR 200.

In essence, we have put COURSE into a many-to-many relationship with itself, much as the previous example put EMPLOYEE in a one-to-many relationship with itself. The ER diagram with the additional PREREQ table is shown in Figure 12.10.

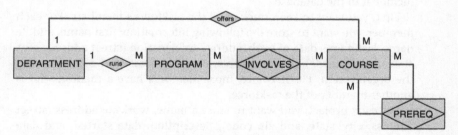

Figure 12.10 ER diagram for the course catalog database using a unary many-to-many relationship.

Recalling that a many-to-many relationship can also be depicted as two one-to-many relationships, another way to depict this exact same arrangement of tables would be as in Figure 12.11.

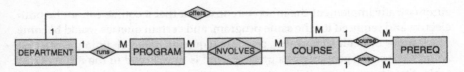

Figure 12.11 Depicted with one-to-many relationships, a unary many-to-many relationship looks the same as a two-to-many relationship.

Note that, displayed in this manner, the binary many-to-many relationship results in exactly the same diagram pattern as a "two-to-many" relationship, for example, the origin and destination airport of a flight in a flight schedule database.

If we had used a synthetic key for COURSE, then the PREREQ and INVOLVES would look simpler, but the overall structure of the database would be the same.

Exercises

12.1 Sustainability taskforce: You have signed on as a member of Sustainability Taskforce, which sponsors ecologically oriented community projects of various kinds (such as building and distributing composters or constructing energy-efficient low-income housing). You have volunteered to start building a relational database to replace the hodgepodge of spreadsheets currently being used to track membership and projects. Assume you have access to a zip code table and plan to include it in the database.

First, you want to keep track of all the taskforce's members. For each member, you want to store the following information: first name, middle name, last name, date of birth, address information (street address, city, state, and zip code), phone number, e-mail address, and date of joining the organization. Furthermore, most members have a mentor, who is another member of the taskforce.

For each project, you want to store a name, worksite address (street address, city, state, and zip code), description, date started, and date ended (blank if the project is still ongoing). Furthermore, you want the database to remember which members are involved in each project: a project can involve as few as 1 member and in some cases as many as 25. A small number of the members involved in each project are designated project leaders; usually there is just one leader per project, but for some larger projects there may be two or three.

Design a database to hold the information described above. Draw an ER diagram, and write a database design outline.

12.2 Company ownership and boards: A government regulatory agency is trying to track the relationships between a large number of companies and individuals. For the purposes of this exercise, assume that the agency is interested only in the present state of these relationships, and not in how they may have changed over time. For each individual, you want to store the social security number, first name, last name, middle name/ initial, date of birth, address, city, state, zip code, e-mail address, and phone number. Assume the agency wants to include a zip code table in the database. For each company, you want to store a tax ID number, name, mailing address, city, state, and zip code. Assume that all individual and company addresses are within the United States.

The agency wants to understand the ownership relationships between the individuals and companies. The system should record the companies in which each individual owns stock, and how many shares are involved. Furthermore, some of the companies hold stock in other companies. You want to record each such situation, including the number of shares held. In addition to stock ownership, an individual may also be related to a company by membership on its board of directors. You want the system to record all such board memberships.

Design a database to hold all this information. Draw an ER diagram, and write a database design outline.

12.3 Products, features, and substitute products: Your firm manufactures a variety of specialized data networking equipment. Each product has a unique model number, a description, and a date introduced. For each product, you also want to the database to keep a pricing history: a set of list prices for the product, each with the date that the price became effective. For each product, you also maintain a list of "features"; each feature has an ID and a description. A product may have many different features, and many different products may have the same feature. For each product, there is a single designated "best substitute" product you offer customers when you are out of stock. You want the database to remember the designated best substitute for each product.

Design a database to store this information. Draw an ER diagram, and write a database design outline. You may add "ID" fields where necessary.

12.4 Biomedical citation index: Your firm maintains a citation index of biomedical journal articles used by a variety of medical research institutes and pharmaceutical firms. Each article is identified by a unique "DOI number"; in addition to this number, you want the database to store each article's title, abstract, date of publication, journal volume number, journal issue number, and journal pages. Each article is authored by one or more researchers. For each researcher, your database should store a family name, given name, date of birth, and current employer. The database should remember which researchers authored each article, and the order they appear in the article writing credits.

Each article appears in a single journal, and each journal is identified by a unique "ISSN" number. The database should be able to identify which journal each article appeared in. Furthermore, for each journal, the database should remember its name and the name of the organization that publishes it. Sometimes journals change names, and one journal "continues" another journal. For example, the *ORSA Journal on Biomedical Computation* might become the *INFORMS Journal on Biomedical Computation* when its publishing organization merges with another organization. The name change makes it a different journal, but the database should be able to remember which journal (if any) "continues" any given journal.

Finally, articles usually contain multiple citations to other articles. For example, an article about clinical treatment of a particular disease might contain citations to dozens of prior research articles about that disease. This information can be very useful to researchers, so the database should be able to store the full pattern of citations between articles. Note that an article not only usually cites many other articles but may also be cited by many other articles.

Design a database to store this information. Draw an ER diagram, and write a database design outline. You may add "ID" fields where necessary.

12.5 SQL queries with a unary relationship: Download the sample database `emp-self.accdb` database from the book website. Write and run SQL code for each of the queries specified below. Make sure all your queries would still work correctly if two different employees can have the same first and last names.

A All cases in which an employee has a higher salary than his or her supervisor. Include the first name, last name, and salary for both the employee and the supervisor.

B The first name, last name, and salary of all supervisors, and the average salary of the employees they directly supervise (labeled *AvgReportSalary*).

C Show the employee first name, employee last name, supervisor first name, supervisor last name, and job title (not *TitleID*) for all employees who have the same job title as their supervisor. Display the list in alphabetical order by employee last name.

D For every employee, list their first name, last name, and the number of other employees that they supervise. This last column should have the column heading *NumberReports* and show a "0" for employees that do not supervise any other employees. The output should be ordered starting with the largest number of people supervised and ending with the smallest. Within this ordering, each group of employees supervising the same number of people should be listed in alphabetical order by last name. (Hint: Employ an outer join and set up the Count () function so that it does not count blanks.)

E A more advanced exercise: Enhance the query of part (a) to show the number of people directly supervised by the employee and the number of people directly supervised by the employee's supervisor, in both cases showing "0" if there are no such people. (Hint: Use the query created in part (d) as if it were a table, a form of query chaining).

12.6 Normalizing employee records: Consider Table 12.6, which contains information about sales representatives. Each sales representative has a backup who automatically gets their calls if they are not available. An employee's backup does not have to be at the same location.

Table 12.6 Data for employee database normalization exercise.

Employee ID	Employee Name	Phone Extension	Location ID	Location Name	Backup ID	Backup Name
101	Yu-ran Chen	2789	L01	Albany	102	William Klimpton
102	William Klimpton	2456	L01	Albany	101	Yu-Ran Chen
103	Latisha Hemmings	3487	L03	Chicago	101	Yu-Ran Chen
104	Mohan Kahn	3876	L03	Chicago	103	Latisha Hemmings
105	Venkat Patel	4678	L02	Atlanta	102	William Klimpton
106	Joseph Hawes	4762	L02	Atlanta	105	Venkat Patel
107	Charles Rowes	7653	L04	Dallas	106	Joseph Hawes
108	John Watson	7329	L04	Dallas	101	Yu-Ran Chen
109	Amy Katsima	7322	L04	Dallas	107	Charles Rowes

Convert this data table into a third-normal-form database without any redundancy except foreign keys, keeping in mind that you may need to use a unary relationship. Draw an ER diagram, and write a database design outline.

12.7 **Movie catalog:** To make the Sickle and Evert movie guide easier to maintain, your firm is trying to create a database from which future editions of the guide will be generated. For each movie, you want to store its title, date of first release, critics' rating (between 0 and 5 stars), motion picture rating (G, PG, PG-13, R, or NC-17), plot synopsis, and critic review. The plot synopsis and critic review are each large text fields. You also assign movies to categories, such as "action," "animated," and so forth. For each category, there is a three-letter code, a name, and a description. A movie may fall into more than one category: for example, *Spaceballs* is both "science fiction" (code SFI) and "comedy" (code COM).

Each movie has exactly one director and any number of actors. The system should be able to list the director and all actors for each movie. Sometimes the same person will both direct movies and act in them. For each person (director, actor, or both), you want to store a first name, last name, middle name/initial, date of birth, nationality, and date of death (if any).

Sometimes a movie is a sequel to another movie: for example, *The Two Towers* is the sequel to *Fellowship of the Ring*. The database should also keep track of such sequel relationships between movies, assuming each movie can be the direct sequel of at most one other movie. Draw an ER diagram, and write a database design outline.

12.8 **Oceanographic institute:** You are volunteering at the Oak Hollow Oceanographic Institute, which is setting up a study of marine species in the Cape May, NJ area. The scientists at Oak Hollow are trying to understand the complexities of the local marine food chain. You want to keep information on scientific staff at the institute and the various local marine species they study. For each staff member, you want to store a first name, last name, date hired, cell-phone number, and e-mail address. Some staff members supervise other staff members, but each staff member has at most one supervisor; you want the database to store the supervisory relationships among staff.

For each species you want to store each species' scientific name, common name, estimated local population, and typical lifespan. For each species, you also want to record multiple observation events, each of which has a date/time, latitude, longitude, comments, and which staff member made the observation. For each species, you also want the database to be able to record which species it is known to prey upon.

For example, the great white shark is known to prey on both harbor seals and dolphins. Naturally, one species may prey on many others and may itself be preyed upon by more than one other species.

Design a database that will store this information. Draw an ER diagram, and write a database design outline. You may add "ID" fields where necessary.

12.9 Salespeople and alternates: You operate a sales organization selling a product to corporate customers. For each salesperson in your organization, you would like to store a first name, last name, base salary, and date hired. You have divided the country into a number of geographic territories, each assigned to a single salesperson. For each territory, you want to store both a description and information indicating which other territories it is adjacent to. For example, the Northern New Jersey territory is adjacent to the Northeast Pennsylvania, Central New Jersey, New York City, and Southeast New York State territories. A salesperson may have more than one territory, but each territory is assigned to a single salesperson. For each customer, you want to store a company name, address, city, state, zip code, and phone number. Each customer lies in exactly one territory. Finally, each salesperson designates a single "alternate" to handle their affairs when he or she is on vacation or sick leave. Design a database to store all this information. Draw an ER diagram, and write a database design outline.

12.10 Pet ownership and genealogy: You maintain ownership and genealogy records for the national basset hound thoroughbred dog registry, keeping information on people and dogs. Each person has an ID number, first name, middle name, last name, address, city, state, and zip code. Each dog is owned by a single person and has a name and a unique ID number. For each dog, you also want to store a name, date of birth, and gender. Finally, for each dog, you want to be able to identify its mother and father, which are, of course, other dogs. Draw an ER diagram, and write a design outline for the required database.

Further Reading

This text is an example-based exploration of relational database design, SQL, and Microsoft Access. We have found our example-centered format to be the best means of entry into the subject for readers without an extensive computing or mathematics background. While providing a good foundation, this format does not support the exploration of every specific aspect of the subject matter. To expand and deepen your knowledge, we suggest the following additional readings.

Database Theory and Design

- Thomas Connolly and Caroline Begg: *Database Systems: A Practical Approach to Design, Implementation and Management*, Pearson, 2009.
- C. J. Date: *An Introduction to Database Systems*, 8th edition, Pearson, 2003. This book, whose first edition was published in 1975, is often considered the "bible" of relational databases. Date's book takes a somewhat abstract, mathematical perspective. Other books of interest by C. J. Date include *Type Inheritance and Relational Theory: Subtypes, Supertypes and Substitutability; SQL and Relational Theory: How to Write Accurate SQL Code;* and *Database Design and Relational Theory: Normal Forms and All That Jazz (Theory in Practice).*
- Mark L. Gillenson: *Fundamentals of Database Management Systems*, Wiley, 2005.
- David M. Kroenke and David J. Auer: *Database Processing: Fundamentals, Design and Implementation*, 13th edition, Prentice-Hall, 2013.
- Gavin Powell: *Beginning Database Design*, Wiley, 2006. While this text does not assume prior knowledge of database design, it is oriented toward those with significant prior computer experience.
- Richard T. Watson: *Database Management: Databases and Organizations*, eGreen Press, 2013.

Introductory Relational Database Design for Business, with Microsoft Access, First Edition.
Jonathan Eckstein and Bonnie R. Schultz.
© 2018 John Wiley & Sons Ltd. Published 2018 by John Wiley & Sons Ltd.

SQL

- Alan Beaulieu: *Learning SQL: Master SQL Fundamentals*, O'Reilly and Associates, 2009. This book covers SQL in general but with a focus on the open-source MySQL database management system.
- Pindaro E. Demertzoglu: *Microsoft Access SQL Comprehensive*, Alpha Press, 2012. A very detailed treatment of SQL, with a focus on Microsoft Access.
- John Viescas and Michael J. Hernandez: *SQL Queries for Mere Mortals*: *A Hands-On Guide to Data Manipulation in SQL*, Addison-Wesley, 2014.

Microsoft Access

- Michael Alexander and Richard Kusleika: *Access 2016 Bible*, Wiley, 2015.
- Matthew MacDonald: *Access 2013: The Missing Manual*, O'Reilly and Associates, 2013.
- Microsoft Official Academic Course: *Microsoft Access 2013 Exam 77-424*, Wiley, 2014.
- Mary Anne Poatsy, Eric Cameron, and Jerri Williams: *Exploring Microsoft Office Access 2016 Comprehensive*, Pearson, 2017.

Management Information Systems in General

- David M. Kroenke: *Using MIS*, 7th edition, Pearson, 2014.
- Kenneth C. Laudon and Jane P. Laudon: *Management Information Systems: Managing the Digital Firm*, 13th edition, Pearson, 2014.

Index

a

advanced query techniques 253
aggregation 110, 151, 228, 230, 235,
    242, 256, 263, 289
  conditions after 237
  criteria after 248
  with grouping 246
  in reports 25
analytical processing 45
AND operator 31, 218, 226
anomalies 63
  deletion 47
  fixing 65
  insertion 47
  update 46
application 3
artificial intelligence (AI) 1
ascending order 28, 240
ASC modifier 240, 261
AS modifier
  in FROM clause 260–262, 286, 288
  in SELECT clause 149, 217,
    232, 238
atomic datum 54, 59, 76, 189, 198
attributes 7, 49, 53–54, 61, 71, 75, 189
Autonumber 12, 34, 36, 57
  keys 119
Avg function 37, 228–229, 237

b

border style property 25
Boyce–Codd normal form 197
bubble diagram 61
business rules 1
Byte datatype 33

c

calculated field 12
  on a form 18, 21
  in a query 29
candidate key 56, 61, 64, 198
Cartesian join 122, 221, 222, 241,
    265, 286
  unintentional 226
cascading deletes 100
cascading updates 100
CBIS (computer-based information
    system) 2
columnar layout 19, 128
columns 7, 12, 53
  order 54
combo box 19, 21, 129, 131, 135–137
  with fixed values 20
composite foreign key 179
composite key 55
composite primary key 56, 62, 70, 77,
    142, 179, 192

Introductory Relational Database Design for Business, with Microsoft Access, First Edition.
Jonathan Eckstein and Bonnie R. Schultz.
© 2018 John Wiley & Sons Ltd. Published 2018 by John Wiley & Sons Ltd.

concatenated key   55
concatenation   55
Count function   228, 230, 257, 267, 289
  in a report   25
course catalog database example   291
create a database   10
cross join   222
Currency datatype   34
  avoiding use of $ signs or
    quotes   108, 243
customer loans database   68

d
data   1
  accuracy   44
  coordination   44
  dispersal   44
  fusion   44
  management   43
  management issues, general   45
  quality   44
  security   44
  warehouse   46
database
  anomalies   63
  design   43
  design guidelines   202
  good design principles   66
  object   7
  relational, basic theory of   53
  relational, fundamentals of   7
Datasheet View
  of a query   27
  for a subform   102
  of a table   14
datatype   8, 54
  Autonumber   12
  Currency   34
  Date/Time   14
  Long Text   13
  matching with autonumber
    key   119
  Memo   13

Number   14
Number, Byte   33
Number, Double   14
Number, Integer   14
Number, Long Integer   14
Number, Single   14
Short Text   13
table of common choices in MS
  Access   32
Yes/No   14
Date/Time datatype   14, 34, 77
  quoting with # characters   31, 107, 221
datum   1, 54
decision support   5, 45
deletion anomaly   47, 64
departmental information systems
  (DIS)   5
dependency
  diagram   61
  partial   62
  transitive   63
DESC modifier   239
Design View   103
  of a form   15
  of a query   31
  of a report   24
  of a table   11, 54
Detail section of a report   24
determinant   61
Documenter   123
Double datatype   14, 33
DSS (decision support system)   5
DVD lending library example
  entity-relationship diagram   72
  with loan history   75
  without loan history   71
dynasets   26

e
e-Commerce   5
EIS *see* executive information
  systems (EIS)
electronic commerce   5

employee database example 279
Enforce Referential Integrity 96
enterprise resource planning (ERP) 5
enterprise resource planning
   systems 5
entities 48, 53, 71
entity-relationship diagram 49, 59
   with many-to-many
      relationships 142
   with multiple relationships between
      the same pair of tables 174
   with subtypes 80
   with unary relationships 283
entity-relationship modeling 48
ephemeral tables 26
ER modeling *see* entity-relationship
   modeling
ERP *see* enterprise resource
   planning (ERP)
ES *see* expert systems (ES)
executive information systems (EIS) 5
expert systems (ES) 5

f
field 7, 49, 53
   calculated 12
   in Form Wizard 19
   properties 13–14
   size 13–14
fifth normal form (5NF) 197
financial services database
      example 189
First function 228
first normal form (1NF) 189
flat file database 7
focus groups example 139
Footer
   Form 17
   Group 25
   Report 25
foreign key 48, 50, 57–58
   annotation 50, 59
   annotation, exact meaning of 82, 174

composite 179
datatype and size 119
name of 82, 174, 283
placement in many-to-many
   relationships 141
setting up in Access 96
in SQL 219, 223
in a subtype 80
for a unary relationship 283
Form 15, 127
   Design View 15
   Form View 15, 20
   nested 101
   Wizard 19, 127, 130
Format
   property of text box 18
fourth normal form (4NF) 197
FROM clause 108, 215, 221, 241,
   260, 262
functional area(s) 4
functional area information systems
   (FAIS) 5
functional dependency 60

g
good database design principles 66
GROUP By clause 153, 231, 242
Group By in query grid 110
grouping
   in a query 110, 114, 151, 153
   in a report 25
Group & Sort feature of
   reports 25

h
hardware 2
HAVING clause 237, 242, 290
header
   Form 15, 20, 129
   group, in a report 23–24
   navigation form 132
   subform 131
hierarchical data 48, 102, 190

i

information   1
  architecture   3
  infrastructure   3
  systems   2
  technology   2
Ingres   7
inner join   105, 122, 218, 222, 225–226
  multiple   109, 225
INNER JOIN clause   105, 122, 153,
    225, 241
input mask   13, 99, 119
insertion anomaly   47, 64
Integer datatype   14, 33
interorganizational system (IOS)   5

j

join   50, 66, 241, 253
  Cartesian   122
  between a Form and Subform   102
  inner   105
  left   253
  line in query grid   104
  multiple   108
  multiple records from same table   260
  outer   105
  right   255
  shortcut   181
  of table to itself   286

k

key
  autonumbering   119
  candidate   56
  composite primary   56
  foreign   57
  simple primary   56
  synthetic   57
knowledge   1

l

Last function   228
Layout View of a form   15

left join   105
LEFT JOIN clause   107, 253, 266, 287
level
  operational   3
  strategic   3
  tactical   4
library example   159
Long Integer datatype   14, 33
  matching autonumber keys   119
long or awkward table name   262
Long Text datatype   13, 33

m

management information system
    (MIS)   5
many-to-many relationship   139
  in Access   147
  equivalence to two one-to-many
    relationships   142
  with 'flavors' of membership   154
  with a quantity field   143
  unary   293
Max function   228
Memo datatype   13
Microsoft Excel   7
Min function   228, 237
MIS *see* management information
    system (MIS)
multi-path pattern of
    relationships   117
multiple joins   108
multiple sorting criteria   28, 239–240
MySQL   7

n

Navigation   132
nested forms   101
nested table view   100
normalization   67, 189
  degrees of   189
  financial services database
    example   189
  first normal form   189

normal forms beyond third   197
office supplies database
    example   198
second normal form   192
third normal form   194
NOT operator   31
Number datatype   14

o

object database   7
office supplies database example   198
    first normal form   200
    second normal form   200
    third normal form   202
one-to-many relationship   49, 60
    in Access Relationship window   96
    and subtypes   81
    two between same pair of
        tables   175, 179
    unary   279
    for zipcodes   117
one-to-one relationship   80
operational level   3
Oracle   7
ORDER BY clause   238, 242
    order of expressions   240
    treatment of blank values   259
ordered lists   161
OR operator   31, 226, 266, 268
outer join   107, 253
    with aggregation   256
    in query grid window   105
outline format for reports   24
outline notation   49, 59

p

parameter value
    request from Access when running a
        query   29
partial dependency   62, 64, 192, 200
plumbing store database
    example   143, 270
    entity-relationship diagram   271

primary key   12, 49, 54–56, 58, 202
    comparing in a query   288
    composite   56
    designating in Access   119
    determining   73, 77
    minimal   56
    only attribute in a table   75
    rules   56
    simple   56
    of subtype   79
    in table mediating a many-to-many
        relationship   142
project teams example   154

q

query   26
    advanced techniques   253
    chaining and nesting   262
    criteria   111, 217
    criteria after aggregation   111
    criteria before aggregation   229
    Design View   27
    grid   27, 104–105, 109–110, 121
    joining records from same
        table   260
    optimization   122, 153, 181, 222,
        225, 233, 242
    running   27, 29, 104, 121, 215
    sequence of operations   241
    sorting   27
    structure   240
    treating as a table in another
        query   263, 268

r

RDBMS *see* relational database
    management system
    (RDBMS)
records   7, 53
redundancy   44, 64, 66,
    189, 264
    bending the rules against   274
    of paths between tables   118

referential integrity   95, 96
  enforcing   96
  and order of entering data into
      tables   120
  in unary relationships   285
relational database management
    system (RDBMS)   7, 54
  fundamentals of   7
relational database theory   53–94,
    190, 279
  basic   53
relations   7
relationship
  many-to-many   139
  one-to-many   60
  two-to-many   174
  unary   279
Relationships window   95, 107
  two-to-many relationships   184
repeating groups   47, 189
Report   26
  View   25
  Wizard   23
Required property of a field   76
reserved word   238
right join   105
RIGHT JOIN clause   107, 255
rows   7, 53
  order of   53, 161
running a query   27

s
saving
  form design   21
  records   99
  Relationships window   97
  Table design   14
second normal form (2NF)   192
  dependency diagram   194
SELECT clause   105, 108, 122, 149,
    215, 242
  in aggregation queries   153
  AS modifier   149

selection criteria in query grid   30
semantically distinct   175
sequence of operations in a query   241
shortcut join   181
short text datatype   13, 32
show box in query grid   30
simple primary key   56
Single datatype   14, 33
software   2
sorting
  in a query   28, 240
  in a report   25
sports league and games database   253
spreadsheet   7
SQL *see* Structured Query Language
    (SQL)
StDev function   228
strategic level   3
Structured Query Language
    (SQL)   26, 31, 215
  basic   215
  displaying   215
  View of a query   31, 105, 215
subtypes   78
sub-windows   17
Sum function   232, 237
synthetic key   57, 70, 77, 118–119,
    142, 146, 180

t
table   7, 53
  characteristics   53
  condensing name   262
  design process   10
  Design View   11, 54
tabs (as opposed to sub-windows)   17
tactical level   4
text box   15, 17, 25
text datatype   13
third normal form (3NF)   194
  dependency diagram   195
  how to recognize   198
transaction   5, 45

numbering   70
processing   45, 47
processing systems   4
transaction processing systems (TPS)   4
transitive dependency   63, 194, 200
True/False datatype   14
tuples   7, 53
two-to-many relationship   174
   in the Access Relationships
      window   184

u

unary relationship   279
   in Access   283
   diagram   283
unsupported join condition   266
update anomaly   47

v
views   26

w
WHERE clause   217, 226–227,
      229, 234
Wizard
   Combo box   21, 129
   Form   19
   Input mask   13
   Report   23

y
Yes/No datatype   14

z
zipcodes   67